ANTONIA AUGUSTA

Portrait of a great Roman lady

Nikos Kokkinos

Foreword by
Fergus Millar

with illustrations by
Franco Vartuca

First published by Routledge in 1992.
This edition published by Libri Publications Ltd in 2002.

ISBN 1-901965-05-8

Designed and typeset by Libri Publications Limited
Printed and bound in Great Britain by Biddles Limited of Guildford

Libri Publications Limited
Suite 296, 37 Store Street
Bloomsbury
London, WC1E 7QF

Portrait of Antonia from the Baiae statue.

To Rikki

Thou hast Hera's eyes and Athene's hands,
the breasts of Aphrodite, and the legs of Thetis.
Blessed is he who looks on thee, thrice blessed he
  who hears thee talk,
a demigod he who kisses thee, and a god he who
  takes thee to wife.

From Rufinus, *Epigrams*
(of uncertain date but possibly
fourth or fifth century AD;
in *Greek Anthology* 5.94, *Loeb
Classical Library*, vol. 1)

CONTENTS

ILLUSTRATIONS

Frontispiece: Portrait of Antonia from the Baiae statue (Kunstgeschichtlichen Institut der Philipps-Universität, Bildarchiv Foto Marburg, C. 408.011)

1 ANTONIA IN HISTORY

2 THE INSCRIPTIONS OF ANTONIA

3 THE PAPYRI OF ANTONIA

4 THE COINS OF ANTONIA

5 ANTONIA AND SCULPTURE

6 ANTONIA AND MINOR ARTS

7 ANTONIA AND ARCHITECTURE

CONCLUSION

FOREWORD

In the late summer of 1986 I was making a journey round Jordan and Syria, and was able to call in at the British excavation at the great mound of Tell Nebi Mend (the ancient Kadesh-on-the-Orontes, and classical Laodicea ad Libanum), which lies at the northern end of the Bekaa Valley, just on the Syrian side of the border. Hearing my name, one of the students taking part in the excavation instantly dived into a back room and produced three offprints of articles which he had recently published in learned journals. I could not but think that it showed a high degree of initiative, not only to take part in the excavation of this remarkable site, but to have some offprints to hand, on the off-chance that a stray professor of Ancient History might come past. I was not wrong in concluding that the student concerned must be an unusual person.

Nikos Kokkinos must indeed count as one of the more striking of the younger contributors to the very lively atmosphere of enquiry and debate which now marks the study of the Graeco-Roman world, and of the original setting and early history of Christianity. Born in Alexandria in 1955, he was educated there, in Greek and Arabic, until 1967, when like so many others his family had to leave, moving back to Greece. His studies in Athens were interrupted in 1976, and he migrated to England, and supported himself for some years before returning to full-time study in 1984–7, when he took an honours degree in Roman Archaeology at the Institute of Archaeology in London. Since then he has been in Oxford preparing a doctoral thesis with me on the history of the family from which Herod the Great came; over a period longer than two centuries more than 100 members of the family can be identified (including the ten ladies who had the luck, good or ill, to be married to Herod himself); and their fortunes during that period vividly illustrate the complexity of the history of the Near East in the period when Roman direct rule was gradually established.

The present book, however, takes us closer to the centre of the stage of Roman history in that same period, and also back, in its origins, to Nikos Kokkinos' work at the Institute of Archaeology. For it began as an undergraduate report there, and is a study, from a number of angles, of what we can know of Antonia, a lady who was a central figure in the transition from republic to empire. Born in 36 BC, the daughter of Mark Antony and Octavia, the sister of Augustus, she was the wife of the favoured elder brother of the later Emperor Tiberius, Drusus, who died on campaign in 9 BC. Her resolute refusal to remarry made her a notable figure in Roman society for nearly half a century until her death in AD 37, under the rule of her grandson, Gaius. For one of her and Drusus' sons was the popular Germanicus, who died or was murdered in AD 19, and one of Germanicus' sons was Gaius, who in his short reign (AD 37–41) showed something approaching genius in throwing away all the hopes which the world placed in him. When he was killed in AD 41, the Praetorian Guard put forward as Emperor another son of Antonia, the scholarly Claudius. And when he was murdered in AD 54, it was to make room for a great-grandson of Antonia, the Emperor Nero.

Enough is known of Antonia's life, all of which was spent very close to the seat of power in the new monarchy, for it to present important material about the position of women in Roman society; the degree of freedom which they could exercise in making moral choices; their control of property; and their direct influence in public life. What is known is set out here, very clearly, and in such a way as to provoke reflection on these questions and others – and not least on the strains and re-evaluations imposed on Roman society by the fact that an 'Imperial' family had suddenly emerged.

None the less the material is not nearly sufficient to allow a real biography, and Nikos Kokkinos neither pretends to be able to offer that, nor seeks to provide some semi-fictional substitute. Instead he does something quite different, which is to look at the way in which the figure of Antonia is reflected, and made visible to us, through a remarkable variety of types of evidence: not just through the main narratives covering the events of the time, but through inscriptions in her honour, coin-types representing her, papyri from Egypt involving the management of her properties, and portraits of her in sculpture. All of these types of evidence have their own problems and limitations; but taken together they illustrate both the sudden centrality of the Imperial house and the variety of forms of expression, in words and in visual representations, which serve to illuminate the Roman world of the early Empire. The significance of all this is heavily underlined by the publication in 1984 of a new inscription recording steps taken in Rome to commemorate Antonia's son Germanicus after his death in AD 19. He had died, or been murdered, in Syria while on a general mission in the East, which happened to fall just half a century after the ill-fated regime there of his grandfather, Mark Antony. Among the honours which the Senate voted in December of AD 19 there was to be a new arch in the Circus Flaminius in Rome, adorned with a statue of Germanicus on a triumphal chariot: 'and at his sides statues of Drusus Germanicus his father, the natural brother of Tiberius Caesar Augustus' (i.e. the reigning Emperor, Tiberius) 'and of Antonia his mother and of Agrippina his wife and of Livia his sister and of Tiberius Germanicus his brother' (the future Emperor Claudius) 'and of his sons and daughters'. Among these were both Gaius, the future Emperor, and Agrippina, the mother of Nero.

The central place of Antonia in Roman public life could hardly be more clearly demonstrated. But at a time when our view of how to understand the early Empire has been transformed by Paul Zanker's book *The Power of Images in the Age of Augustus*, it is specially significant that this is the only known text of an iconographic 'programme' for a Roman arch. The bronze tablet from which the text comes was actually found not in Rome but in southern Spain. In a whole variety of ways the name and the image of Antonia were to be diffused all round the Empire. The study of what our evidence for her consists of can therefore, at a different level, be understood as a significant contribution to the understanding of the early Roman Empire itself.

Fergus Millar
Camden Professor of Ancient History,
Brasenose College,
Oxford University

PREFACE

My primary concern for some years has been the study of Christian origins and the life of Jesus, and this has gradually led me to the historical and archaeological exploration of the Herodian family of Judaea, individual members of which I have examined directly or indirectly.[1] Agrippa I has recently been in my focus, since although he rose to power after the crucifixion of Jesus he was his exact contemporary. In the search for connections between Agrippa and known historical figures, my attention was drawn to Antonia Minor (later Augusta) who had been his great friend and protector.

Looking more closely into the life of Antonia, I realised that although historical references and material evidence have been handed down to us from antiquity, there has been little modern work on her. Apparently no university thesis has ever been written, nor has a general book been published, and even periodical articles are scarce.

Short entries on Antonia are included in most dictionaries and encyclopaedias, but the main authority remains Stein's entry in the *Prosopographia*, which perhaps is now equalled by Raepsaet-Charlier's *Prosopographie*.[2] Antonia is briefly alluded to in works on the Julio-Claudians, Tiberius, Germanicus, Caligula and Claudius, and also in works on Roman women and broader historical themes.[3] Her involvement in the fall of Sejanus has been discussed in particular, but Gaggero's elaborate and out-of-date article seems to be the only general historical account of her.[4]

Nor has much been done to bring together the relevant archaeological material. Of the inscriptions relating to Antonia only the 'portrait-inscriptions' have been looked at, and even then only cursorily, though inscriptions of her household staff were considered to some extent by Treggiari.[5] For the relevant papyri there is no definite survey but they were used constructively by Parassoglou.[6] The coins have been dealt with comprehensively only recently, and the same may be said for the tokens (*tesserae*).[7] Most work has been concentrated on iconography. The first attempt was by Bernoulli, who was followed by Rumpf and Poulsen.[8] Again only in recent years have more detailed studies been published by Polaschek and Erhart.[9] Finally, excavation finds and museum acquisitions of Antonia's portraits have initiated various discussions, the most extensive being those of Benoit, Clavel, Simon and Andreae.[10]

Clearly, there is room for a historical-archaeological book on Antonia. Limitations of space and time rule out anything definitive, but I have tried to survey all areas of research, while examining more closely certain elements of the non-literary record, particularly where they throw light on the available literary evidence.

I hope I have shown how archaeological material can be used in the study even of individual personalities of antiquity. By consistently supplementing, verifying and correcting the historical sources (which are often fragmentary or misleading) we may undoubtedly improve our understanding. After all, excavated physical remains represent what somebody once did, not what some contemporary or later writer says they did.

The interdisciplinary approach employed puts our *grande dame* in context. For the first time her dramatic life and its bearing on the lives of other members of the Imperial family can be seen from different perspectives. At first I examine the written history with minimum assistance from other sources. I then turn to the investigation of all types of material relating to her, divided into categories, in order to contrast their information, value and independence. In conclusion I present the current state of knowledge, with special emphasis on new standpoints that have been developed. Antonia's profile may thus be said to have been built 'archaeologically', from the ground up, as it were. Such a systematic approach may be useful for scholarly treatments of other important ancient figures.

I have taken care to explain technical terms in the text to avoid the need of a glossary (which readers often fail to consult). I have tried to give a hermeneutic presentation (by locating places, qualifying names and expounding concepts), sometimes even at the risk of departing from the main subject. The expert has to bear with me at these points. They are useful to the general reader. In fact I hope the attention paid to this, together with the English translations of ancient texts and the large number of illustrations, will make an otherwise academic publication of interest to a wider readership.

Much of the material presented is contained in a report submitted to the London Institute of Archaeology on 1 May 1987, marking the 1950th anniversary of Antonia's death (1 May 37). That report, however, was only a basis for the present book. Apart from a major revision, the research is wider, the documentation more extensive, the texts have been translated and the number of illustrations has doubled.

Antonia Augusta has become a reality to me only through the help of teachers, colleagues and friends. None of those mentioned below should be held responsible for any interpretations or errors, which are solely my own.

From the Institute of Archaeology in the University of London I am especially grateful to Professor John Wilkes for directing the earlier version and to Mark Hassall for his constant encouragement. My supervisor at Oxford, Professor Fergus Millar, has offered valuable criticism and rescued me from not a few blunders. I am honoured that he should have written a foreword.

Special thanks are due to Miss Susan Wright of the Caerleon Museum, Wales, for grappling with the work as if it were her own. She has read it through patiently and made many suggestions. Her contribution cannot be overstressed. To Peter James and Dr Ian Thorpe of University College London I am indebted for the trouble they took to read through the manuscript and suggest alternative expressions, and even more so to Colin Haycraft of Duckworth for his numerous corrections. Without the help of Franco Vartuca of the Cooperativa Archeologia Lombarda at Brescia, the task of illustration would have been very difficult. His enthusiasm, imagination and hard labour have been a positive enrichment.

For consultation, permissions and supplying photographs I am grateful to the following: Professor B. Andreae (Kunstgeschichtlichen Institut der Philipps-Universität); Mr P. Attwood (Coins, British Museum); Professor D. Barag (Jerusalem

University); Dr D. Brown (formerly Ashmolean Museum, Oxford); Dr A. Burnett (Coins, British Museum); Mr J. Busuttil (Museums Department, Valletta); Dr M. Ceresa (Biblioteca Vaticana); Miss A. Claridge (British School at Rome); Dr R. Coles (Papyrology, Ashmolean); the late Professor K. Erim (New York University); Dr A. Frendo (Pontifical Biblical Institute, Rome); Dr Z. Karapa-Molizani (Epigraphical Museum, Athens); Dr D. Klose (Staatliche Münzsammlung, Munich); Mr C. Lazos (Athens); Dr F. Manera (Museo Nazionale Romano); Dr A. Mantis (Acropolis Museum, Athens); Miss G. Matheson (John Rylands Library, Manchester); Mr P. Paraskevaides (Mytilene); Mr S. Qedar (Jerusalem); Dr J. Rea (Papyrology, Ashmolean); Professor J. Reynolds (Cambridge University); Miss V. Scott (British School at Rome); Professor J. Vardaman (Cobb Institute of Archaeology, Mississippi); Dr L. Vattuone (Museo Vaticano); and Dr M. Wappner (Museo Capitolino). My apologies are offered to any whom I have inadvertently omitted.

I am grateful too to the staff of the following libraries and institutions: the Hellenic and Roman Societies; the Institute of Archaeology; University College London; the British Library; the Department of Coins in the British Museum; the Egypt Exploration Society; the Palestine Exploration Society; the Ashmolean, Oxford; the Bodleian, Oxford; the Bibliothèque Nationale, Paris; the British School at Rome; the German Institute at Rome; the Gabinetto Fotografico Nazionale, Rome; the Fototeca Unione, Rome; the Soprintendenza Archeologica di Roma; the Musée Archéologique, Cimiez; the Museo Arquelógico de Sevilla; the Archaeological Society, Athens; the National Museum of Athens; the American School of Classical Studies at Athens; the German Institute at Cairo; the Albright Institute at Jerusalem; the Fogg Art Museum, Harvard; and the Kelsey Museum, Michigan.

Last but not least, for her endurance, her understanding and the sacrifice of her personal interests to enable me to pursue my own, I dedicate this book to my wife Rikki. No one deserves it more.

N. K.

London, August 1988

There has been a long delay in the publication of *Antonia* due to unforeseen circumstances, involving not less than the change of publishers; despite the fact that it had been advertised and planned to appear (with some 300 illustrations) around 1989. I would particularly like to thank Leslie Gardner and Richard Stoneman for seeing the book successfully through the press under the cover of Routledge. I am also grateful to Heather McCallum, Sue Bilton, Jenny Overton, Joanne Tinson and Jo Smart for all their efforts.

No systematic attempt to update the bibliography has been made, but nothing earthmoving concerning Antonia has caught my attention in the period 1988–91. I have thus decided to make no alterations. Nevertheless, the chance should not be missed here to mention two major works recently published in London (Batsford): one by A. A. Barrett on *Caligula* (1989); and another by B. Levick on *Claudius* (1990). Both are masterly expositions of Roman Imperial politics in the first century AD, and variously touch upon Antonia *en passant*. Further, the English translation of D. Schwartz's *Agrippa I* (1990) now published in Tübingen (J. C. B. Mohr), is of some relevance, but note my review of this book in volume 82 (1992) of the *Journal of Roman Studies*.

N. K.

London, October 1991

PREFACE TO 2002 EDITION

It is hard to believe that a decade has passed since the first publication of *Antonia*. The book may have had a successful life as a hardback but it seemed to be crying out for a paperback edition – not least due to its original price tag (in the middle double figures), unaffordable to many general readers and most students. This was the moment that Anna Lethbridge stepped in. Libri Publications offered the right environment in which *Antonia* was to be reincarnated, now with a soft cover that can be had without having to break one's bank. But Anna did something even more useful. She urged me to write a new chapter looking at the aftermath of my initial conclusions. Though more work in a subject one considers long-finished and 'done' is not easy to accept, I was convinced to go back and assess the impact that *Antonia* had in the 1990s. In the process I have had to update my research to a reasonable degree, which was quite a task. This is what the 'Review Chapter' is all about. With these new pages of reactions and second thoughts the book has now been enriched. I can only be pleased with the result, and hope it to remain in circulation for years to come. Thanks should also go, once more, to my colleague (and frequent proof reader) Peter James, to my iron lady agent Leslie Gardner, and to my wife Rikki for her inexhaustible devotion.

N.K.
London, 2001

INTRODUCTION

Despite the myth of the Amazons – the female warriors thought to have lived at the very edges of the known world – which seems to have been invented only to show how bad things can be when women get the upper hand, there is no evidence in antiquity for the existence of matriarchal societies.[1] The Greeks knew of two famous Assyrian queens of remote times, Semiramis and Nitocris, who were regarded as incidental and alien. The only public role a woman could be seen playing in Greece was that of priestess or similar functionary.[2] The Greeks themselves later experienced, among others, the Argive Telesilla (a rebel aristocrat) and the Cyrenian Aretaphila (a royal matron); but their stories were told only as paradigms of female bravery in times of crisis.[3]

Aristotle in the fourth century BC made an interesting comparison between Spartan women (undoubtedly the most liberated women ever known in Greece) and fierce and warlike nations living beyond the Celts and believed to be governed by women (*gynaikokratoumenoi*). But this comparison was probably based either on travellers' tales of distant barbarians, or on a misunderstanding of the habits and laws of foreigners: for example, the 'dowry' among German tribes which, according to Tacitus at the beginning of the second century AD, was brought by the husband to the wife rather than the other way round; or, the 'Law of the Britons', mentioned by the Syriac writer Bardesanes at the end of the same century, that women in Britain had the right to have many husbands at one time, in contrast to all oriental custom.[4]

We might be tempted here to draw a parallel with the 'wild' British women fighting frantically against the Romans in

1

Anglesey, 'in robes of deathly black and with dishevelled hair', or, even better, with the British queens – such as Cartimandua, who captured the anti-Roman Caratacus, thus furnishing an adornment for the triumph of the Emperor Claudius, and the remarkable Boudicca, who resisted the Roman conquest until her death.[5] Yet we know so little about these women or the circumstances in which they ruled that no generalisation is possible. Besides, women playing major roles in Britain are recorded only in the first century, an exceptional period, as we shall see.

Better documented precedents are the notorious Hellenistic queens. The Seleucid and Ptolemaic women who sat on the thrones of Syria and Egypt in the first three centuries BC, have always been regarded as unique examples of true female independence in ancient times. However, not even the most capable of these reigned without at least a titular male consort, brother, or son.[6] In any case, one reason why Cleopatra VII made such an impression on her contemporaries outside Egypt and became the centre of a bizarre legend, was that she was a woman. While there is no suggestion that *all* women were underprivileged *all* the time in *all* walks of Graeco-Roman life, this female apparition on the main political stage, cluttered with male players, must have looked extraordinary.

Roman history too is almost exclusively male history – women play no visible part in its major events. Even in its less important episodes they are scarcely involved. It is true that history, biography, poetry and satire were all written by men, but this only shows that women were not readily encouraged to write. If a few did, following the conspicuous example of Sappho in the sixth century BC, their works have unfortunately not survived. Nevertheless, in Roman law, women could not vote, were not magistrates or senators, did not serve as judges or even speak in court, and did not hold military commands or take part in public life. They seem to have been largely restricted to the home, though a few aristocrats succeeded every now and then in influencing the careers of the men in their family. For the Late Republican period (80–44 BC), as Dixon rightly pointed out:

> the argument is not that, say, Servilia and Fulvia had
> political power, but that the social and economic position of
> a Claudia or Aemilia was such that she was implicated, by
> means of ties of family and patronage, in actions which a

modern commentator would term political . . . if the term 'politics' is synonymous with the suffrage, the magistracies and membership of the senate, these were purely male preserves. If 'politics' is, rather, to be taken in the sense of the pursuit and exercise of real power, it alters the question of female involvement.[7]

In Roman history, however, there is one notable exception which merits analysis: the century between the deaths of Julius Caesar and Nero (44 BC–AD 68). During this period there appeared in 'politics' a number of female figures who, like Cleopatra, became the centre of legends, not only bizarre but often dramatic. Women, for some reason, seem now to have been able to achieve more. Though none of them of course ever attained a political position *per se*, their power and influence were far-reaching; their interests were often sought far beyond their homes, while the business they contracted had been hitherto the prerogative of males. What is significant is that they were recognised for their power, or the services they provided, and venerated both by the state and the populace. This was unprecedented in the annals of Rome.[8] Let us remember the warning given to the Romans, in an often quoted passage, by Cato the Elder, consul in 195 BC. He had bitterly opposed the repeal of the Oppian Law which limited the ownership of property by women:

> Our ancestors permitted no woman to conduct even personal business without a guardian to intervene on her behalf; they wished them to be under the control of fathers, brothers, husbands . . . Give loose rein to their uncontrollable nature and to this untamed creature and expect that they will themselves set bounds to their licence! . . . It is complete liberty or, rather, if we wish to speak the truth, complete licence that they desire. If they win in this, what will they not attempt? . . . The moment they begin to be your equals, they will be your superiors.[9]

The vital turning-point must have been the establishment of the Empire. The new system of affairs required many changes. Society, economy, religion and the law stood in need of reshaping. The architect of the Empire, Augustus, began a long-term revision and refinement. Fundamental changes to the legal standing of women were not made, but enough space was now allowed so that the privileged at least could gain power uncontemplated before. We are almost led to conclude that it was mainly the acquisition and use of economic power by women of wealthy backgrounds that brought about this 'revolution' in attitudes. Similar reasons in the past had helped to open new horizons for the female Hellenistic elite.[10]

Beyond doubt the two greatest Roman women in this category were Livia Augusta and Antonia Augusta. Antonia, the subject of this book, was the celebrated niece of Augustus, sister-in-law of Tiberius, mother of Claudius, grandmother of Caligula and great-grandmother of Nero. Of the two women the first, Livia, is usually looked upon as the more important, apparently because she was the wife of Augustus. It will become increasingly evident in the course of this book that Antonia not only equalled Livia in status in the later part of her life, but on many counts (social, political, economic) even surpassed her. From the outset, therefore, it may be claimed that from one point of view Antonia was the greatest lady the Empire ever produced.

It was Finley who said that although the Roman world was not the only historical society in which women lagged behind in politics and business, it is not easy to think of another civilisation without a single important woman:

> no truly regal queen, no Deborah, no Joan of Arc, no Florence Nightingale, no patron of the arts . . . Where were the rebels among the women, real or fictitious – the George Sand or Harriet Beecher Stowe, the Hester Prynne or Tess of the D'Urbervilles?[11]

The answer can now be given. As I shall argue, there appeared in Roman society one woman who would have envied little in these heroines: not only a beautiful, gentle, educated and revered member of the Imperial family, but a vivid, tireless, fearless and compassionate woman, a skilled organiser with a business sense whose political motivations and actions changed the course of history.

All this is relevant to powerful and rich women. Poor women remained utterly silent – they found no shade beneath the Roman sun. For them there was only one hope of equality, which had recently been proclaimed by the strange teaching of a new sun that rose in the East:

> Have you never read that the Creator made them from the

4

beginning male and female? . . . For this reason a man
shall leave his father and mother and be made one with his
wife; and the two shall become one flesh. It follows that
they are no longer two individuals: they are one flesh.[12]

Jesus' attitude towards women was without question 'revolutionary': that is, by all current standards, western and oriental.
Evidently this had been appreciated by his female followers, who
came from among the rich and the poor alike. He attended to
them personally: the strong, the weak and even the adulteress.[13]
He offered his 'kingdom' to women, accepting them as equal
human beings from whatever background: Judaean, Samaritan,
Galilaean and even Greek-Phoenician.[14]

Modern sceptics have argued that, if this was Jesus' real message to women, it must have been badly distorted by the time it
reached Rome. The culprit is the Apostle Paul, who had to be
seen as a rigid moralist, a spiritual dictator and a male chauvinist. Yet the argument is primarily based on a few epistles attributed to him, whose authenticity has been seriously questioned in
the past.[15] In the most authentic of his letters the 'good tidings'
seem to remain clear:

There is no such thing as Jew and Greek, slave and freeman, male and female; for you are all one person in Christ
Jesus.[16]

1

ANTONIA IN HISTORY

The person most instrumental in contracting the treaty of Tarentum (Taranto, in south Italy) in the early summer of 37 BC, when Octavian (later the Emperor Augustus) and Mark Antony agreed to renew the Triumvirate, was Octavia Minor.[1] As Octavian's sister and Antony's wife, she was in the best position to intervene, and it was her persistent desire for a reconciliation between the two men that achieved the temporary truce. She was with child at the time (Antonia Minor – 'the younger') and had already borne Antony one daughter (Antonia Maior – 'the elder').[2] Antonia Minor seems to have been conceived in Athens (in early May 37 BC), where Octavia and Antony had resided until the early summer of that year.[3] She was born in Rome (31 January 36 BC). After the treaty of Tarentum, while returning to the East, Antony had sent her mother back from the island of Corcyra (Corfu) to the Roman capital.[4]

Antony himself proceeded to Syria, to prepare for war against the Parthians, spending the winter of 37/36 BC at Antioch, where he summoned Cleopatra to marry him. The ambitious queen of Egypt, whose vision of ruling the Roman world had led her to seduce Antony and bear him twins (Cleopatra Selene and Alexander Helios), now succeeded in winning him over completely. It was largely this ultimate union that made Antony withdraw from his natural environment and gradually forced him to his final downfall.[5] Cleopatra in Syria must have been left pregnant, since in the spring of 36 BC, when she returned to her kingdom, she became the mother of another boy (Ptolemy Philadelphos).

Octavia at Rome meanwhile gave birth to Antonia in the

6

Figure 1 Portrait of Octavia found at Smyrna and now kept in Athens.

Figure 2 Limestone statue of Mark Antony in the Cairo Museum.

Figure 3 General view of the west side of the Agora excavations at Athens, with the seating of the Temple of Hephaistos on Kolonos Agoraios.

Figure 4 General view of the Roman Forum, with the Palatine buildings rising to the right.

Figure 5 A war galley (probably a *quadrireme*) as it appears on a relief from Praeneste (late first century BC), now in the Museo Vaticano, which may commemorate Augustus' victory over Mark Antony and Cleopatra.

house of Antony, which she occupied in spite of Octavian's objections. From here she was ejected in 32 BC when Antony sent her the official divorce.[6] The family then moved to Octavian's court on the Palatine (see p. 148). Next year (31 BC) saw the famous battle of Actium, in which the fleets of Antony and Cleopatra suffered a crushing defeat, and the following year (30 BC) they committed suicide in Alexandria.

Antonia, who was then six, never knew her illustrious father. She grew up among the Roman Imperial family, with her sister (Antonia Maior), half-sisters (Marcella Maior, Marcella Minor and Cleopatra Selene) and half-brothers (Marcus Marcellus, Iullus Antonius, Alexander Helios and Ptolemy Philadelphos – see Family Trees 1 and 2). As an aristocratic young lady she would have been taught how to run a household rather than how to do its work, though spinning and weaving (*lanificium*) was an enjoyable and profitable skill favoured by the rich.[7] She would have learnt how to dress and primp properly, how to sweeten her breath, walk gracefully, dance well and emulate the best poetry.[8] In fact the education provided for her must have been of the highest quality: we know that her mother Octavia employed well-known Greek philosophers as instructors for her children.[9]

Antonia's uncle Octavian, now the victorious Emperor Augustus, assigned money to her from her father's property, presumably in Italy. She also inherited from Antony many of his social and business relationships in the East and a number of his estates in Egypt, and perhaps elsewhere (see p. 71).[10] At this stage, since the power of the head of the family (*patria potestas*) had ceased to exist (i.e. there was no father), Antonia would have passed according to Roman law into the *tutela perpetua* (that is, she would have acquired a guardian-tutor). The guardian's permission (*auctoritas*) was needed for major pledges, transfers of property or other substantial economic activities. This state of affairs would have remained until the power of a husband (*manus mariti*) had descended upon her.[11]

On 5 December 19 BC, five years before the legal age, the elder Drusus, the son of Augustus' wife Livia (by her first husband, Ti. Claudius Nero), held the quaestorship. He was born either on 14 January, the birthday (*dies natalis*) of Mark Antony, or in March–April 38 BC, and now at the age of nineteen, on the threshold of a public career, he seems to have been ready for marriage.[12] Antonia, then seventeen, had already passed the normal age at which young aristocratic women were wed, but she may have been waiting for Drusus.[13] According to Crinagoras, a Greek poet of the palace, the marriage took place in early spring (probably in 18 BC) not long after her birthday:

> Roses used to flower in spring, but we now in mid-
> winter burst scarlet from our buds,
> smiling gaily on this thy natal morn
> that falls so nigh to thy wedding.
> To be seen on the brow of the loveliest of women is
> better than to await the sun of spring.[14]

Her first pregnancy was also commemorated by the poet, though the child must have died at birth or in its infancy.[15] Suetonius says that Drusus had 'several' children by Antonia, but only three survived him: Germanicus, Livilla and Claudius.[16]

Germanicus, the first child to reach maturity, was born on 24 May 15 BC and therefore had been conceived in the late summer of 16 BC.[17] This year Drusus represented Augustus in the gladiatorial games given on the occasion of the Emperor's

Figure 6 Antonia and Drusus on the southern relief of the Ara Pacis.

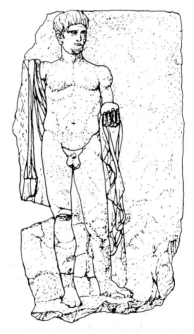

Figure 7 Germanicus on a relief from Aphrodisias.

12

departure for Gaul. Attending to the praetorian duties of his brother (later the Emperor Tiberius) who had followed Augustus, Drusus remained with his wife in the city.[18] Germanicus seems to have been born in Rome, assuming that Antonia did not follow Drusus in his campaign against the Raetians in 15 BC.[19]

Livilla's birth, some time between 14 and 11 BC, probably also took place in Rome, but it may have been somewhere else if Antonia accompanied Drusus on any of his military operations during this period. Drusus seems to have joined Augustus in Gaul and Spain in 14–13 BC. That Antonia was present with her husband in Spain may be suggested by an inscription found at Ulia (Montilla) thought to date around 12 BC. (see p. 42).[20] Drusus went to war in Germany in 13 BC,[21] but he was back in Rome for the foundation-day (4 July) of the Ara Pacis, that splendid monument of the Augustan age, on which he is depicted with Antonia and Germanicus (see p. 115). He was sent to Gaul to organise the census of 12 BC where he took the opportunity to establish the Altar of Rome and Augustus at Lugdunum (Lyons).[22] He continued his mission in Germany, becoming the first Roman general to sail the North Sea. He also supervised the construction of huge canals, the Fossae Drusinae, connecting the Rhine with the Yssel. On his return to Rome in 11 BC he was appointed praetor of the city with responsibility for jurisdiction (*praetor urbanus*; in Greek *astynomos*).[23]

The absence of Antonia's daughter Livilla from the relief on the Ara Pacis suggests that she was born in 12 or 11 BC. On the other hand, if it was slightly earlier, she would have been too young to be carried in this tiring procession. This is certainly more consistent with the date of her first marriage (often confused in literature), to Gaius Caesar, the adopted son of Augustus, in 1 BC when she should have been at least twelve.[24]

Antonia's youngest child Claudius was born on 1 August 10 BC, at Lugdunum, on the very day of the great altar's dedication.[25] Claudius must have been conceived late in 11 BC, while Drusus was with Antonia in Rome, as we saw. Evidently Antonia had accompanied Drusus to Gaul, shortly after the death of her mother Octavia, at whose funeral he delivered the oration.[26]

Drusus became consul in 9 BC when he attacked the German tribes and reached the Elbe.[27] During his return to the Rhine, he died unexpectedly either in a riding accident or of some disease.

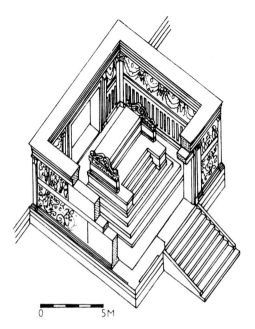

Figure 8 Axonometric view of the restored Ara Pacis Augustae.

Figure 9 The altar of 'Rome and Augustus' inaugurated in 10 BC at Lugdunum, as depicted on the reverse of a brass sestertius.

14

Figure 10 A reconstruction (frontal view) of the Mausoleum Augusti built in 28 BC.

Baseless rumour had it that he met his end through poisoning, for which Augustus was to blame.[28] His body, escorted on foot by Tiberius (who had rushed to Drusus from Rome in record time), was brought to Rome to be cremated in the Campus Martius; his ashes were deposited in Augustus' grandiose Mausoleum.[29]

Drusus' death had a shattering effect on Antonia. Ovid (to whom the Latin elegiac epicedium, which may have been read at the funeral, is sometimes attributed) describes her as tearing her hair, screaming like a madwoman and attempting suicide; or again, in depression, embracing her children as the only pledges left to her of her husband. Words hardly sufficed to console her:

> What shall I say of thee, most worthy consort of thy Drusus, worthy daughter-in-law of Drusus' mother? A pair well suited: the one a hero among youths, the other that hero's darling, as she was his. Queen among women wert thou to him, and daughter of Caesar, nor didst thou seem less than the wife of mighty Jove. Thou wert his freely given, his last and only love, thou wert his pleasant repose from weary toil. Thy absence did he, dying, in his last words bewail, and his tongue, though cold, strove to pronounce thy name.[30]

Antonia's love for Drusus never waned, and despite her youth (she was only twenty-seven) and pressure from Augustus (including legal implications: the *Lex Iulia de maritandis ordinibus* allowed her only three years' exemption from the obligation to marry again), she never remarried.[31] She became a 'one-man woman' (*univira*), a model of matronly behaviour, the symbol of family love. It is probably she who is depicted as the personification of Piety (*Pietas*) on coins struck under Tiberius and later 'restored' by Titus (see p. 95).

Antonia decided to remain in the house of her mother-in-law, Livia, and even in the room she had shared with Drusus (see p. 148). In the words of Valerius Maximus, a historian of the reign of Tiberius with a strong rhetorical and philosophical bias:

> in the same bed, on the part of the one (Drusus) the vigour of youth was extinguished, while on the part of the other (Antonia) the experience of widowhood dragged on into old age. Let this bedchamber be taken as representing the extreme case of such experiences.[32]

Antonia devoted herself to the education of her children, but this should not be seen as a dedication to merely domestic interests.[33] On the contrary, she strongly influenced Roman politics and even became involved in private business transactions away from home (see p. 84). After her husband's death, the number of her children would have enabled her to avoid returning to the legal control of a guardian–tutor. According to Augustus' new law, the *ius liberorum*, a widow with three children gained automatic exemption (*excusatio*) from guardianship (*tutela mulierum*). Now at last she could operate as a free agent.[34]

For the next twenty-five years we have no direct historical information about Antonia, but during this time she witnessed momentous political developments, particularly in respect to her elder son's career. In AD 4 Germanicus was solemnly adopted by his paternal uncle Tiberius, and in 12, at the age of only twenty-six, he rose to the position of consul, the highest magistracy the city had to offer. In 14, the year best remembered for the death of Augustus, Germanicus was further elevated to the proconsular command of Gaul and Germany (*imperium proconsulare*). Finally, in May AD 17, at the request of the new Emperor Tiberius and after a triumph held to celebrate his victories over the German tribes, the Senate conferred on him powers overriding the decisions of all governors in the eastern provinces (a *maius imperium*).[35]

This event marked the beginning of what turned out to be a long and extraordinary journey (fig. 15, p. 24), not only on state affairs but on private business and pleasure, undertaken by Germanicus together with his family and entourage. Although the journey has been discussed at length, the extent to which descendants of Mark Antony participated in it and the sentimental value which it inevitably held for them, have not been fully appreciated.[36] While it ended in tragedy, this 'exodus' from Rome to the old realm of Antony in the East, not long after the death of Augustus, must have been popularly recognised as symbolising the family's imminent return to power. Indeed this was to happen in less than two decades. That Antonia herself apparently joined Germanicus on at least a part of the journey, has escaped attention, basically because it was ignored by the main historian Tacitus, whose silence is taken a priori as evidence. But dedications to her along the same route, evidently dating from the same period and mentioning her as 'benefactress' (*euergetis*), clearly suggest that she was one of this special Imperial group (see pp. 43–5).

After crossing from Italy to Dalmatia to meet his cousin the younger Drusus (the son of Tiberius) and sailing down the Illyrian (Adriatic) and Ionian coasts, Germanicus arrived at Nicopolis in southern Epirus (in western Greece). There, on 1 January AD 18, he entered the consulship for the second time.[37] The nearby site of Actium, where Antony had lost the crucial battle to Augustus, was visited almost immediately; for Antonia's family it must have been a moving experience. They then proceeded to Patrae and Athens, where Antony and Octavia had spent the most romantic part of their married life together (the fruit of which was almost certainly Antonia's conception). Subsequently they crossed via Euboea to Lesbos, where Germanicus' wife (the elder Agrippina) gave birth to Julia Livilla.[38]

Livilla was one of the three well-known sisters of Caligula. The other two, the younger Agrippina and Drusilla, had been born in succession in the previous two years, and they too, *pace* Tacitus, may have been taken along by the family.[39] Caligula himself was undoubtedly present, but Germanicus is said to have left behind his older sons, Nero Caesar and Drusus Caesar, in the care of his brother Claudius, though Magie, on the basis of epigraphical evidence, presumed that they also made the

Figure 11 The Augustan victory monument at Nicopolis, built on the slope of the hill consecrated to Apollo, with its unusual *rostrata* collection from the captured ships of Mark Antony.

journey.[40] An alternative, as we shall see, is that some of the children did not complete the full journey, returning to Rome (with their grandmother Antonia) a year earlier than their mother.

After leaving Lesbos the Imperial vessels made for the northern outskirts of Asia Minor and reached the Euxine Sea, going perhaps as far as the colony of Sinope. They then returned to the Aegean and, bypassing the island of Samothrace, sailed south to several coastal towns until they arrived at Rhodes.[41] The family brought aid and encouragement to the Asian communities, who welcomed them with extravagant honours; a number of inscriptions and coins have been collected from a chain of locations around this area.[42] Germanicus now headed for Armenia, probably via Lycia, Cilicia and Cappadocia, but his family may have remained in the Aegean, for the trip was difficult and dangerous. Agrippina had children to look after (including a newborn baby) and Antonia was now fifty-three.

Figure 12 View of the theatre and harbour at Mytilene on Lesbos.

The reunion may have taken place in Syria upon Germanicus' return, probably via Commagene. In Artaxata, the capital of Armenia, Germanicus appointed Zeno (whom he renamed Artaxias) as the new king, perhaps because they were cousins.[43]

After Germanicus' visits to the cities of Syria, which included a venture as far east as Palmyra, where important economic reforms and other business of his are on record, Antonia may have joined him in his move south.[44] If her attendants on this journey included her good friend Berenice I (the Herodian princess) and the latter's son Agrippa I (the future king of Judaea), who had lived in Rome close to Antonia since 4 BC, the occasion would have been ideal for an excursion to Palestine.[45] Among other places, she may have visited Caesarea Maritima, the magnificent city of Herod the Great in which the Drouseion tower had been erected to the memory of her husband. She may even have taken the road to Jerusalem, where a fortress built next to the Temple was named Antonia after her father.[46] In a previous mission to the East, parallel in many ways to that of Germanicus, Gaius Caesar, the adopted son of Augustus, had visited Jerusalem. Germanicus may to a certain extent have followed in Caius' footsteps. Livilla, the daughter of Antonia, had accompanied her first husband Caius. She too on that occasion must therefore have visited the Holy City.[47]

In the narrative of Tacitus the Imperial family can be traced again only during their stay at the Nabataean court, apparently in Petra, the capital of King Aretas IV. There Germanicus and Agrippina were offered 'massive golden crowns', and the other members of the party 'lighter specimens'. This crowning could have been taken to signify the submission of the Nabataean kingdom to the descendants of Antony. He had once given parts of this kingdom to his children by Cleopatra.[48]

The ultimate destination was the fascinating land of the Nile, which they reached at the beginning of AD 19. Here, on the pretext of a famine to which relief had to be brought, Alexandria, prohibited to Roman senators, was entered by Germanicus without the Emperor's consent.[49] If a speech of Germanicus as transmitted by a papyrus is to be taken at face value, his mother Antonia and some of his children do not seem to have come as far as Egypt, and perhaps not to Nabataea either (see p. 82). From this point onward the group was reduced in size. In the Greek metropolis of Alexandria, we can point to at

Figure 13 A reconstruction of the Pharos at Alexandria, the famous lighthouse which stood some 120 m in height, originally built in the third century BC.

least one act of Germanicus. Since 'whenever he came upon the tombs of distinguished men, he always offered sacrifice', a rich sacrifice at Mark Antony's tomb would have been in order.[50] Even though Antonia was apparently absent, this ought to have been the most memorable event of the journey. It may even have silently marked the 'half-centenary' from the defeat at Actium and the death of Antony.

On 26 January AD 19, preparations had begun for sailing up the great river. Germanicus paid a visit to the Arsinoite district to view the 'artificial' lake of Moëris and its fantastic canal network[51] – it is a safe inference that he attended to the affairs of his and Antonia's estates in this area (see p. 71). Famous places, attractive even today for their antiquities, were next to be seen: Thebes (Karnak, Luxor and Medînet-Habu), Elephantine and Syene (Assouan) at the southernmost border of the Augustan Empire.[52] At Thebes, excited by the hieroglyphics which were cut on piles of masonry, Germanicus ordered the senior local priests to explain some. One inscription, containing mainly fabulous Pharaonic conquests attributed to Ramesses II

21

Figure 14 Augustus presented as a Pharaoh adoring Isis from a relief at Tentyra in Upper Egypt.

(conventionally 1290–1224 BC), was translated for him. It is sufficiently interesting to cite Tacitus' version here as a comparison with or contrast to the expansion of the Augustan Empire:

> Once the city contained seven hundred thousand men of military age, and with that army King Rhamses (Ramesses), after conquering Libya and Ethiopia, the Medes and the Persians, the Bactrian and the Scyth, and the lands where the Syrians and Armenians and neighbouring Cappadocians dwell, had ruled over all that lies between the Bithynian Sea on the one hand and the Lycian on the other.[53]

Germanicus returned to Syria, and on 10 October AD 19 he suddenly died, poisoned, it was claimed, by Gnaeus Piso,[54] an ambitious consular recently appointed to the command of Syria, 'a man of ungoverned passions and constitutional insubordination'.[55] Piso's colleague in the alleged crime was his wife Plancina, whose high lineage and great wealth had inspired his excesses. She may herself have been involved in a kind of 'black magic', particularly fashionable among women of the upper class in the reign of Tiberius, perhaps under the influence of oriental cults.[56] This may explain, first, the mildness of Piso in AD 16 towards magicians and astrologers,[57] and second the suspiciously odd circumstances made manifest in the room where Germanicus stayed. Upon examination of the floors and walls, disturbing paraphernalia, according to Tacitus, were revealed:

the remains of human bodies, spells, curses, leaden tablets engraved with the name 'Germanicus', charred and blood-smeared ashes, and other implements of witchcraft by which it is believed the living soul can be devoted to the powers of the grave.[58]

Whether or not Tiberius gave instructions to the murderers was never established. Suetonius believed this story; Dio implied it; Tacitus was uncertain; Josephus either refrained from comment or, more probably, had not heard about it.

At first a spurious report announcing Germanicus' recovery spread in the city of Rome, causing the assembled crowd to chant that night: 'Safe is Rome, safe too our country, for Germanicus is safe' (*Salva Roma, salva patria, salvus est Germanicus*). But at thirty-three the prince was dead. This was the second major setback for Antonia after the loss of Drusus. Her son's popularity, which exceeded even her husband's, generated frenzied mourning throughout the Empire which must have deepened her sorrow, if not driven her to hysteria.[59] In Suetonius' description:

> On the day he passed away the temples were stoned and the altars of the gods thrown down, while some flung their household gods into the street and cast out their newborn children. Even barbarian peoples, so they say, who were engaged in war with us or with one another, unanimously consented to a truce, as if all in common had suffered a domestic tragedy. It is said that some princes put off their beards and had their wives' heads shaved, as a token of the deepest mourning; that even the king of kings suspended his exercise at hunting and the banquets with his grandees, which among the Parthians is a sign of public mourning.[60]

Antonia, it seems, did not attend the cremation of Germanicus in Antioch. Agrippina brought her husband's ashes to Italy, early in January AD 20 according to Tacitus, or perhaps in mid-December AD 19 (see p. 38).[61] Nevertheless Antonia's participation in Germanicus' eastern mission, ignored by Tacitus, may explain why she was able to help avenge Piso's conspiracy – for which she received official thanks. It may also provide us with a further reason for distrusting the record that she took so little part in the funeral at Rome:

> I fail to discover, either in the historians or in the government

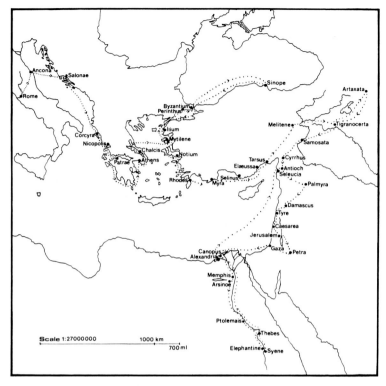

Figure 15 Approximate and partly assumed route of Germanicus'
eastern journey in AD 18–19.

Phase A: Rome via Athens and Mytilene to Sinope
Phase B: Sinope via Rhodes and Elaeussa to Artaxata
Phase C: Artaxata via Antioch and Petra to Alexandria
Phase D: Alexandria–Syene–Alexandria–Antioch

journals, that the prince's mother, Antonia, bore any striking part in the ceremonies.[62]

Tacitus thought that ill-health was the reason, or a spirit broken with
grief. Again, she may have been confined to the palace by Tiberius
and Livia who were abstaining from public appearances, giving the
false impression that they were equally distressed. The historian was
unaware of the real events. New epigraphic material, recently discovered in southern Spain, suggests that Antonia was active in Rome
during the funeral (see p. 39). In fact the inadequacy of Tacitus'
research on the subject of Antonia can be demonstrated further by

24

his persistent confusion of the two sisters of the same name.[63]

Antonia remained influential throughout Tiberius' reign. She maintained a remarkable court in Rome, supervising a circle of young foreign princes and princesses, which included members from the royal families of Judaea (Agrippa I), Commagene (Antiochus IV), Thrace (Pythodoris II and her brothers), Armenia (Tigranes V), Mauretania (Ptolemy) and many more. Even the Parthian 'king of kings' felt obliged to send his son Darius as a hostage to her household.[64] Her contribution to Roman politics in this respect was outstanding. The young 'hostages' became familiar with Roman culture, but above all Antonia's patronage gave the Imperial family an effective means of interfering in the internal affairs of these dynasties, so vital for the preservation of the borders of the Empire.[65]

In the last decade of Tiberius' reign Antonia's 'political' influence was at its greatest, especially after the death of Augustus' wife Livia in AD 29 made her the leading lady of the palace. Antonia now supervised her grandson Caligula, as well as her son Claudius who had previously been under the control of Livia, his grandmother.[66] Among people of high rank upon whose devotion she could rely were the wealthy consulars Lucius Vitellius and Valerius Asiaticus. The first, father of the future Emperor Vitellius, gained the consulship three times, while the second gained it twice.[67] Although the available sources do not indicate exactly how these men won Antonia's confidence and friendship, it must have been through the help they gave her in achieving her 'political' goals. Such goals would have been the promotion of the interests of male members of her family.

It was at about this time (AD 31) that Antonia uncovered the great conspiracy and saved the lives of her brother-in-law Tiberius and her grandson Caligula (see pp. 42, 91–5). The Jewish historian Josephus, our primary source for her involvement in this matter, is very explicit:

(Antonia) on her own had done a very great service to Tiberius. For a great conspiracy had been formed against him by his friend Sejanus, who at that time held the greatest power because he was prefect of the praetorian cohorts. Most of the senators and freedmen joined him, the army was bribed, and so the conspiracy made great progress. Indeed, Sejanus would have succeeded if

25

Antonia had not shown more craft in her bold move than Sejanus did in his villainy. For when she was informed of the plot against Tiberius, she wrote him a full account of it and, entrusting the letter to Pallas, the most trustworthy of her slaves, sent it to Tiberius at Capri. Tiberius, being informed, put Sejanus and his fellow-conspirators to death. As for Antonia, whom he had previously held in high regard, he now valued her even more and put full confidence in her.[68]

Sejanus was an able opportunist who succeeded in reaching the top of an equestrian career to become *praefectus praetorio*.[69] Remembering the words of the outspoken writer Cremutius Cordus, who once said of him that 'he had not only been set on our backs but had actually climbed there', the philosopher Seneca gives us a glimpse of his true character:

> Sejanus was decreed a statue which was to be placed in the theatre of Pompey, which Caesar was restoring after a fire; Cordus cried out: 'Now the theatre is really destroyed!' Should it not make one burst with rage that Sejanus be set over the ashes of Gnaeus Pompeius, that a treacherous soldier be consecrated in the building of the greatest general? Consecrated too was his signature, and the ravening dogs, vicious to all, whom he kept as his personal pets by feeding them on human blood, began to bay all around Cordus, who was already trapped.[70]

A little before his fall Sejanus was further elevated to the position of consul, granted proconsular powers (*imperium proconsulare*; in Greek *anthypatikê exousia*) and even had hopes of receiving those of tribune of the people (*tribunicia potestas*; in Greek *dêmarchikê exousia*).[71] His plans seem to have been to strike at the principate, by eliminating Caligula, one of the principal Imperial candidates, and, inevitably, by destroying Tiberius himself.[72] Eight years earlier (14 September AD 23), he had taken a similar action against the younger Drusus, the son of Tiberius, the previous candidate. As was subsequently revealed by Sejanus' wife Apicata and other witnesses, he had killed Drusus by poisoning him after seducing his wife Livilla, the daughter of Antonia.[73] On 31 October AD 31, Sejanus was executed by the decision of the Senate, informed by a letter from Tiberius after he had received Antonia's warning in Capri, where he then resided.[74] His body was hurled down the

Figure 16 The Castra Praetoria on the reverse of a gold aureus of
Claudius minted in Rome (AD 41–2), showing a soldier on guard. The
  building was constructed in AD 21–3 at the instigation of Sejanus.

Gemonian Stairway (*Scalae Gemoniae*) leading from the Capitol
to the Roman Forum, where it was abused for three days by the
rabble and later thrown into the Tiber. The satirist Juvenal put
it thus:

> The head of the people's darling glows red-hot, great
>   Sejanus
> Crackles and melts. That face only yesterday ranked
> Second in all the world. Now it's so much scrap-metal,
> To be turned into jugs and basins, frying-pans, chamber-
>   pots.
> Hang wreaths on your doors, lead a big white sacrificial
> Bull to the Capitol! They're dragging Sejanus along
> By a hook, in public. Everyone cheers. 'Just look at that
> Ugly stuck-up face', they say. 'Believe me, I never
> Cared for the fellow.'[75]

   On the accession of Caligula in AD 37, Antonia's importance as
the first lady of the Empire was further highlighted. She was
now raised to all positions previously held by Livia: granted the
title 'Augusta', appointed priestess of Augustus and offered the
privileges of the Vestal Virgins.[76] Although there has been some
doubt about whether the title 'Augusta' was used during her

27

lifetime, it was certainly employed in the reign of Caligula (see pp. 46, 98).[77] However, the favour shown to her at first lasted only a few weeks. Caligula soon began to reject her advice, refuse her private audience and even threaten her life. She knew his character and the extremes he could go to: she had herself caught him, while he was still a minor, violating his sister Drusilla.[78] On 1 May AD 37, at the age of seventy-two, the great lady, preferring to die with dignity, was driven to suicide. Some believed that in fact she was poisoned by Caligula. He was seen observing her cremation from his dining-room with indifference.[79] We have no record of where her ashes were put, but Caligula probably allowed them to be deposited in the Mausoleum of Augustus, where he had previously put those of his mother, the elder Agrippina.[80] If so, Antonia's last dwelling was highly appropriate since it was also shared by her eternal husband Drusus.

Antonia was celebrated for her beauty and virtue.[81] She was looked upon, among others, as the goddess Venus (see p. 50) and was represented in particular as Venus the Ancestress (*Genetrix*), the mother of the Roman people and the Imperial family (see p. 116). Her gentle nature became proverbial: Pliny relates that she was not even accustomed to spit! Her generosity was illustrated when she lent a large amount of money to the troubled young Agrippa I and later offered material comfort to him while he was imprisoned by Tiberius.[82] On another occasion, for his own protection, she forbade her son Claudius to give a frank account of the Empire's early years, when in his youth he was encouraged by Livy to write a chronicle. This prohibition made him realise the political danger of telling the truth about the period after the death of Julius Caesar (that is, the years of Augustus' rise to power), and he had to shift his narrative to later times where he made a fresh start at the end of the Civil War – thus producing only two books for the early history but forty-one for the later.[83]

However, although in other respects Antonia's reputation was that of a wise and courteous woman, some spiteful remarks about Claudius are attributed to her. She is said to have called him 'a monster of a man, not finished but merely begun by Mother Nature' and when anyone appeared stupid enough she declared that he was 'a bigger fool than Claudius'. Perhaps Augustus' contemptuous opinion of her son, only thinly disguised in his

Figure 17 A *carpentum*, the highly ornamented two-wheeled carriage drawn by two mules and used by the powerful women of Rome. The type here is funerary, reconstructed from representations on coins of the elder Agrippina and Antonia.

OSSA
AGRIPPINAE M AGRIPPA
DIVI AVG N EPTIS VXORIS
GERMANICI CAESARIS
MATRIS C CAESARIS AVG
GERMANICI PRINCIPIS

Figure 18 The tombstone of the elder Agrippina, the wife of Germanicus and mother of Caligula, referring to her 'bones' which Caligula placed in the Mausoleum of Augustus.

letters to Livia, suggesting that Antonia might read them, may have increased her frustration with Claudius.[84] At all events, Antonia apparently had her other side, as a harsh woman and strict mother. So rigid were her moral standards that when her own daughter, Livilla, inexcusably fell for Sejanus, who had pretended to be in love with her, Antonia's sense of duty made her starve Livilla to death. In Antonia's eyes, Livilla, a mature woman and mother of Tiberius' grandchildren, had defiled herself and her family with a common adulterer, exchanging her honourable and present hopes for dishonourable and uncertain ones.[85]

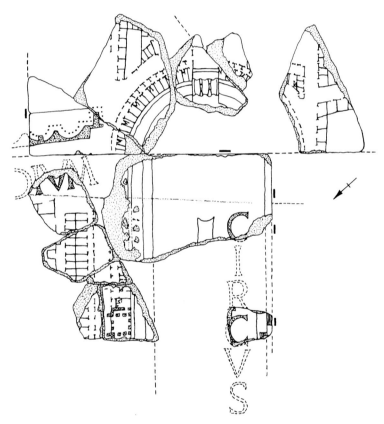

Figure 19 Plan of the Circus Maximus as seen in the surviving fragments of the famous marble map of Rome (Forma Urbis) dated to the third century AD.

When Claudius assumed power in AD 41 he immediately arranged public offerings to the shade of his mother. He reconferred on her posthumously the title 'Augusta' and introduced games on her birthday, at which her portrait was borne on a carriage in the Circus Maximus.[86] A large number of Antonia's inscriptions, coins, sculptures and luxury objects come from this time in which Claudian family propaganda was generated (see pp. 131–2). Roman coins depict her as Ceres, the patron goddess of harvest and marriage, and proclaim her 'Priestess of the Divine Augustus' (*sacerdos divi Augusti*) or 'Constancy of Augustus' (*Constantiae Augusti*). On Greek coins she is named 'Antonia Sebaste' (that is, 'Venerable'), which means 'Augusta' (see p. 98). Our sources do not mention any posthumous formal consecration in Rome, but this may have taken place, for a temple dedicated to her (apparently as *Diva Augusta*, that is, Goddess Augusta) seems to have been built there by Claudius (see p. 119). Shrines associated with her are known in various places, including Naples and Athens, where a joint cult of Antonia and her husband Drusus had already been established.[87] Further, Antonia had been worshipped in various cities of the Empire (such as Lepcis Magna) under the spectrum of the Imperial Cult, the wider cult of the Emperor and his family (see pp. 45, 49, 110, 121). Lastly, it is worth noting that a basilica in Rome had earlier been dedicated to Antonia and her sister.[88]

Among the members of Antonia's household staff we should mention M. Antonius Pallas, her famous freedman, who was killed by Nero for his massive wealth. His origins seem to have been in Greece, perhaps in Arcadia, the mountainous area of central Peloponnese, because when he was offered public thanks by the Senate, he was complimented on his descent from the royal family of that region.[89] Evander, the mythical king of Arcadia, had named his son Pallas after an ancestor.[90] The zenith of Pallas' career occurred at the end of Claudius' reign when he accepted praetorian insignia, while haughtily refusing fifteen million sesterces. These facts were engraved on a bronze tablet which was affixed to the mailed statue of the deified Julius Caesar. They were also inscribed on Pallas' tombstone which was read and criticised half a century later by the younger Pliny:

'To him the Senate decreed in return for his loyal services to his patrons (Antonia and Claudius), the insignia of a

Figure 20 A lead water-pipe mentioning Antonia Caenis, unearthed on
her estate, and now kept at the Museo Nazionale Romano.

praetor, and the sum of fifteen million sesterces, but he
thought fit to accept the distinction only' . . . this inscription more than anything makes me realise what a ridicu-
lous farce it is when they (such honours) can be thrown
away on such dirt and filth, and that rascal could presume
to accept and refuse them . . . such people will think they
have really achieved something when their lucky chance
has brought them no more than ridicule.[91]

Pallas was the slave who was sent to Tiberius in Capri with the
crucial letter accusing Sejanus mentioned earlier. Antonia had
dictated this letter to her trustworthy freedwoman Antonia
Caenis, later famed as the mistress of the Emperor Vespasian.[92]
The Greek historian Dio relates how after completing her writing task she was ordered by Antonia to erase the message
entirely, for safety reasons. Caenis replied:

It is useless, mistress, for you to give this command; for not
only all this but also whatever else you dictate to me I
always carry in my mind and it can never be erased.[93]

The notorious brother of Pallas, Ti. Claudius (erroneously
known as M. Antonius) Felix, who married three princesses
(perhaps by deceiving them with the story of his royal descent!),
became procurator of Judaea and tried the Apostle Paul, should
no longer be regarded as a freedman of Antonia; he was freed
by Claudius.[94] Josephus mentions Protos, a rich freedman
whom Antonia inherited from her friend Berenice I of Judaea,
the mother of Agrippa I. He also refers to Alexander the
Alabarch (that is, a customs official) of Alexandria (brother of
the Jewish philosopher Philo) who served as procurator, pre-

sumably of her Egyptian estates. Antonius Hiberus, a descendant of another of her freedmen, became consul in AD 133.[95]

Many members of Antonia's household are also known from inscriptions, including several doctors: Celadus, Pindarus, Hieron.[96] The Greek eclectic physician and philosopher Galen refers to the eye ointment prescribed by Florus (another of Antonia's doctors) after her eyes had been singed by the harmful 'remedies' of other practitioners. The composition of this ointment, apart from being expensive to produce, may have been unusual even for Antonia's time and its preparation seems to have required some skill:

> 47 drachmas of acacia; 47 drachmas of dried roses; 47 drachmas of lotus honey; 24 drachmas of cyprus-tree powder; 2 drachmas of mandrake apples; 24 drachmas of crocus; 6 drachmas of opium; 2 small cups of hyoscyamine seeds, or as much as 24 drachmas; 4 drachmas of myrrh; 4 drachmas of burned and washed copper; 40 drachmas of gum; 3 glasses of white wine and as much rain-water. Having mixed the wine with the water add the roses, the lotus honey, the hyoscyamine seeds and the mandrake apples [etc. and then boil and cool?]. But the crust must remain wet for three to five days. Afterwards, having poured the fluid out, use it for the preparation of the medicine and when this is transformed test it out.[97]

Scribonius Largus, the Roman physician who accompanied Claudius on his British campaign, mentions a salve often used by Antonia for her colds. While it was intended for severe flu and aching tendons, it had the ability when smeared on to warm up the chilled body and prevent the limbs from catching cold.[98]

It has been suggested that the Greek poet Thallus may have been a freedman of Antonia and, together with Honestus, another poet and a compatriot, may have resided in her famous Campanian villa. Pliny, by the way, records the extraordinary fact that it was in a fishpond there that she kept her favourite lamprey adorned with earrings. After her death it passed, like her house in Rome, to Claudius (perhaps via Caligula) and then to the younger Agrippina, the mother of Nero.[99]

Now we have set Antonia's life in its historical context we can examine more closely her unwritten history from information derived from non-literary and archaeological material.

2

THE INSCRIPTIONS OF ANTONIA

Archaeology is constantly adding to our knowledge of the past with a plethora of different types of evidence. One important category is inscribed materials. The continuing discovery of inscriptions is the best assurance we have that our understanding of the ancient world will never be static. Through writings on stone, bronze, pottery and other durable materials, in addition to papyri and coins, we have direct access to various aspects of antiquity. Equipped with such primary, or 'documentary', evidence, the modern historian can verify, supplement, or correct the written record.[1] If our information had depended on the literary sources, we should not have been able to write the life of Antonia with any confidence.

According to my estimate there are at least sixty-one inscriptions bearing on the history of Antonia, nineteen directly and forty-two indirectly (see Registers A and B). By 'direct' inscriptions I mean those commemorating Antonia exclusively,[2] as against 'indirect' inscriptions which commemorate others but make mention of her in passing.

DIRECT

Of the direct inscriptions eleven are in Latin (A.1–3, 8–11, 13, 14, 16, 19), seven in Greek (A.4–6, 12, 15, 17, 18) and one in Neo-Punic (A.7). Thirteen are apparently 'portrait-inscriptions' (A.1–7, 10, 12, 15–17, 19), six belonging to 'portrait groups' (A.1, 2, 7, 10, 17, 19).[3] The remaining six are a building dedication (A.18), and fragments of *Senatus Consulta* (A.8, 9) and *Fasti* and *Acta* (A.11, 13, 14).

The direct inscriptions were found over a wide area (see fig. 109,

p. 167). Of those in Latin seven came from Italy: Rome (A.8, 13, 14, 19), Ostia (A 11), Marruvium (A.2) and Herculaneum (A.16); two from southern Spain: Ulia (A.1) and Siarum (A.9); one from southern France: Cemenelum (A.3); and one from Greece: Corinth (A.10). Of those in Greek, four came from Turkey: Aphrodisias (A.12, 18), Ilium (A.5) and Sardis (A.17); two from Greece: Helicon (A.15) and Lesbos (A.4); and one from North Africa: Ptolemais (A.6). The Neo-Punic inscription was also discovered in North Africa, at Lepcis Magna (A.7).

With regard to epithets and titles ascribed to Antonia, the earliest direct inscription (*c.* 12 BC) mentions her simply as 'daughter of Marcus' (*M(arci) F(ilia)* – A.1). Apart from the epigrams of Crinagoras (dated here to 18 BC, see p. 11) and, as we shall see, perhaps one or two indirect inscriptions (B.1, 2 – possibly dating before 18 BC), the text from Ulia (Montilla) in Spain is the earliest record of Antonia that has come down to us. Only once later is she referred to as 'daughter of Marcus and wife of Claudius Nero Drusus' (*M(arci) F(ilia) Cl[au(di) Neronis Drusi Ger(manici) uxor]* – A.3), for she is usually called 'wife of Drusus' (*[uxor] Drusi*; or *gynaika Drousou* – A.2, 4–6, 19). She is also variously given as 'niece of Augustus' (*adelphidê Sebastou* – A.5), 'mother of Germanicus, Claudius and Livia [= Livilla]' (*mêtera Germanikou, Klaudiou kai Leibias* – A.5), 'mother of Germanicus' (*mater Germanici Ca[esaris]*; or *'[m gr]m'nyqm* – A.8–9, 7) and 'mother of Claudius' (*matri Ti(berii) Claudi Caesaris*; or *[Klaudi]ou Kai[saros Se]basto[u . . . mêtera]* – A.16, 17, 19). She is acknowledged in Lesbos and Ilium as 'benefactress' (*euergetis* – A.4, 5) and in Ilium and Aphrodisias as 'goddess' (*thea* – A.5, 18). In AD 37 she is mentioned for the first time as 'Augusta' at Corinth (A.10) and in the following year at Rome (A.13). On inscriptions (apart from coins) we find her as 'priestess of the divine Augustus' (*sacerdos divi Augusti* – A.19) only in AD 51–2.

The direct inscriptions provide valuable information, particularly the fragments of the *Acta Arvalium* (A.13–14), the *Fasti Ostienses* (A.11) and the *Tabula Siarensis* (A.9). The first fragment of the 'Acts' of the Arval Brethren to mention her was found in 1867 in their sacred grove, on the Via Campana at the fifth milestone from Rome, and is dated to AD 38.[4] In this grove the ancient priestly brotherhood honoured Dea Dia, the corn-goddess, with a supreme festival in May during which some version of the old (and by then obscure) ritual-hymn the *Carmen*

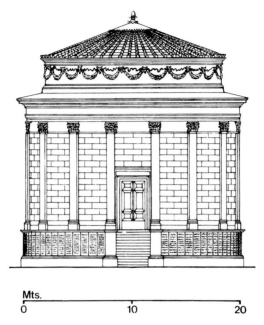

Mts.

0   10   20

Figure 21 A reconstruction of the round building next to the sacred grove of the Arval Brethren. This was probably the temple dedicated to Augustus, on the walls of which the brotherhood's acts were affixed.

Arvale may have been chanted. A round building discovered next to the site may have belonged to the Caesareum, the temple dedicated to Augustus and his family, which is often mentioned in the inscriptions found on the spot.[5] The Arval 'Acts' identify Antonia's birthday as 31 January. Before this discovery we knew only that she was born some time in 'midwinter'. A second fragment, a copy of the first, dating to AD 39 was found in 1884 on the Via dei Baullari, but it is badly preserved.[6]

Antonia is also mentioned in a part of the *Fasti* from Ostia, the city's calendar (or register of magistrates and other public records), found near the Forum in 1916. The day of her death is given as 1 May.[7] From this we learn that she lived only six weeks into the reign of Caligula, which commenced on 18 March AD 37, the day he was hailed Imperator by the Senate (*dies imperii*).[8] The short time needed to drive Antonia to suicide (if she did commit suicide), rouses our curiosity about the circumstances of her death.

In fact if we consider Caligula's movements during his first month, Antonia must have known him as emperor for an even shorter period. He arrived in Rome only in the night of 28 March (Tiberius' body was brought into the city on 29 March), to prepare for the funeral on 3 April. He then went off immediately to the islands near Campania, in the most unsuitable weather, to retrieve the ashes of his mother and brother.[9] His return to Rome can hardly have taken place in less than ten days, which brings us to the middle of April and leaves only two weeks before Antonia's death on 1 May.

However, as we have seen, the great lady was aware of her grandson's evil character and, after only two weeks under him, she decided to be out of the way before he had the pleasure of removing her. The breaking-point must have been the threat to her life,[10] which Caligula may have made on the last day of April. By way of parallel, we have the story of Lucius Arruntius, a prominent consular, who took his own life as soon as Tiberius fell sick: that is, at the beginning of March. He frankly declared:

> I cannot in my old age become the slave of a new master like him (Caligula).[11]

Of course, this presupposes that Arruntius knew that Caligula would succeed Tiberius. At this stage, it might not have been difficult to guess. Whether or not the story is entirely true, it helps explain the speed with which Antonia made her decision.

The remains of two bronze tablets discovered in 1982 near Siarum (close to Seville in southern Spain), a small town in Roman Baetica, and published under the name of *Tabula Siarensis*, are important documents for the early principate. They contain some of the senatorial decrees (*senatus consulta*) announcing the honours to be conferred on Germanicus officially distributed after his death to Roman and Latin communities throughout the Empire.[12] Details were previously known only from a summary in Tacitus and from remains of three other bronze tablets (one of which survives in the Vatican).[13] The first fragment of *Tabula Siarensis*, which concerns us here, has thirty-seven lines of text arranged in a single column and refers to Antonia twice (lines 7, 20). Its main theme is the erection of triumphal arches in memory of Germanicus.

In the first the Emperor Tiberius is invited to select from various honours put forward by the Senate in consultation with

Livia, the younger Drusus, Antonia Minor and apparently the elder Agrippina. Since this fragment is dated 16 December AD 19 and since it implies that Agrippina had just arrived at Rome from Syria (carrying the ashes of her loved one), Tacitus may be slightly incorrect in his estimate of a date for her return early in January AD 20. Other epigraphic evidence to be examined later will show that the mother of Germanicus, despite the opinion of Tacitus, seems to have joined her son in at least a part of his eastern mission. The historian is also ill-informed when he suggests that Antonia would not have contributed to the ceremonies of the funeral. He claims that there was no mention of her in the work of earlier writers, or in the *Acta Diurna*, the government's official journal (see p. 24). On the contrary, the senatorial decree for Germanicus' posthumous honours (which must have been reported in the *Acta Diurna*) shows that she was by no means neglected at this critical moment.[14]

The second mention of Antonia in the decree is at an equally

Figure 22 Fragment I of the bronze tablet from Siarum (*Tabula Siarensis*) in southern Spain.

significant point. It occurs during the description of the first monumental arch:

> It has pleased (the Senate) that a marble arch shall be erected in the Circus Flaminius at [public] expense, in the place where statues [have already been] dedicated to the Divine Augustus and to (the members of) the Augustan House by Gaius Norbanus Flaccus, along with gilded reliefs of the conquered nations and [with an inscription] on the front of the arch (stating) that the Senate and Roman People had dedicated this [marble] monument to the memory of Germanicus Caesar . . . {a long list follows – presumably also to be stated in the inscription – of the positions held by Germanicus, his achievements in wars and the honours received}. Above this arch a statue of Ger[manicus Caesar] shall be placed, (with him) in a triumphal chariot and at his sides shall be statues of his [father Drusus Germanicus], the natural brother of Tiberius Caesar Augustus, and of his mother Antonia [and of his wife Agrippina] and of his sister Livia (= Livilla) and of his brother Tiberius Germanicus (= Claudius) and of his sons and [daughters]. {Mainly following the restoration in Lebek 1987}

Two other arches were to be erected, both outside Italy, in two corners of the Roman world: on the mountain of Amanus in Syria, where Germanicus' last command was based, and on the banks of the Rhine, where the cenotaph (*tumulus*) of his father, the elder Drusus, was built after his death.[15] It should be added that Germanicus had already been celebrated (with his cousin the younger Drusus) by an arch on one side of the Temple of Mars the Avenger (*Ultor*) in the Forum of Augustus. This was dedicated in AD 19 when the news arrived that Germanicus had appointed Zeno to the throne of Armenia.[16] Thus the *Tabula Siarensis* not only illuminates Antonia's role in the preparation of the funeral, but provides new evidence that her statue was set on top of the Arch of Germanicus in the Circus Flaminius.[17] Of the general area around this race-course, or hippodrome, we shall say more later (pp. 53–5).

We gain further information about Antonia and the building of an arch from another inscription (A.19). Since it dates to AD 51–2, it is the latest to mention her directly. It was originally

Figure 23 The text which accompanied Antonia's statue on the Arch of Claudius, now in the Museo Capitolino.

placed on the Arch of Claudius, which bore statues that were accompanied by appropriate texts and had been ordered by the Senate to celebrate Claudius' conquest of Britain.[18] It was located on the ancient Via Lata (now the Via del Corso) and was used to carry the Aqua Virgo (constructed by Marcus Agrippa in 19 BC), one of the nine aqueducts of Rome at that time, across the street towards the centre of the Campus Martius, not far from the Circus Flaminius. Among surviving pieces belonging to this monument (ruined before the ninth century) one is notable: a fragment of the dedicatory inscription famous for its reference to the submission of 'the eleven kings of Britain'.[19] A similar

Figure 24 A reconstruction of the Arch of Claudius across the Aqueduct Virgo.

arch was erected in Gaul, because, according to Dio, it was from there that Claudius crossed to Britain, but also perhaps because the Emperor was born in Gaul (see p. 13).[20]

With the addition of Antonia's image to the Arch (or arches) of Claudius, the tradition of triumphal dedications for the Antonian-Claudian family seems to have come to an end. This tradition had begun at the time of the elder Drusus, whose 'marble arch adorned with trophies' was erected shortly after his death in 9 BC to commemorate his German victories. The arch stood on the Via Appia, possibly a little north of its junction with the Via Latina, but it is probably not the one seen today known as 'Arco di Druso'.[21] Coins of Claudius struck in gold and silver, dated to AD 41–2, show on the reverse a triumphal arch with the legend *De Germanis*. Although only a symbolic representation, it may well be the Arch of Drusus. Support for this identification may be gained from some undated Claudian coins of similar reverse type also struck in gold and silver and bearing on the obverse the head of Drusus. Claudius' father, together with Antonia, was honoured in AD 41, the probable date of these coins. This was the year of the victory against the German tribes the Chatti and Chauci which yielded Claudius the well-merited title of *imperator*.[22] The same kind of arch, ascribed here to Drusus, appears on later coins of Claudius but with the legend *De Britannis*, since by then the conquest of Britain had been achieved. This has given numismatists the false impression that the arch is that of Claudius. Yet these types all predate its

Figure 25 The arch (probably of Drusus) seen on the reverse of a brass sestertius of Claudius, minted in Rome in AD 41.

completion in AD 51–2. At best, therefore, they announce its planned construction along the traditional lines set by the Arch of Drusus and evidently those of Germanicus.[23]

The inscription from the valley of the Muses at Mount Helicon in Greece (A.15) is also of some consequence. It was found in 1889 at the village of Hagia Trias not far from Thespiae, one of the chief towns of ancient Boeotia, where visitors came to see Praxiteles' magnificent statue of Eros.[24] The text represents an epigram cut on the base of a statue of an 'Augusta' (*Sebastê*) and written by the Greek poet Honestus. Antonia is not named, but the content makes the attribution highly likely:

> Augusta, who can boast of two divine sceptred Caesars,
> set light to twin torches of Peace;
> fit company for the wise Heliconian Muses,
> a choir-mate of intellectual counsel, her genius saved the
>   whole world.
> By Honestus.

Cichorius was the first to suggest that this is a reference to the widow of Drusus and her contribution to the fall of Sejanus.[25] Nicols, in his attempt to dissociate Antonia entirely from the affair of Sejanus, had to reject this interpretation. But his reasons are weak. The reattribution of the Salus coin (as well as the Iustitia and Pietas coins) supports Cichorius (see pp. 90–4). Also, the papyrus mentioning the first estate of Pallas that we know of in Egypt, and dated to the time of Tiberius, might suggest that this freedman of Antonia earned the land for his part in the downfall of Sejanus (see p. 84). Further, Nicols is surely wrong to discount the clear testimony involving Antonia: that of Josephus (see p. 25).[26] Nevertheless Cichorius' identification of the 'two Caesars' mentioned by Honestus as Caligula and Tiberius Gemellus need not be correct; an alternative solution will be put forward later.

The inscription from Ulia in Roman Baetica was discovered built into the great doorway of the medieval castle at Montilla (A.1). Assuming that it belongs to a group of dedicatory inscriptions which are thought to be contemporaneous, it has been dated around 12 BC. Doubts have been thrown on the integrity of this group of stones, however. The text of Antonia may

therefore belong to a slightly earlier period. Even if it is only a
year or two older, it may support the hypothesis that she visited
this part of the Empire (see p. 13). Admittedly the inscription is
brief and, unlike those of Antonia from the East, contains
nothing to show that she was actually present. Yet the mere fact
that she was chosen for commemoration in the Western Empire
at such an early date requires some explanation – such as that
she took part in a tour made by Drusus in 14–13 BC when
Augustus was in Spain.[27]

The inscription from Thermis on the island of Lesbos, found
reused in the fountain next to a church (A.4), and the inscription from Ilium, the ancient Troy (Hissarlik), a round base
discovered in the Turkish cemetery of Halileli (A.5), strongly
imply that Antonia accompanied Germanicus on his mission in
AD 18. Both places are specifically named by Tacitus as being *en
route*.[28] The reference to her as 'benefactress' (*euergetis*) suggests
that she gave help to these communities, apparently during her
visit. The inscription from Ilium, commissioned by one Philo
son of Apollonius, a beneficiary of Antonia, is the longest direct
text about Antonia on stone that we know of and must be
translated here:

> To Antonia the
> niece of the divine
> Augustus, who became the wife
> of Drusus Claudius,
> the brother of the
> Emperor Tiberius Augustus,
> son of Augustus, (and) the mother
> of Germanicus Caesar
> and of Tiberius Claudius
> Germanicus
> and of Livia (= Livilla) the goddess Aphrodite
> Anchisias (= wife of Anchises, father of Aeneas),
> having provided the fullest and greatest
> principles of the most divine family.
> Philo, son of Apollonius,
> to his goddess and benefactress
> at his own expense.[29]

The assumption that she took part in what in this book has been

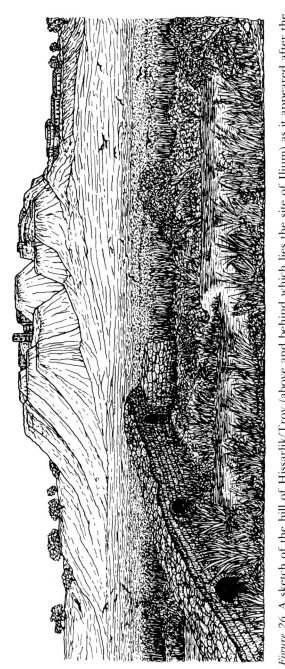

Figure 26 A sketch of the hill of Hissarlik/Troy (above and behind which lies the site of Ilium) as it appeared after the excavations of 1879. The bridge in the foreground is on the ancient Scamander, the houses and magazines in the background were those of Schliemann.

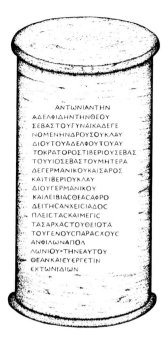

Figure 27 An imaginary reconstruction of the inscribed round base from Ilium, based on known descriptions and size.

ΑΝΤѠΝΙΑΝΤΗΝ
ΑΔΕΛΦΙΔΗΝΤΗΝΘΕΟΥ
ΣΕΒΑΣΤΟΥΓΥΝΑΙΚΑΔΕΓΕ
ΝΟΜΕΝΗΝΔΡΟΥΣΟΥΚΛΑΥ
ΔΙΟΥΤΟΥΑΔΕΛΦΟΥΤΟΥΑΥ
ΤΟΚΡΑΤΟΡΟΣΤΙΒΕΡΙΟΥΣΕΒΑΣ
ΤΟΥΥΙΟΣΕΒΑΣΤΟΥΜΗΤΕΡΑ
ΔΕΓΕΡΜΑΝΙΚΟΥΚΑΙΣΑΡΟΣ
ΚΑΙΤΙΒΕΡΙΟΥΚΛΑΥ
ΔΙΟΥΓΕΡΜΑΝΙΚΟΥ
ΚΑΙΛΕΙΒΙΑΣΘΕΑΣΑΦΡΟ
ΔΕΙΤΗΣΑΝΧΕΙΣΙΔΔΟΣ
ΠΛΕΙΣΤΑΣΚΑΙΜΕΓΙΣ
ΤΑΣΑΡΧΑΣΤΟΥΘΕΙΟΤΑ
ΤΟΥΓΕΝΟΥΣΠΑΡΑΣΧΟΥΣ
ΑΝΦΙΛѠΝΑΠΟΛ
ΛѠΝΙΟΥ•ΤΗΝΕΑΥΤΟΥ
ΘΕΑΝΚΑΙΕΥΕΡΓΕΤΙΝ
ΕΚΤѠΝΙΔΙѠΝ

allegorically called the 'exodus' of the Antonian–Claudian family is supported to some extent by other evidence: an indirect text from Athens (B.15), a coin from Clazomenae (F.1) and even sculpture, carved precious stones and decorated silver plate. All these will be investigated later.

Of about the same date, and perhaps reflecting the general atmosphere created by this journey, are two direct inscriptions from Ptolemais in Roman Cyrenaica and Lepcis Magna in Roman Africa (now both Libya).[30] The first (A.6) was noticed early in the nineteenth century incorporated in the wall of an Arab fortress (Kasr-el-Askar), but it is very fragmentary. The second (A.7) was unearthed in 1934 in the Old Forum of the sumptuous city of Lepcis and is the only extant record of Antonia in a language other than Latin or Greek.[31] Written in Neo-Punic, it is a 'group portrait-dedication' to Rome and Augustus, Tiberius, Julia Augusta (Livia), Germanicus, Drusus Caesar, the elder Agrippina, Livilla, Antonia Minor ('*nṭ'ny*') and Vipsania Agrippina (see p. 110). This inscription was clearly connected with the Imperial Cult which had penetrated Lepcis Magna as early as *c.* AD 18.[32]

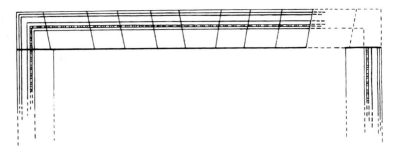

Figure 28 A reconstruction of the Monumental Gate (Porta) of the Temple of Rome and Augustus in the Old Forum at Lepcis Magna. The Neo-Punic inscription was cut on the upper stone blocks.

Two similar dedications to Antonia may be dated to the time immediately after Sejanus' fall. It was then that Antonia's vital services to the throne had become an open secret. During the panegyric climax that followed resolution of the crisis, many new inscriptions honouring her and Tiberius would have been generated by grateful followers of the Imperial regime in towns inside and outside Italy.[33] The first (A.2), from Marruvium, the chief town of the land of the Marsi, was discovered in 1752 close to San Benedetto.The second (A.3), an extremely fragmentary text, from Cemenelum (Cimiez), the capital of the small Roman province of Alpes Maritimae, was excavated in 1963 inside the second hot room (*caldarium*) of the city's North Baths (see p. 122).[34]

Similarly, a slightly later wave of texts for Antonia, which would have been written after the enthronement of Caligula and Antonia's elevation to the position of Augusta, is represented by the example from Corinth (A.10). This is a slab of white marble discovered in 1915 east of the Agora at the south of the Julian Basilica, and its date can be calculated with a measure of accuracy. It is dedicated to the young Tiberius Gemellus (called here 'Tiberius Caesar') and to Antonia. Now, since Gemellus was adopted by Caligula at the very beginning of his reign (to be put out of the way a little later) and since Antonia died within six weeks of her grandson's accession, the inscription probably dates to April AD 37. Coins struck at Corinth under Caligula (F.6) commemorate Antonia as 'Augusta', as this text does.[35]

The remaining direct inscriptions are probably products of the early reign of Claudius. One from Herculaneum (A.16), the

Figure 29 The inscription from Corinth.

Campanian town destroyed with Pompeii by the eruption of Vesuvius in AD 79, was found in 1731. It is on the base of a statue raised by one L. Mammius Maximus, no doubt another beneficiary of Antonia and perhaps remotely related to L. Mammius Pollio, the consul designate in AD 49.[36] The proximity to this place of her villa at Bacoli (if she did not possess a villa even closer) could explain her popularity in the region (see p. 154). A further inscription from Sardis (A.17), the capital of Lydia and one of the 'Seven Churches' of the Apocalypse, was recovered in 1910 on the north side of the temple of Artemis. There may be an earlier connection between Antonia and this city through her journey with Germanicus in the East, whether or not she had physically been to Sardis. Hanfmann, on the basis of an inscription and a coin, thinks that the 'ill-starred prince' could have come here some time before AD 17. But if we consider the schedule of Germanicus at the beginning of Tiberius' reign, this seems unlikely. The right time for such a visit, especially since the family 'brought relief' to the provinces they passed through,

Figure 30 The inscription from Sardis.

Figure 31 An anniversary of the Asia Minor Earthquake Relief, as commemorated on the reverse of a brass sestertius of Tiberius minted in Rome some time after AD 22/3, possibly in AD 27.

would be AD 18, immediately after the great earthquake which shook Lydia with results comparable to a biblical catastrophe.[37] In the narrative of Tacitus:

> twelve important cities of Asia collapsed in an earthquake, the time being night, so that the havoc was the less foreseen and more devastating. Even the usual resource in these catastrophes, a rush to open ground, was unavailing, as the fugitives were swallowed up in yawning chasms. Accounts are given of huge mountains sinking, of former plains seen heaved aloft, of fires flashing out amid the ruin. As the disaster fell heaviest on the Sardians, it brought them the largest measure of sympathy, the Caesar promising ten million sesterces, and remitting for five years their payments to the national and imperial exchequers. The Magnesians of Sipylus were ranked second in the extent of their losses and their indemnity. In the case of the Temnians, Philadelphenes, Aegeates, Apollonideans, the so-called Mostenians and Hyrcanian Macedonians, and the cities of Hierocaesarea, Myrina, Cyme and Tmolus, it was decided to exempt them from tribute for the same term.[38]

Of the twelve cities mentioned as badly hit only Myrina and

Cyme, in the area of Aeolis, were on the coast. Since both lie opposite the island of Lesbos we can assume with some confidence that they at least were visited by Germanicus and his group. Sardis is located quite a distance inland, and it would have been difficult, though not impossible, to reach it on the same occasion, unless of course a special visit was arranged. The centre of the upheaval happened to be the capital of the region, which was therefore in need of considerable help and encouragement.

Finally the two inscriptions discovered at Aphrodisias in Caria (Kehre in Turkey), an important nucleus of the Imperial Cult in Asia Minor, particularly in the Julio-Claudian period, seem also to be of Caligulan/Claudian date.[39] Aphrodite, the patron goddess, was the mythical mother of Aeneas, whose descendants had founded Rome and from whom Augustus and his successors claimed to have sprung. The first inscription (A.12), a small marble statue base, was found in the southern portico of a building-complex recently excavated and identified as the Sebasteion, the temple dedicated to the early emperors and Aphrodite. The dedicator, one Hermias, uses a formula which strongly suggests that he was a priest of the cult of Antonia. According to Reynolds we are not compelled to believe this, because parallels may not exist. Yet in the direct inscription from Ilium (A.5), two indirect ones from Athens (B.15, 38), a coin from Clazomenae (F.1) and possibly a papyrus from Egypt (C.12), parallels can be found, and we shall look at them later. Thus we are forced to entertain the idea that, apart from being worshipped under the umbrella of the Imperial Cult, Antonia may have possessed her own sanctuary at Aphrodisias and a priest who administered it.[40]

The institution of such a cult is compatible with the second inscription (A.18) as interpreted here. This also comes from the southern portico of the Sebasteion and was inscribed on an architrave belonging to a major rebuilding phase dating from the time of Claudius. Although damaged at a critical point, it does inform us of the person largely responsible for the work, one Tiberius Claudius Diogenes, who evidently gained Roman citizenship under Claudius. The dedication is made to Aphrodite, to an uncertain divine Augusta who seems to personify the goddess, to Claudius and to the citizens. Reynolds feels that Livia would suit the 'Augusta' in question; but in such a

Figure 32 The dedication of Hermias from Aphrodisias.

context it is more likely to be Antonia.[41] At the time she was the deified mother of the reigning Emperor, the real 'mother of Rome' (in line with Aphrodite the mythical mother of Aeneas), who had, as the text from Ilium said, 'provided the fullest and greatest principles of the Imperial family' (if this translation is accepted). She was the one whose beauty equalled that of the goddess whom she often represented in art (see p. 116). Livia was not famous for such qualities, and she usually personified the goddesses Hera or Demeter. Before Antonia only Julia, the daughter of Augustus, seems to have been called Aphrodite. Similarly, Livilla, Antonia's daughter, as though she had inherited the title from her mother, was identified with the same goddess and became in her own right 'a sovereign beauty'.[42]

Whether or not the Antonian-Claudian family visited Aphrodisias in AD 18 is an open question. As with Sardis, its distance from the coast would have required a lengthy interruption in the long sea-voyage. Germanicus, however, did search for religious centres at which he could pay his respects, even though the only clear example is that he went from Notium to the grove of Apollo at Claros, about two miles inland:

> (he) anchored off Colophon, in order to consult the oracle of the Clarian Apollo. Here it is not a prophetess, as at Delphi, but a male priest, chosen out of a restricted number of families, and in most cases imported from Miletus, who hears the number and the names of the consultants, but no more, and then descends into a cavern, swallows a draught of water from a mysterious spring, and – though

50

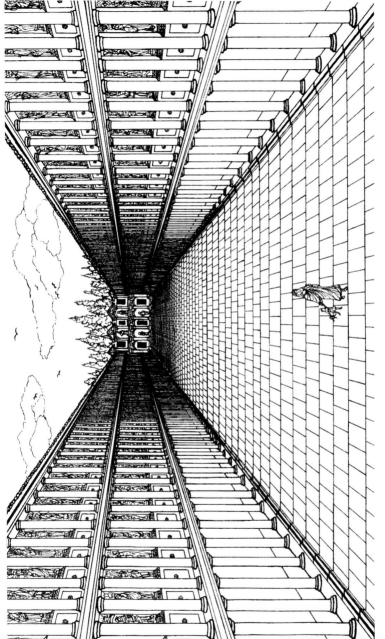

Figure 33 A reconstruction of the Sebasteion at Aphrodisias.

ignorant generally of writing and of metre – delivers his response in set verses dealing with the subject each enquirer has in mind. Rumour said that he had predicted to Germanicus his hastening fate, though in the equivocal terms which oracles affect.[43]

Germanicus also consulted the oracle of Apis at Memphis in Egypt. There, every twenty-five years or so, a young bull replaced an old one and became an object of worship, after having being led into the city and conducted to a sacred chamber by a hundred priests. This sacred bull, it was thought, foretold events by manifest signs:

> some of those who approach him he evidently rejects by unfavourable signs, as once he turned away from Caesar Germanicus when he offered him food, and thus prophesied what soon after came to pass.[44]

According to Magie Germanicus reached Alabanda in Caria, which is half-way from the coast to Aphrodisias, as well as Eumeneia of Phrygia, far beyond, in the interior of Asia Minor.[45] If so the city of Venus/Aphrodite might also have been visited.

INDIRECT

Thirty-eight of the indirect inscriptions (B.1–14, 16–33, 35, 37, 39–42) are in Latin, three in Greek (B.15, 36, 38) and one is bilingual (B.34, Latin–Greek). Except for the graffiti from Pausilypon in Campania (B.39–41), all Latin inscriptions are epitaphs, and except for one from Cirta in North Africa (B.37), all were found in Rome. Two of the Greek examples came from Athens, one a 'portrait-inscription' (B.38), the other inscribed on a theatre seat (B.15), and a third, a building dedication, from Naples (B.36). The bilingual example, an epitaph (B.34), is also from Athens.

As for epithets and titles, one inscription (B.1) which may date to before Antonia's marriage (that is, before 18 BC) calls her 'minor', one (B.15) which seems to date *c.* AD 18–37 calls her 'goddess' (*thea*), and eight (B.35–42) dating after AD 37 call her 'Augusta' or 'Sebaste'. All other indirect texts might in theory date to any period of her life if they name her simply 'Antonia', or after marriage if they refer to her as 'wife of Drusus' ([*uxor*] *Drusi*). Though it is generally true that inscriptions mentioning the 'wife of Drusus' probably date to after 9 BC (the death of Drusus) and before AD 37 (Antonia's acquisition of the title 'Augusta' and her death), most of them may belong to the last ten years of Tiberius' reign, when Antonia kept the most important household in Rome.

A unique document bearing on the history of Antonia is the inscription found in Rome (B.2) in the area between the Via Appia and the Via Latina:

> Caius Portumius (*sic*) Helenus,
> freedman of Caius,
> (his ashes are placed here by)
> Calpurnia Anapauma,
> jester in the basilica
> of the two Antonias.[46]

There seems to be a minor error in this text in the transcription of the name of Helenus' patron, which should have been 'Postumius' rather than 'Portumius'. A Roman senator called Quintus Postumius is known to have been put to death on the orders of Mark Antony in 31 BC, but a connection cannot easily be surmised.[47] The inscription seems to have come from a burial ground mainly belonging to members of the Imperial household. Calpurnia Anapauma, who set up the epitaph (possibly the girlfriend of Helenus), was employed as a jester (*nugari*) in the basilica of the two Antonias.[48]

Now, the construction of this building surely dates to earlier times, perhaps when Antonia and her sister were young and still living together, that is, before 18 BC. It may have been erected as a compliment to Octavia, their mother. The Porticus Octaviae, a rectangular colonnaded portico adjoining the Theatre of Marcellus and enclosing the Temples of Jupiter the Stayer (*Stator*) and Juno, was dedicated to Octavia by her brother Augustus before 23 BC.[49] Hence the basilica may date as early, Antonia being less than thirteen and her sister less than sixteen. On the other hand, the basilica may have been dedicated to the 'two Antonias' by Octavia herself. We know that she built a library in memory of her son Marcus Marcellus in the Porticus Octaviae, which also enclosed a senate-house (*curia*) and a school (*schola*) or schools (*scholae*).[50] Consequently, the basilica may have been located close by the portico in the vicinity of the Circus

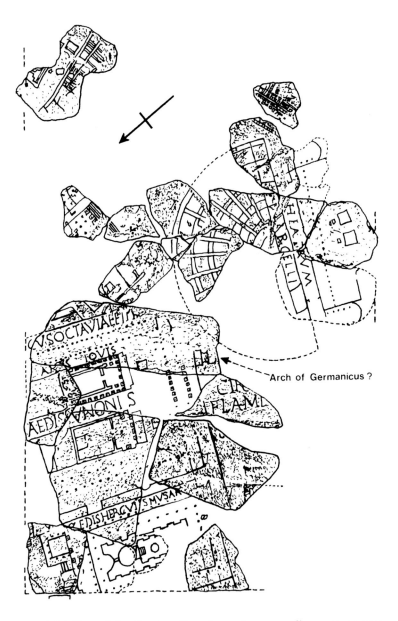

Arch of Germanicus ?

Figure 34 Plan of the Porticus Octaviae and surrounding area, as seen in the surviving fragments of Forma Urbis (noted is the possible location of the Arch of Germanicus).

54

Flaminius. That this building has yet to be identified may be because the Forma Urbis, the startling Severan marble map of Rome (at the beginning of the third century AD), is very fragmentary around this area.[51]

The inscription from Athens found in the Theatre of Dionysus under the Acropolis (B.15) was cut on a stone seat (*cuneus primus dexter, ordo III*) reserved for the 'Priestess' of the 'Goddess Antonia'. Women commonly attended productions of the highly acclaimed Greek tragedies and comedies; special seats in this theatre were assigned to priestesses but perhaps also to women who had in some way earned the gratitude of the people.[52] The inscription's date seems to be in the reign of Tiberius, in the earlier rather than the later half, and it implies that a kind of a shrine, requiring a priestess, was dedicated to Antonia in Athens. In fact, as postulated by Graindor, a cult of Drusus and his wife had been established there from an earlier period.[53] When Antonia was later proclaimed Augusta, we hear of her 'high priest' (*archiereus*), Tiberius Claudius Novius, the son of Phileinos, whose inscription (B.38) was also discovered on the Athenian Acropolis:

> The council of the Areopagus and
> the council of the six-hundred
> and the people (honoured) Tiberius Claudius
> Novius, son of Phileinos,
> general of the hoplites
> for the fourth time and priest of the Delian
> Apollo for life and president
> of the great Augustan Panathenaea
> and the Augustan Caesarea
> and high priest of Antonia
> Augusta, friend of Caesar and
> friend of his country, for his virtue.
> During the time of the priestess Junia Megiste,
> wife of Zeno from Sunium.
> Epagathus, son of Aristodemus from Thriasia
> made it.[54]

The dating of this text is also interesting. We know that Novius became general or *stratêgos* for the 'eighth' time in AD 61. Had he taken up this annual office in consecutive years, his 'fourth'

Figure 35 The Theatre of Dionysus in Athens.

Figure 36 The inscription of Novius from the Acropolis at Athens.

56

appointment would have been in 57, under Nero. But this is contradicted by other epigraphic evidence referring to him as *stratêgos* for the 'fourth' time while Claudius was still in power; that is, in or before 54. We also know that his 'first' tenure occurred in the year of the games in honour of Claudius, probably those held on the Emperor's return from Britain in 44; that is, Novius would have been made general for the 'fourth' time at the earliest in 47. Therefore the inscription in question appears to date between AD 47 and 54.[55]

The information provided by both these indirect Athenian texts – the anonymous priestess of Antonia and her high priest Novius – can now be correlated with what we learn from the direct inscription from Aphrodisias (A.12), already examined. Hermias would have been the priest of Antonia's cult at 'the city of Venus'. Further, the reference to Antonia as 'goddess' at Ilium (A.5) and, as we shall see, at Clazomenae (F.1) and perhaps Egypt (C.12) may imply that her cult also existed in those places. The extent of her veneration in the East could thus be assumed to have been considerable, though it is difficult at present to understand its exact relationship to the wider Imperial Cult.

In the West we hear of no personal priests of Antonia but – to say nothing of her alleged temple in Rome (see p. 119) – a contemporary shrine of some kind (B.36) was dedicated to her in Naples.[56] Two of her freedmen (?) or functionaries were responsible for its construction: Paneros and Sibaris, perhaps a married couple. Of course, whether the cult at Naples was connected with Antonia's 'guardian spirit' (*iuno*) while she was alive, or was her posthumous cult of 'Goddess Augusta' (*Diva Augusta* – if such existed under Claudius), we have no way of knowing. The latter would be the equivalent of the eastern cult of Antonia, but with the major difference that her consecration was accepted in the East during her lifetime.

The latest indirect inscription (B.42) dates to *c.* AD 73–4 when Dio records the death of Antonia Caenis, an exotic product of the Julio-Claudian era who became the mistress of the Flavian Emperor Vespasian. She was the freedwoman and secretary (*a manu*) of Antonia Augusta, whom Antonia used when writing to Tiberius about Sejanus (see p. 32).[57] This funerary text, inscribed on a great marble altar found close to the Porta Pia in Rome, was erected to the memory of their patroness by Aglaus, a freedman of Caenis, and his children:

> To the spirits of the departed,
> Antonia Caenis
> freedwoman of the Augusta.
> Excellent patroness.
> Aglaus (her) freedman with Aglaus
> and Glene and Aglais
> his children.

The erection of the altar precisely on this location was not coincidental. Major property of Caenis (including her estate) has been reported in an area opposite Porta Pia, where the Villa Patrizi used to be located and where impressive baths that took the name of Caenis (*Balineum Caenidianum*) were established later.[58]

The majority of the indirect texts concern members of Antonia's city domestic staff (*familia urbana*) and were set up to honour the dead. Most were cut on the small marble slabs labelling the urns which were placed in niches arranged in

Figure 37 The inscribed altar of Caenis, now in the Bardini collection at Florence.

columbaria. These 'dove-cotes' or burial chambers were financed by funerary societies formed among slaves in large households, with their masters' support.[59] According to my estimate, from inscriptions alone we know of at least twelve of Antonia's freedmen and freedwomen and over thirty of her slaves and slave-girls. For many of them the information includes the type of work they performed in the household.

As far as administration is concerned, the head of the financial sector (and in fact of the entire working body) was the steward (*dispensator*), a position held at that time by Laphirus (B.31); one of his assistants (*vicarius*) being Celadus (B.4).[60] The accountant (*tabularius*) was Optatus (B.24) and one of his clerical assistants (*adiutor tabularii*) could have been M. Antonius Ianuarius (B.37) from Cirta in Numidia (North Africa) who became a freedman. His inscription, cut on a burial chest, has been recently assigned by Weaver, quite rightly, to Antonia.[61] Weaver is wrong, however, in thinking that Ianuarius was the only one of her freedmen we know of outside Italy; M. Antonius Tertius (B.34) from Athens was another. A freedman of Antonia named Macrinus was once buried by an Aemilius Ianuarius (B.13). Though it is by no means clear, the latter probably belonged to the same household, and if so we may wonder whether any relationship existed between the two Ianuarii.

The staff was divided into administrative units (*decuriae*), and we are aware of a servant in charge of such a unit (*decurio*),[62] M. Antonius Pindarus, later freed by Antonia (B.35), in addition to Eros (B.16) the treasurer of another unit (*decurio quaestorum*). The general office was run by the secretary (*a manu*) Diadumenus (B.31), whom Antonia Caenis might have succeeded after his death in this position. In the dining-room we know of Liarus (B.23), the cupbearer of cold drinks (*glaber a cyato*). In reception worked Maritimus (B.32) the usher (*rogator*) and Tyrannus (B.30) who screened the guests (*ab admissione*). With this last post Antonia anticipated later emperors and, unless there is a gap in the evidence, she must have been the first to create it.[63]

As for the personal staff,[64] in the bedroom we know of Pamphila (B.8) the dresser (*ornatrix*), Chia (B.25) the masseuse (*unctrix*) and a craftswoman Athenais (B.9), the mender of Antonia's clothes (*sarcinatrix*). Of the professionals working in

Figure 38 An old engraving of the area between Porta Appia and Porta Latina. Columbarium Codini I is seen on the right at the top.

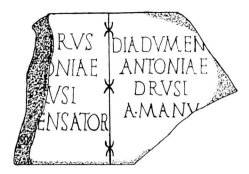

Figure 39 The double epitaph of Laphirus the 'steward' and Diadumenus the 'secretary', now in the Museo Capitolino.

the household, in the medical department we know of another Celadus (B.19), the doctor and surgeon (*medicus et chirurgus*) whose unfortunate wife, a slave of Antonia called Chreste, died when she was very young (even by Roman standards – see below):

> (To) Chreste the fellow-slave
> and wife. Celadus (slave) of Antonia
> (the wife) of Drusus, doctor and surgeon.
> Well-deservingly made it.
> She lived 17 years.

Two other slaves, trained as doctors, are on record: Hieron (B.14) and Pindarus (B.10); the latter may be identical with the synonymous freedman (B.35), whom we saw at one time in charge of an administrative unit. On education, Onomaste (B.9) seems to have run the library (*a bybliot.*), though her attachment to Antonia's *familia* is not absolutely clear. On entertainment, the

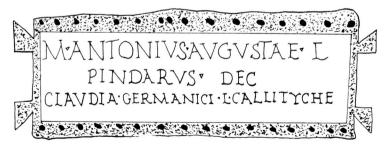

Figure 40 The epitaph of Pindarus the 'administrator' in Columbarium Codini II.

Figure 41 Cupbearers serving drinks as depicted on a Roman relief from Trier. Note the wine vessels on and beneath the single-legged table.

Figure 42 A Roman lady and her servants in the process of primping (*cultus*) as shown on a relief from Newmagen, now in the Museum of Treve.

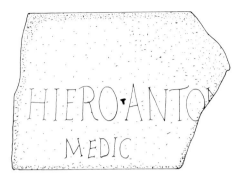

Figure 43 The epitaph of Hieron the 'doctor' in Columbarium Codini II.

Figure 44 The inscribed sarcophagus of Tertius from Athens, now kept in the Epigraphical Museum.

Figure 45 Litter-bearers in funerary procession as seen on a relief from Amiternum and now in Aquleia.

63

freedwoman Quintia (B.32) was the female singer of the court (*cantrix*), while the freedman M. Antonius Tertius (B.34) was the male vocalist (*paianieus*). The latter's inscription, from Athens, is interesting if only as the one text connected with Antonia that was written bilingually: in Latin and Greek.[65]

Among the outdoor staff we know of yet another Eros (B.1), the litter-bearer (*lecticarius*). It goes without saying that the Lady Antonia had possessed a litter (*lectica* or *ferculum*) for her activities around the city, carried on foot by a number of bearers. On festive occasions, however, she would have mounted the *carpentum*, a two-wheeled covered and extravagantly ornamented carriage drawn by animals. This was a mark of the highest distinction accorded only to certain matrons, the Vestals and some priests. For example, Messalina, the wife of Claudius, was granted the privilege of using it inside the city walls only by a vote of the Senate.[66] The funerary *carpentum* of Antonia, and the one used after her death for carrying her image to the games, will be discussed later (pp. 89, 124–6).

Another slave of Antonia working outside the household was Cerdus (B.18), a temple-keeper (*aeditimus*). Incidentally the temple mentioned is that of Venus, which I would identify as the one on the Capitoline (*Aedes Capitolina Veneris* or *Venus Erucina*); the appropriate goddess to be respected by Antonia, who according to popular consent personified her. In this temple Livia dedicated a statue of a son of Germanicus who died in infancy, called Gaius Caesar (like Caligula) and apparently born (unlike Caligula) at Tibur (modern Tivoli). The Emperor Galba subsequently consecrated in the temple a necklace of pearls and precious stones.[67]

Finally, the administrator (*procurator*) of Antonia's villa at ancient Bauli (see p. 154) may have been one Diadumenus Antonianus, who appears to be her freedman. Three graffiti (B.39–41) found on the inner wall of an aqueduct in Pausilypon (Posillipo), opposite Bauli across the Bay of Puteoli, refer to him (DIADVMENI·AVG·L·PROC·ANTO-NIANI) and his son Macrinus. Macrinus, according to these texts dated to AD 65, was the steward (*dispensator*) of an estate at Pausilypon belonging to Pollius Felix, the wealthy patron of the poet Statius.[68] Hirschfeld was the first to propose the connection of Diadumenus with Antonia and her villa.[69] We can

Figure 46 The epitaph of Eutychia, a freedwoman of Antonia, in the Museo Vaticano.

now supplement his view by observing that both names are attested in Antonia's indirect inscriptions and they may be showing a secondary form of relationship. We met the freedman Macrinus (B.13) who was buried by an Aemilius Ianuarius, as well as Diadumenus (B.31), Antonia's secretary (*a manu*).

The remaining indirect inscriptions record the names of people connected with Antonia without mention of any particular qualifications: they are simply slaves, slave-girls, freedmen and freedwomen. The following should be noted among others: Arsames (B.3), Ant[h]us (B.5), Eutychia (B.6), Lamus (B.7), Cerus (B.11), Cerialis (B.12), Thalia (B.16), Amoebes (B.17), Corymbus (B.20), Thethis (B.21), [Eu]ropa (B.22), Hilarus (B.26), Napes (B.27), Nebris (B.28), Xenus (B.29), Statira (B.29), [M]alche (B.29) and Iucundus (B.33).

Figure 47 The epitaph of Hilarus the slave, now in the Museo Capitolino.

As for ages at death of members of Antonia's staff found on inscriptions we know of only four. The slave-girl Chreste who died at seventeen we have already mentioned (B.19). The slave Anthus was twenty (B.5). The freedman [M. Antonius?] Lamus (B.7) was thirty-two. The slave-girl Nebris, whose ashes were apparently deposited in the *columbarium* by her boyfriend, died at thirty-five (B.28):

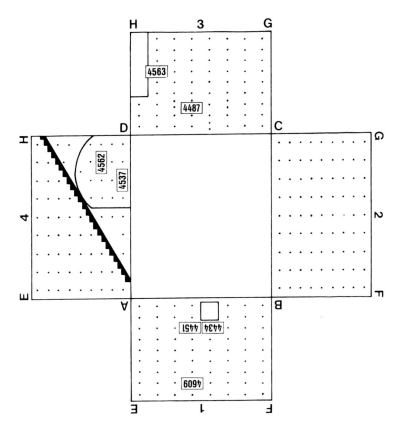

Figure 48 Plan of the interior of Columbarium Codini II. Noted are the locations of the inscriptions belonging to members of Antonia's domestic staff.

> Nebris (slave-girl) of Antonia
> (the wife) of Drusus. Here she lies.
> She lived 35 years.
> Lychius (her) companion,
> made this to her from his own (resources).

These ages should not be regarded as excessively young, especially for the class of people we are dealing with. It has been estimated that throughout the Roman period life expectancy at birth averaged about twenty-five to thirty, allowing for the high rate of infant mortality. From adolescence onwards the sur-

Figure 49 The epitaph of Eros, a slave of Germanicus, who was buried by Cerialis, the slave of Antonia, in Columbarium Codini II.

vivors are thought to have halved every ten years, so that only half of those who reached fifteen would live to twenty-five, and a quarter to thirty-five.[70]

In 1847 a group of indirect texts (B.9–14, 16, 22, 35) was found in Columbarium II of the vineyard Codini between the Via Appia and the Via Latina in Rome. This *columbarium* belonged to the family of Marcella Minor, the half-sister of Antonia (see Family Tree 2). Its life-span must have been quite long. According to epigraphical evidence the work on it was completed in AD 10, when the urns were divided among the shareholders of the company which had built the place.[71] Antonia's doctor, Pindarus, was buried there it seems side by side with [L?]ichiscus, a slave of Germanicus (B.10); while one of her slaves, Cerialis, undertook to bury Eros, another slave of Germanicus (B.12). Both burials therefore may date from the time the prince was still alive, that is, before AD 19. Similarly, Pindarus the *decurio* and freedman of Antonia (B.35) was deposited in the same chamber by Claudia Callityche, a freedwoman of Germanicus; but this was after Antonia had been named Augusta, that is, after AD 37. Above all we must note the connections between members of Antonia's staff with those of Germanicus' (B.10, 12, 35), the elder Agrippina's (B.20) and Marcella Minor's (B.11). These are an important indicator which will help us later to identify these households as parts of the same establishment on the Palatine (see p. 150).

3

THE PAPYRI OF ANTONIA

Few archaeological discoveries have attracted as much attention in modern times as the Greek papyri unearthed from the rubbish-heaps and sands of Egypt. Amazingly these documents provided not only parts of classical works known previously only in later copies, but parts of writings believed to have been lost for ever. The earliest texts of certain books of the New Testament have been exclusively retrieved from papyri.[1] Thanks to the durability of papyrus, preserved in the dry climate of the land of the Pharaohs, we now own a golden library of information concerning the Graeco-Roman world. Thousands of private and official letters, decrees, wills, contracts, leases, accounts, petitions, memoranda, on anything and everything, are today at our disposal to afford us a better understanding of ancient society.

Papyri have certainly taught us important lessons about the Imperial family, from state matters even to relationships between individuals. For example, it was only recently that we learned that Quinctilius Varus, the famous consular whose three legions, of about 15,000 men, were lost in the unprecedented German massacre of AD 9, was the son-in-law of Marcus Agrippa, the kinsman and right-hand man of Augustus.[2]

According to my estimate there are thirteen papyri which bear either definite or probable witness to the history of Antonia (Register C) and a further twenty-four (perhaps twenty-five) which may possibly qualify for inclusion in this study (Register D).

Figure 50
General view over the southern part of House C59 at Karanis, during the American excavations of the 1920s.

DEFINITE AND PROBABLE

All thirteen papyri of Antonia are from Egypt; they were found in the area of two nomes (districts), the Arsinoite (C.1, 3, 5–11, 13) and the Oxyrhynchite (C.2, 4, 12). With one exception (C.4) which is bilingual, its signature and date given in Latin, they are written in Greek. There are three petitions (C.3, 6, 7), three leases (C.9–11), two registers (C.5, 8), an account (C.1), a possible fragment from municipal *Acta* (C.2), a transfer (C.4), an edict (C.12) and a receipt (C.13). The first seven, which date to the time of Tiberius, refer to Antonia simply as 'Antonia' (C.1, 5), 'Antonia (the wife) of Drusus' (C.3, 4, 6, 7), or 'mother (of Germanicus)' (*mêtera* – C.2). The other six, which date from the reign of Claudius to that of Antoninus Pius, refer to her as 'Antonia Sebaste' (the title may have been omitted from C.11 and C.13 – if indeed these belong to Antonia) or as 'goddess' (*thea* – C.12).

The papyri of Antonia are invaluable for the historical record. Above all they confirm a fact that could only have been guessed at previously: namely, that she possessed in Egypt landed wealth or, as the Greeks had it, *ousiai*. This term had the meaning 'property' and, like any other property, the Julio-Claudians' was normally referred to as *ousia*. Just as the Latin-speaking world continued to employ the word *patrimonium* when referring to all kinds of property, so in Egypt *ousia* meant 'property' and 'estate', not necessarily 'Imperial property' or 'privileged estate'. This was the rule both before and after the creation of the *ousiakos logos* or *patrimonium principis*, by which the Flavians, for the first time, defined the Imperial wealth. Clearly, therefore, any land is Imperial only when it carries the name of an emperor or of a member of his family, or can be shown (after Flavian times) to be part of the *ousiakos logos*.[3]

Perhaps the most important asset of the Roman Emperor was his estates, which were enlarged by means of inheritance, gifts, confiscations and acquisition by conquest, or diminished by various forms of alienation.[4] Relatives of the Emperor and members of his *familia* owned land in their own right which was administered separately and privately. For example, we know of the agents (*procuratores*) who managed Livia's lands in the Roman provinces of Gallia Narbonensis, Sicily and Palestine.[5] Josephus reports an agent (*epitropos*) of Antonia, presumably in charge of her estates in Egypt. He was Alexander the Alabarch (see p. 32), perhaps the richest Jew who ever lived in Alexandria, and who paid to have the gates of the Jerusalem Temple decorated with gold and silver.[6]

According to Dio, Augustus assigned 'money' to Antonia and her sister from their father's property, probably from the liquidation of Antony's possessions in Italy and perhaps elsewhere. Antony is known to have inherited wealth even from people he had never met. He may also have owned land in Asia Minor, part of which could have passed to Antonia, whose popularity in the East is illustrated by inscriptions, coins, sculptures and minor artworks. Primarily, however, we now know (from papyri) of Antonia's extensive holdings in Egypt, and it is natural to assume that initially, at least, some of them belonged to her father, whether directly inherited or presented to her by Augustus.[7]

Though it cannot yet be conclusively proved that Antony owned land in Egypt given to him by Cleopatra, it is a preferable assumption, I believe, to the one recently made: that Antonia acquired her estates through purchase, in the same way that members of the Imperial family and other associates obtained their land.[8] As has been pointed out by Crawford, it is hard to believe that a free market for land ever functioned for Romans in Egypt, a province that was closely and jealously guarded by the Emperor from the start. The Egyptian holdings of members of the Imperial family are normally understood as 'gifts', one way by which the Emperor's property was reduced in size.[9] The Emperor's interest would be better served by grateful subordinates, and anyhow land given as a gift was often returned to him through inheritance. Augustus' will stated that in the last twenty years of his life he had received from friends' wills one billion four hundred million sesterces![10]

Another part of her Egyptian estates Antonia may have inherited from her husband Drusus, if he held property in this province, as he may have done since his mother Livia had possessions there, as did his son Germanicus.[11] Antonia may also have inherited from devoted friends, members of royal families and clients of Rome, who possessed land in Egypt from the Ptolemaic period. We know for a fact that Berenice I of Judaea, the mother of Agrippa I, named Antonia in her

Figure 51 Augustus being formed by the god Khnum on the potter's wheel, as depicted on an Egyptian relief.

will and she could have owned estates there. A possible descendant of hers (apparently via Julia Berenice her notorious granddaughter of the same name) had Egyptian property. The journeys of Herod the Great, Agrippa I and Agrippa II to the countries neighbouring their own are well recorded. Salome I (the sister of Herod the Great and mother of Berenice I), made Livia heir to her most productive land in Palestine.[12]

An important papyrus (C.9) informs us that two estates, one belonging to Antonia and another jointly shared with Livia, passed after Antonia's death to Claudius – perhaps via Caligula, but perhaps directly, since it can be demonstrated that Caligula and Claudius jointly owned land in the province;[13] in any case both emperors must have been the chief, if not the only, beneficiaries under Antonia's will. Pertinent to what we have

Figure 52 A Nilotic rural estate from a painting at Pompeii.

said above concerning Berenice, the papyrus also tells us that these particular estates were inherited from one G. Iulius [Alexandros], who seems to have died between AD 26 and 28 and whose identity has yet to be discovered.[14]

Rostovtzeff suggested that he was G. Julius Alexander, the son of Herod the Great and Mariamme the Hasmonaean, but this was rejected by Fuks on the grounds that Herod's son had been executed in c. 8 BC. Fuks proposed Alexander the Alabarch (Antonia's procurator); but he was also rejected on the grounds that he was alive under Claudius.[15] I suggest that, if the word after 'Alexandros', in the seventh line of a papyrus referring to him, is read 'of royal descent' ([ba]si[likou]), he was probably a member of the Herodian family.[16] But since Alexander the son of Herod (Rostovtzeff) cannot qualify, the hypothesis will be put forward that he was G. Julius Alexander II (the synonymous son of Alexander), grandson of Herod, who may have died c. AD 26–8. He was the son of Alexander by Glaphyra, the Cappadocian princess, and the brother of Tigranes V, king of Armenia, who was executed in Rome in AD 36.[17]

From the 'definite' and 'probable' papyri of Antonia we learn that she owned land in all three divisions of the Arsinoite nome (in the area of Fayûm), one of the seven administrative units (nomoi) into which Middle Egypt was divided (under Augustus there were some thirty nomes in the entire province).[18] In the division of Herakleides, on the north and east shore of Lake Moëris, her property consisted of farmsteads in the villages of Philadelphia and Ptolemais Nea (C.5), palm groves in Psenyris (C.11) and wheatfields in Karanis (C.13).[19] In the division of Themistus, on the south and west sides of the lake, it consisted of farmland in Euhemeria (C.6, 7, 9) and Herakleia (C.10). In the division of Polemon, to the south, her holdings must have been considerable, since in the village of Tebtunis a whole district was called after her (C.1). Other land of hers is known in an Arsinoite village called [..].kh[o]u (C.3) as well as at an unspecified place in the area (C.8). She possessed flocks in the Oxyrhynchite nome, where she seems to have had extensive grasslands, as well as in the Kynopolite nome, where a large number of sheep and goats were pastured (C.4).

Interesting, as well as characteristic, information is supplied to

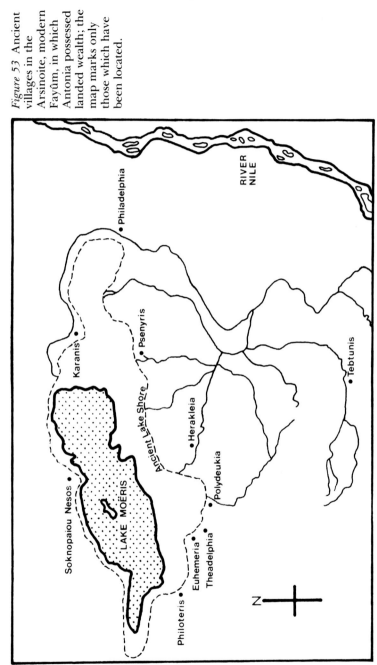

Figure 53 Ancient villages in the Arsinoite, modern Fayûm, in which Antonia possessed landed wealth; the map marks only those which have been located.

RIVER NILE

Philadelphia

Karanis

Psenyris

Soknopaiou Nesos

LAKE MOÉRIS

Herakleia

Philoteris

Euhemeria

Theadelphia

Polydeukia

Ancient Lake Shore

Tebtunis

N

us by these papyri, some of which are worth examining more closely.

On 11 November AD 22 (C.3), Dionysius, a supervisor of Antonia's land in the Arsinoite village of [..].kh[o]u, posted a petition in which he complained to Dionysodoros, the chief officer of the nome (*stratêgos*), about damages caused by someone else's sheep to a farmer's store of wheat on her estate. The farmer, who seems to have leased the land from Antonia, and on whose behalf Dionysius acted, was Chaeremon son of Sarapion. The herdsmen, Horus son of Thiaouaretias, Petesouchus son of Labatatos, and Psosneus, must have been entitled to graze their flocks in some nearby fields, but evidently they let them go illegally into the estate. We do not know whether an order for punishment of this particular misdeed was ever issued by the local authority, but considering the thoroughness of the Graeco-Roman adminis-tration and policing in Egypt, it probably was. A frequent dis-agreement between farmers in the Near East, generating a constant flow of official complaints, has been the abuse of land divisions and the damage caused to crops. It should come as no surprise that such arguments were as frequent in ancient as they are in modern times.

On 3 February AD 23 (C.4)[20] Cerinthus, a slave of Antonia, requested from Chaereas, the *stratêgos* of the Oxyrhynchite nome, permission to transfer flocks of sheep and goats from the grassland of Antonia there to grassland (apparently also belong-ing to his mistress) in the Kynopolite nome across the Nile:

To the Chief Officer Chaereas,
from Cerinthus, slave of Antonia (the wife) of Drusus,
Since I wish to transfer
from the Oxyrhynchite to the Kynopolite
nome, for the sake of pasturage,
three-hundred-and-twenty sheep and
one-hundred-and-sixty goats and the lambs and kids
that may (in the meantime) be produced,
– which I have on the register in the Oxyrhynchite in the
    present
ninth year of Tiberius Caesar Augustus –
I am submitting this memorandum in order that you
may write to the chief officer of

the Kynopolite for mention to be made of the indicated
  sheep
and . . . on the register . . .
I, Cerinthus, slave of Antonia (the wife) of Drusus,
submitted this in the 9th year of Tiberius
Caesar Augustus, on the eighth day of Mechir.

{Appended to this in different handwriting is the following fragmentary letter}

Chaereas to Hermias, Chief Officer of the Kynopolite,
  many greetings.
Cerinthus the slave of Antonia (the wife) of Drusus, has
  submitted to me a return,
wishing to . . .

As is clear, Chaereas promptly got in touch with Hermias, the
stratêgos of the Kynopolite nome, to put Cerinthus' request before him. The reply, which would probably have been in the
affirmative, since Imperial property was involved, is lost to us.
These grasslands lying on both sides of the river must have been
viewed by Germanicus a few years earlier when he sailed up the
great river to Upper Egypt. As noted (p. 21), it is a safe inference
that he attended to the business of his and his mother's landholdings, especially in the area of Fayûm. This document is also
interesting for its signature and date, which are written in Latin,
one of the earliest examples on papyrus of cursive writing (that
is to say, the business type of script, with small, joined characters
– as opposed to the literary 'capitals').

On 14 November AD 36 (C.6)[21] Aunes, a state farmer from the
village of Euhemeria who (besides working for the local authority) also worked privately on Antonia's land, notified the local
chief of police of the theft of his pig, worth eight drachmas,
under audacious circumstances:

To Gaius Errius (read Arrius) Priscus,
Chief of Police,
from Aunes son of
Anchorimphis, inhabitant of
Euhemeria, state farmer.
– I also farm the
estate of Antonia (the wife) of Drusus –
On the 18th of the present month

Figure 54 Head of a man from the
Fayûm, as painted on his coffin-lid.

Neos Sebastos, in the 23rd (year) of
Tiberius Caesar Augustus,
there was stolen from me a pig
of reddish skin, worth 8 (drachmas),
by certain bandits
at my very door.
I therefore request that you give written
    instructions,
for an inquiry into
the matter. Farewell.
Aunes, aged 35 (years), with a scar on his left thumb

The father of Aunes may have been the same person as
Anchorimphis the son of Anchorimphis who worked as a farmer
in an estate of Germanicus which had passed later to Tiberius.[22]
Bad fortune seems to have run in the family, for Anchorimphis
two years earlier (1 April AD 34) had made a report to the same
chief of police about the theft of his pig, somewhere in the
village.

On 27 April AD 37 (C.7)[23] Petermouthis, another inhabitant of
the village of Euhemeria, a state farmer and tax collector who
also worked privately on the land of Antonia, complained to a
locally stationed Roman centurion that he had been assaulted by
two shepherds who refused to pay damages to him for the

77

grazing done by their flocks. Petermouthis stated that as he was
being fiercely beaten up he lost his belt and forty drachmas:

> To Gaius Trebius Justus,
> centurion,
> from Petermouthis, son of
> Heracleus, inhabitant of Euhemereia,
> state farmer
> and public tax collector.
> – I also farm (the estate of) Antonia
> (the wife) of Drusus –
> On the 2nd of the present month Pachon,
> in the 1st (year) of Gaius Caesar
> Imperator, while I was talking
> to the shepherds Papontos,
> son of Orsenouphis, and Apion
> known as Capareis,

Figure 55 A Nilotic rural estate from a painting at Herculaneum.

about damages
owed me for the
grazing-down done by their
flocks, they gave me
a lot of beating, announcing with impudence
that they would not pay. And I (also)
lost 40 silver (drachmas) which I had with me
from the sale of opium, and a belt.
I therefore request that I receive
redress, so that nothing
falls upon the state.
Farewell.

As it happens, on the fourth day after Petermouthis' assault and
before even his bruises had faded away, in Rome his landlady
Antonia died (1 May)! It is also significant that although only
forty days had passed since Caligula assumed power (18 March)
this document is already dated according to the era of the new
'leading citizen' or *princeps*. The news of his accession must have
reached even remote locations of the Empire in record time.[24]

In AD 56/7 (C.10)[25] Papus the son of Tryphon who was living
in the farmstead of Antonia at Herakleia applied to become a
lessee (*misthôtês*) of an estate belonging to Ti. Claudius
Doryphorus. The latter was a notorious favourite of Nero, but
also Nero's victim.[26] The estate had passed to Doryphorus from
(Ti. Claudius?) Narcissus, another crafty imperial freedman,
famed for many things: for having sorted out the mutiny in
Gaul a little before the invasion of Britain, for being able to
watch even in his sleep over Claudius' safety and for having his
image cherished by the father of the Emperor Vitellius.[27] The
terms of the lease were very favourable for Papus: while paying
an annual rent he was to receive from his landlord Doryphorus
not only the usual advance of seed-corn but a grant of money
towards the tillage and upkeep of the embankments.

In AD 126–8 (C.11) two brothers from Soknopaiou Nesos,
Stotoetes and Onnophris, applied for the lease of an estate in the
village of Psenyris, which was once part of the Emperor
Vespasian's property (*patrimonium principis*) and, before that, of
Antonia's *patrimonium*. Apparently the estates of Antonia as well
as those of Germanicus, Antonia the daughter of Claudius,
Pallas the freedman, etc., were incorporated into Vespasian's

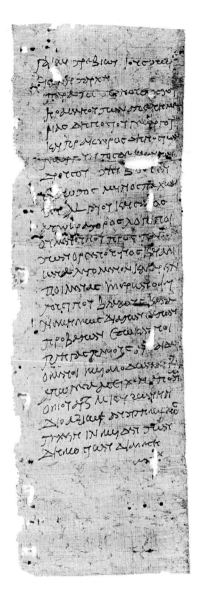

Figure 56 The papyrus of
Petermouthis from Euhemeria.

share of the Flavian *ousiakos logos*, whereas estates of other
members of the Imperial family were included in that of Titus.[28]

Yet another significant papyrus (C.12)[29] thought to refer to
Antonia is an edict issued in AD 147/8 by M. Petronius

Honoratus, prefect of Egypt. In this a triennial contest was announced, to be held in honour of the Goddess Livia and another deified member of the Imperial family whose name is lost. This was probably Antonia Augusta, in honour of whom (together with Livia) horse-races were instituted by Claudius in Rome and, no doubt, subsequently in the provinces.[30] Nothing further is known of these games in Egypt though they seem to have had considerable local importance. At the town of Oxyrhynchus, of which practically nothing is known in written history apart from information derived from innumerable papyri,[31] we may imagine that the day of the Livian-Antonian Games also involved religious and theatrical festivities. Its theatre would have staged appropriate plays, perhaps in an

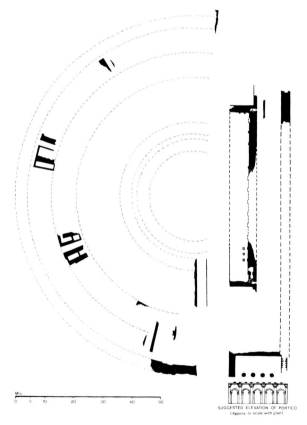

Figure 57 A reconstructed plan of the Roman theatre at Oxyrhynchus.

81

atmosphere as syncretistic and curiously mixed as the building's own architecture, described by Petrie as astounding for featuring Greek, Roman, Syrian and Egyptian styles.[32] Further, we may note that the year in which, according to the papyrus, the games were held (AD 147), was the 110th anniversary of the death of Antonia, not quite a centennial commemoration though certainly comparable to the ancient *saeculum* (110 years) upon which the Secular Games (*Ludi Saeculares*) were based.[33]

Lastly, a fragmentary papyrus (C.2),[34] falling into the category of 'pamphleteering' literature and perhaps belonging to the Alexandrian *Acta*, is of some consequence. Palaeographically dated to the first half of the first century AD, it concerns a speech of an unnamed *imperator* given upon his arrival at Alexandria. The choice can only be between Gaius Caesar (the adopted son of Augustus) and Germanicus. The latter fits the details in the text better and its precise date would therefore be shortly after AD 19.[35] The relevant part of the speech containing information on Antonia is translated here:

> I, who have been sent, as I said, by my (adopted) father to regulate the overseas provinces, I have a most difficult assignment, first because of the sea-voyage and due to having been separated from my (adopted) father (= Tiberius) and grandmother (= Livia) and mother (= Antonia) and siblings (= Claudius, Livilla) and children (= only Nero Caesar, Drusus Caesar, the younger Agrippina and Drusilla) and intimate friends . . .

As observed by Turner, the reference to the hardships of the travelling and family separation reads oddly coming from the victor of the German campaigns, a man now in his thirties.[36] We have to see the words of Germanicus throughout this document as rhetorical exaggeration. He knew how to please the audience not only by praising their famous city but, on a more personal level, by composing a melodrama about being torn from the embrace of his relatives. This can hardly have been so painful, however, if only because his wife (the elder Agrippina) and, despite the generalising nature of his claim, at least two of his children (Caligula and Julia Livilla) were still with him (see p. 18)! Certainly the available data argue for the absence of his mother from the Imperial group that entered Egypt, but in view of the apparent element of exaggeration there is no need to

Figure 58 Head of a woman from the Fayûm, as painted on her coffin-lid.

suppose that Antonia did not follow Germanicus on any part of his long journey. That she did has been suggested earlier from other evidence. It might be a reasonable compromise to deduce that she departed for Rome from Palestine (if not from an earlier point – see p. 20), taking with her the younger of Germanicus' children. To a certain extent this scenario may satisfy the indications provided by all three sources: the inscriptions, the papyrus and Tacitus.

POSSIBLE AND IMPROBABLE

Twenty-four papyri that may concern Antonia's estates, dated between about AD 90 and 222/3, were written, buried and recovered in the Arsinoite nome (D.2–25). They consistently refer to property called 'Antonian' (*Antonianê*) and Mark Antony could well have been the original owner of it. This 'ousiac' land may have passed jointly to both Antonias and continued to be known as Antonian.[37] Unfortunately papyrologists automatically attribute all relevant evidence to Antonia Minor, supposing that her sister Antonia Maior (grandmother of the Emperor Nero) had no interest in Egypt; yet we know of Nero's landholdings there, some of which may have been passed on to him from Antonia Maior.[38] We should note at this point that other material from the wider Empire, with no clear content or context, may similarly in the past have been attributed to the wrong Antonia.

Given that the estates mentioned as 'Antonian' belonged to Antonia Minor, her property in Egypt must have been vast. Together with the property of her son Germanicus it would have made them (as far as can be determined by papyri) the richest members of the Imperial family. To the places already mentioned in which Antonia possessed landed wealth we could now possibly add the following (see fig. 53, p. 74): in the division of Herakleides, the villages Soknopaiou Nesos (D.5, 15, 22–4) and Patsontis (D.7); in the division of Themistus, the villages Theadelphia (D.3, 4, 9, 13, 14, 17, 18, 20), Polydeukia (D.9), Philoteris (D.11) and Bernikis Aigialou (D.12); in the division of Polemon, the village Boukolon (D.6).

These estates produced a variety of goods; there were further palm groves (D.6, 11), vineyards (D.17) and pastures for sheep and goats (D.2, 5, 14, 21). Interestingly enough, Antonia's private economy was expanded also to cover fishing; her fondness for fish-keeping has already been noted (see p. 33). In the village of Soknopaiou Nesos,[39] on the north shore of Lake Moëris, she owned fishing-boats which were regularly leased out (D.15, 22–4). Of course, such boats would have been equally useful for transferring crops between various stores, from one side of the lake to the other and even down the Nile to Alexandria. Antonia thus in a way maintained a tradition that went back to the Hellenistic period. Then the uppermost layer of Ptolemaic society which, as papyri show, included many female courtiers in addition to queens, owned ships for the transport of state grain.[40]

We may be able to trace further lands connected with Antonia if some of the estates of M. Antonius Pallas were also initially owned by her.[41] Pallas was freed by Antonia between AD 31, when he is last attested as slave, and 37, the year of her death. He passed into the 'clientage' (*clientela*) of her son Claudius – a further reminder of the content of Antonia's will. Pallas must have begun accumulating wealth in Egypt immediately after his manumission (if not while he was a slave) since a papyrus mentioning property belonging to him dates to Tiberian times. Perhaps it was Pallas' participation (via Antonia) in the fall of Sejanus that earned him his freedom and his first Egyptian estate.[42]

Figure 59 An old photograph of Lake Moëris.

Finally, an improbable reference to Antonia Augusta in another papyrus (D.1) has been ascribed to her, but ought rather to be assigned to Claudia Antonia the daughter of Claudius. The word 'daughter' (*thygatêr*) is known in papyrology in connection with her, even without the name of her father next to it.[43] Antonia Augusta is nowhere mentioned on papyri as 'daughter' (that is, of Mark Antony) and there are only two inscriptions referring to her thus (A.1, 3), both of which predate the papyrus under consideration by many years. On the other hand, if it could be ascribed to her we would be able to assert from this document not only the existence of further land belonging to Antonia in the village of Boubastos (in the Herakleidian division of the Arsinoite nome), but also some direct link with the 'elusive' possessions of Mark Antony in Egypt.

4

THE COINS AND TOKENS
OF ANTONIA

Ancient coins have been described as the most lasting and most 'vocal' monuments of antiquity. As metal objects of a determined standard, issued by a competent authority, they help us grasp the mechanics of ancient economies. They are also manifestations of the artistic tradition and outlook of their time. Though small and containing limited information, they are by no means of negligible interest to the historian and archaeologist.[1] In fact, coins are universally treated as historical documents of the first degree. For the history of the Roman Empire, they are an inexhaustible source. A vast number were minted both in Rome and in the provinces, many thousands of which survive, and they were often used by the emperors to advertise their achievements and propagate their intentions.[2] For research into the lives of individual members of the Julio-Claudian family they are an indispensable tool.

In my view there are three main types of Roman coin commemorating Antonia and a further five which may be attributed to her (Register E). There are also eleven, or perhaps twelve, types of provincial issue from the East (Register F), as well as seven tokens (*tesserae*) that have been tentatively assigned to her (Register G).

ROMAN COINS

The three main coin types of Antonia were minted posthumously in Rome, early in the reign of Claudius (E.6–10). The first was struck both in gold (aureus, E.7) and silver (denarius, E.8). It bore on the obverse a bust of Antonia wearing the corn wreath of Ceres, patron goddess of harvest and marriage. The

87

inscription reads ANTONIA AVGVSTA, the title reconferred on her by Claudius.[3] Ceres, the equivalent of the Greek Demeter, shared a temple with Liber (Dionysus) and Libera (Persephonê or Korê) on the slope of the Aventine facing the Forum Boarium. This was burnt down in 31 BC, rebuilt by Augustus (who had then been initiated in the mysteries of the Eleusinian triad), and dedicated in AD 17 by Tiberius.[4] To this important cult apparently belongs the annual festival conducted by Roman women in August, called the 'Greek Initiation' by Cicero. So fundamental was the adoration of Ceres/Demeter that Claudius even tried to transplant her mysteries from Eleusis to Rome.[5] The depiction of Antonia as this goddess was a high honour, though one very much in line with her productive nature and her aspect as matron or *materfamilias*. Incidentally, in the well-known imagery of Demeter holding a torch and searching for her fallen daughter in Hades, some may have seen Antonia exploring the darkness of the other world looking for Livilla, her beloved but fallen daughter, whose existence she sadly had to terminate.

On the reverse of the same coin the personified female figure of Constancy (again representing Antonia) is depicted, standing holding a long torch in her right hand (like Demeter but also suggesting a priestess) and a cornucopia in her left (suggesting plenty and happiness). The inscription reads CONSTANTIAE AVGVSTI, meaning the 'constancy' of the new Augustus. This personification had a special reference to Claudius' 'courage' or 'resolution' in civic life – the quality that had enabled him to bear the trials of his early life. Antonia in the role of Constancy or Imperial Firmness indicated (somewhat ironically in view of the Emperor's disabilities and Antonia's remarks about him! – see p. 28) whence Claudius' *constantia* was derived: apparently from his mother, a woman of marked strength and determination.

The second type of Antonia's coins was also struck both in gold (E.9) and silver (E.10). It used the same obverse as the first but a new reverse, bearing two lighted torches bound below their flames by a ribbon. The legend now reads SACERDOS DIVI AVGVSTI, a direct reference to the priesthood granted to Antonia by Caligula.[6] An identical description of her as 'the Priestess of the Divine Augustus' is found on a very rare type but relevant to this issue (E.11), showing on the reverse a carriage (*carpentum*), probably of a funerary kind. This is hard to fit into

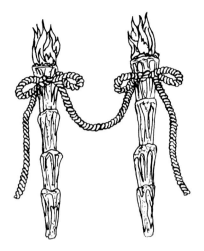

Figure 60 Twin lighted torches as they appear on the coins of Antonia.

the series minted at Rome and it seems to be of eastern origin (Caesarea in Cappadocia). Further, although listed under Claudius, it might well belong to the reign of Caligula.[7] Such a date would be more natural if the procession involving the *carpentum* represents Antonia's funeral in AD 37. We cannot fail to compare this coin with coins of Livia and the elder Agrippina, both associated with funerary *carpenta* (cf. fig. 17, p. 29), which will be mentioned later.

The third main type, dated to AD 41, was struck in brass and was known to the Romans as *orichalcum* (dupondius, E.6). It bore on the obverse a different portrait of Antonia but the same

Figure 61 A brass dupondius minted in Rome under Claudius, depicting Antonia on the obverse.

inscription as the other two. On the reverse Claudius was depicted standing, togate and veiled, holding a small ladle for libation (*simpulum*) in his right hand. The inscription TI·CLAVDIVS·CAESAR·AVG·P·M·TR·P·IMP·S C is rendered thus:

> Tiberius Claudius Caesar, Augustus, Pontifex Maximus, (holding) Tribunician Power, Imperator. (Struck) by Decree of the Senate.

Certain varieties of this type exist: with the addition P·P (*pater patriae*), 'Father of his Country', at the end of the inscription, a title received by Claudius not earlier than AD 42;[8] a hybrid with the head of Claudius instead of Antonia on the obverse; some countermarked issues (i.e. restruck by a later authority) and ancient imitations; as well as modern forgeries. Further, a sestertius with ANTONIA AVGVSTA on the obverse and S·C·IMP·T·CAESAR·P·VESP·F·AVG·RESTIT on the reverse has also been reported as a forgery.[9] Its reverse inscription translates:

> (Struck) by Decree of the Senate. The Imperator Titus Caesar, Augustus, Pontifex, son of Vespasian, restored.

This pretended to place the coin (apparently without success) within the series cut by the Emperor Titus and known as the 'Restoration', by which the Flavians glorified the memory of several members of the Julio-Claudian family.

In view of some Roman (not to mention provincial) issues struck earlier, which could be attributed to Antonia (although with reservations), it is unwarranted to maintain that Imperial coins honouring her began to be circulated only under Claudius. Apart from the *carpentum* coin referred to above, which could be a product of Caligula's reign, there are three types of Tiberian dupondii (internally dated to AD 22–3) that have been difficult to interpret. They are known by the female busts on their reverses which carry the legends SALVS AVGVSTA (E.1), IVSTITIA (E.2) and PIETAS (E.3). In 1923 Mattingly led the way to an identification of these issues:

> It has been generally agreed that these three personifica-
> tions are not without reference to some actual person or
> persons. Livia may be easily recognised in Salus Augusta.
> Antonia has been seen in Pietas . . . The portraits of the

Iustitia and Pietas coins are like one another and not very like Salus Augusta; and it is therefore possible that Antonia, as well as Livia, was honoured. But it is perhaps better to suppose that we have variant studies in the portraiture of Livia.[10]

As a result, whereas the identification of Iustitia and Pietas remained *sub judice*, with a measure of preference towards Livia, the Salus portrait became the basis of all subsequent iconographic studies of Livia.[11] Later, however, Mattingly, influenced by Grant and Sutherland, radically changed his mind:

> If, as now appears probable, the *aes* coinage of Tiberius with the date AD 22/23 (TR.P.XXIIII) was not all struck in that actual year, a new meaning of the date must be found: what else can it be than the date of the 'senatusconsultum' that regulated the coinage for some years ahead? The main reason for dating part of this issue later than AD 22/23 lies in some of its reverses. The sestertius with the reverse S.P.Q.R. IVLIA AVGVST . . . should refer to the death of Livia in AD 28, the dupondius with reverse SALVS AVGVSTA . . . (of Antonia not Livia . . .) to Antonia's share in frustrating the designs of Sejanus.[12]

The *aes*, small-denomination bronze coins, seem therefore to have continued to be produced after AD 22–3 without changing their date, representing the decree of the Senate (*senatusconsultum Caesaris auctoritate*) from which the revival of the *aes* coinage as a whole originated.[13] The sestertius of Livia (who died in AD 29 not in AD 28) must be dated to AD 29/30, and in showing a funerary *carpentum* is clearly comparable with two other issues: the one to the memory of the elder Agrippina and the other to that of Antonia, perhaps from an eastern mint (E.11), which we have already seen.[14]

By analogy we can argue that the Salus Augusta coin has to be dated to AD 31/32 and refers to the 'Safety' and 'Salvation' of the Imperial family achieved by Antonia in her exposure of Sejanus' conspiracy. If so there is good reason to associate with it the epigram of Honestus (A.15 – see p. 42) in which an 'Augusta' is said to have 'saved the whole world': that is to say, Antonia who saved her family and hence the world. This 'Augusta', according to Honestus, could 'boast of two divine sceptred Caesars'. The phrase has been taken to mean 'two young godlike Caesars': that

Figure 62 A brass dupondius minted in Rome under Tiberius, depicting 'Salus' on the reverse.

is, as Cichorius suggested, Gaius Caesar (Caligula) and Tiberius Caesar (Gemellus).[15] Such an understanding would place the text approximately between AD 32 and 37.

Alternative theories are possible, however. On the one hand, given that the date to be followed is actually the very beginning of the reign of Caligula, AD 37 (cf. inscription (A.10) and coin (see p. 98) from Corinth), the young Caesars may rather be Germanicus and the younger Drusus. It was now that the retribution inflicted by Antonia for the death of both princes was remembered (cf. this trio in a sculpture from Nomentum under Caligula – p. 127). On the other hand, in the Greek parlance of the Roman Empire the phrase 'two divine sceptred Caesars' may rather imply 'two emperors and gods', whom one can readily identify with Caligula and Claudius. The epigram then would be placed at the outset of Claudius' reign. Antonia was the only Augusta who became mother of a family that produced two emperors (regardless of the fact that one of them proved to be a ruthless monster). Moreover, it should be pointed out that in the words of Honestus she 'set light to twin torches of peace', and, interestingly enough, on the reverse of the SACERDOS coins of Antonia we see two bound lighted torches (fig. 60, p. 89). Since these coins are dated to *c.* AD 41, they may be regarded as an appropriate commemoration of the tenth anniversary (*decennium*) of Sejanus' fall. Honestus' poem (hitherto dated to Tiberian times) may then have been inspired by the celebrations held on this Claudian anniversary.

The only problem in placing the Salus coin in context with the punishment of Sejanus would be the title 'Augusta' which was granted to Antonia, to the best of our knowledge, by Caligula in AD 37. For the sake of argument, we can explain 'Augusta' on this coin as referring to Salus herself (the equivalent of the Greek Hygeia) rather than to Antonia, her personification (cf. Pax Augusta). Yet, for the sake of clarity, we cannot entirely avoid the following question: could Antonia have been previously honoured with this title under Tiberius? This question is definitely worthy of consideration. Tiberius seems to have had every reason to confer the title on his sister-in-law.[16] First, after the death of Livia in AD 29 the position of 'Augusta' remained vacant and Antonia was surely next in line to occupy it. Second, after the execution of Sejanus in AD 31 there must have been some urgency to bestow the highest honours on Antonia.

Although at present it is difficult to prove that the Senate or Tiberius did name her 'Augusta', a vague statement in Suetonius may point in this direction. According to him it was a known fact that before Claudius granted her the title posthumously, 'she had declined (it) during her lifetime'. Modern scholars have thought that Antonia's rejection must have followed the offer made by Caligula. Caligula, however, is nowhere said to have 'offered' the title to her. He 'conferred' it on her, explicitly by a decree of the Senate.[17] Inscriptions and coins seem to prove this (e.g. A.10, 13, 15; E.11; F.5, 6). Further, as we are now aware, Antonia lived only six weeks under Caligula (and only two actually under his direct rule – see p. 37), an extremely short period which should have been mentioned more specifically by Suetonius. His phrase 'during her lifetime' may well imply an earlier point in Antonia's life rather than her last two weeks. Would it therefore be reasonable to assume that she had been nominated for the title of 'Augusta' in AD 29 (after the death of Livia), or even better at the end of AD 31 (after the execution of Sejanus), and that she declined the title until the accession of her grandson in AD 37?

Such an interpretation would inevitably require a readjustment in our understanding of some of Antonia's inscriptions, currently dated after Caligula solely because this title appears on them. Also, it would provide us with grounds for assigning her various elusive provincial issues: for example, the Spanish coins from Emerita (Mérida) and Carthago Nova (Cartagena), the first under Tiberius with SALVS AVGVSTA included in the legend, the second under Caligula with SAL·AVG.[18] The latter has been attributed in the past to Caesonia, the wife of Caligula, but this is difficult to accept since there are no coins depicting her and the one discussed here is dated to AD 37, when she had yet to marry the young Emperor.[19]

Following Mattingly's argument further, the other two dupondii (Iustitia and Pietas) would also now represent Antonia as 'Justice' and 'Duty'. Grant thought[20] that the coin of Iustitia celebrates the tenth anniversary (*dicennium*) of her altar (*ara Iustitiae Augustae*) in AD 22/3, but since there is nothing to prevent us from dating the *aes* series later than AD 23, the anniversary in question may actually have been the twentieth (*vicennium*) in AD 32/3. This would accord with Antonia, who would then be the 'justice' exacted upon Sejanus with his punishment late in AD 31. Iustitia was the Roman equivalent to Dikê, one of the Horae of Greek mythology, the goddesses of Seasons, Time and Justice. Dikê reports to Zeus the wrongdoings of men; similarly

Figure 63 Dikê fighting Adikia from a vase painting.

Antonia reported to Tiberius the plot against his life. Dikê catches an evil-doer; likewise Antonia caught Sejanus.[21] This event may be reflected later in the popular belief of the islanders in Malta, who said of Paul, when a snake fastened on his hand, that the divine Dikê (or Iustitia) 'will not suffer a murderer to live'; to their surprise he shook the snake off into the fire. Another parallel from the perspective of the New Testament, and even closer to the episode of Antonia and Sejanus, is Jesus' 'peace-makers', an idea certainly not alien to the Roman concept of Peace with Justice.[22]

For Pietas, the personification accords perfectly with Antonia's character and her symbolism of 'family unity'. This coin has on its obverse the following inscription S·C, DRVSVS· CAESAR·TI·AVGVSTI·F·TR·POT·ITER·, or in English:

(Struck) by Decree of the Senate. Drusus Caesar, son of Tiberius Augustus, (held) Tribunician Power twice.

The issue evidently commemorated Drusus Caesar, the son of Tiberius, and it would make sense for it to have been minted on the *decennium* of his death (AD 33). The simultaneous depiction of Antonia on the reverse would then bear witness to the exposure of Drusus' murderer, Sejanus. It is of interest that Mark Antony in 41 BC had silver denarii struck with the image and name of Pietas, through an intermediary in the person of his brother. The process suddenly came to a halt, however, until the time of Tiberius when again we find Pietas on coins and altars.[23] In the case of Antony's brother, as with Antonia, Pietas is not the personification of 'Piety' in general, but is expressive of true and self-sacrificing attachment of kinsman to kinsman. It is also interesting that later the Emperor Titus, though curiously omitting in his 'Restoration' series the coins of Antonia, did select and 'restore' both Iustitia and Pietas.[24]

If this identification is accepted, we may, again, proceed to suggest the reattribution of some elusive provincial issues, such as the three coins from an uncertain village in North Africa, from Dium in Macedonia, and from Caesaraugusta (Zaragoza) in Spain, all with the legend PIETAS AVGVSTA. The last bears a bust of Pietas, imitating the Roman dupondius, which is strikingly similar to the bust of Antonia on provincial coins from Crete and Thessalonica (see below).[25]

Finally, there are two Roman coin-types under Caligula where connection with Antonia may also be suggested: first, a sestertius with Pietas on the obverse struck in AD 37/8 (E.4), and again in AD 39/40 and AD 40/1; and secondly, an *as* with Vesta on the reverse struck in AD 37/8 (E.5), but also in AD 39/40 and AD 40/1.[26]

The Pietas type will follow the same argument we presented under Tiberius. The small draped figure on the obverse, upon which the seated Pietas is resting her left arm, which has been identified by Mattingly as a 'priestess', may represent Antonia, herself the 'Priestess of the Divine Augustus'.[27] This view is supported by the depiction of Caligula on the reverse, who sacrifices at an altar in front of the Temple of Divus Augustus, an Ionic hexastyle building (that is, with a six-column façade). This once stood to the south of the Basilica Julia in the area of the Roman Forum.[28]

That the Vesta type may be connected with Antonia is implied by the fact that Caligula granted her 'all the privileges of the Vestal Virgins', which could thus have been advertised. The Vestal privileges had great honour and prestige and had been increased by Augustus himself.[29] Although Antonia did not live long enough to exercise many of them, she may briefly have profited by some. From the long list of Vestal rights, Antonia would now be maintained at the public cost (given that the state had not already been charged for services she provided in the past: for example, the supervision of foreign princes). She would be entitled to make a will (though as an Imperial matron and a widow exempted by the *ius liberorum*, she seems already to have possessed this otherwise male prerogative – see p. 17). She would be able to give evidence in a court of justice without taking an oath (though she may already have been allowed to do this in the cases of Piso and Sejanus). Further, she could now demand the release of any prisoner she came across; she could ask for anyone to be put to death who had passed under her litter while she was being carried through the streets of Rome; and she would be exempted from the law of the Twelve Tables, which forbade burial within the sacred boundary (*pomerium*) of the city.[30]

Vesta was the Roman hearth-goddess, equivalent to the Greek Hestia, as prominent in family worship as Antonia. The centre of her cult, also in the Roman Forum, was located in the impressive Augustan round building, conceivably a stone imitation

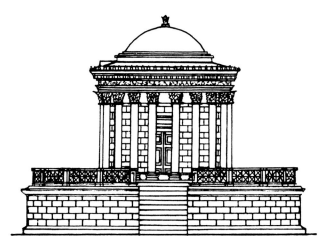

Figure 64 A reconstruction of the Temple of Vesta in the Forum Romanum.

of the ancient round hut. Inside it there was no image but a central undying fire. Not until the time of Hadrian was an ornamented tabernacle (*aedicula*) built behind the temple to accommodate the statue of the goddess. Also, curtained off from the rest of the building there was a mysterious store-room (*penus*), thought to contain various sacred objects. As only the Vestals could enter it, we may assume that Antonia, who had been granted all their privileges, would have been drawn by natural curiosity to examine its interior.[31] In Imperial times Vesta was served by six Virgins who were employed from childhood, when aged between six and ten, and held their position for some thirty years, during which time they were obliged to remain chaste.[32]

PROVINCIAL COINS

The eleven main types of provincial bronze coins of Antonia cover a wide area in the Greek Imperial world (F.1–6, 8–12; see fig. 109, p. 167). Four types come from Thessalonica in Macedonia (F.2–5) and one from each of the following: Corinth in Achaea (F.6), Gortyna(?) in Crete (F.12), Alexandria in Egypt (F.8), Caesarea(?) in Cappadocia (F.11), Clazomenae in Ionia (F.1), Ilium in Troas (F.9) and Tomis in Moesia Inferior (F.10).

With regard to dates and titles for Antonia, the Corinth coin (F.6) and one from the Thessalonica series (F.5) provide evidence for the use of AVGVSTA or SEBASTE during the reign of Caligula (AD 37–41). The other three types from Thessalonica, with the goddess Nikê or Victoria (F.4), the wreath (F.2) and the horse (F.3), which are undated and mention simply ANTONIA, it would be tempting to place during the time of Tiberius; preferably in his last decade (cf. Register B). All three designs (although commonly found in the Greek environment) must have been carefully selected by the die-cutter, since they symbolise acts and virtues clearly linked to Antonia, especially after the events of AD 31: victory, salvation, reward, chastity and love.

Another undated coin is from Clazomenae (F.1), close to Smyrna (Izmir in Turkey), a town which used to lie on an island a few hundred feet from the shore, connected with it by a causeway.[33] This refers to Antonia as 'goddess' (THEA), depicts on the reverse Cybele or the Great Mother (*Magna Mater*), and may be dated on technical affinities earlier in Tiberius' reign, perhaps as early as AD 18. If so, it would be the earliest coin of Antonia yet discovered and it could be associated with her (and Germanicus') visit to the East, as well as her cult around this area (cf. THEA in Athens, B. 15, B.38; Ilium, A.5; Aphrodisias, A.18; and Egypt C.12). Further, it would also indicate the existence of a 'mature and individualised' portrait of Antonia (fifty-three years old in AD 18) in the first part of the reign of Tiberius, as will be seen later (p. 121). The choice made on this coin to juxtapose Antonia with Cybele, a goddess worshipped by the people of Clazomenae, was highly significant. While it seems that Antonia was popularly reckoned to be the 'Great Mother' of the Imperial family, the major cult of Cybele in Rome was centred in a temple on the Palatine, next door to Antonia's own residence (see p. 150). This temple was completely rebuilt by Augustus in AD 3 and it enshrined the magnificent statue showing the goddess seated on an elaborate throne flanked by lions. On her left knee with her left hand she held the enigmatic oriental drum (*tympanum*), supposed to represent the globe of the earth, or the musical instrument (*cymbalum*) used by the priests at her holy rites.[34]

The coin from Tomis (Constantza in Romania) is also undated (F.10), but the title SEBASTE (disregarding at present the

Figure 65 The Temple of Magna Mater on the Palatine from a Roman frieze, probably belonging to the Ara Pietatis Augustae.

theory that Antonia might have been granted this title earlier – see p. 93), seems to date to Claudian times.[35] We should note in passing that Tomis was the place where Ovid died, having been exiled there by Augustus, some years after he wrote (if indeed he was the author) the 'consolation' to Livia and Antonia for the death of Drusus (see p. 16).[36] Germanicus' journey into the Black Sea in AD 18 would have brought him almost within sight of this city. All other coins either belong or are assumed to belong to the time of Claudius. The most precisely dated is the coin from Alexandria (F.8 = AD 41/2).

All provincial issues bear busts of Antonia, except the Ilium coin (F.9) which depicts her seated statue, perhaps in the fashion of the great goddess Hera or Juno (see p. 117).[37] Caligula appears on one of the Thessalonica types (F.5), a coin encountered in a number of varieties.[38] Claudius appears on the coins

99

Figure 66 A bronze coin minted in Alexandria under Claudius, depicting Antonia on the reverse.

of Alexandria (F.8), Ilium (F.9) and Gortyna(?) (F.12), and the elder Drusus, facing his wife Antonia, again on the Gortyna(?) specimen (F.12). Finally, Messalina is depicted on the coin from Caesarea(?) (Kayseri in Turkey – F.12), a city previously known as Mazaca and the capital of King Archelaus of Cappadocia.[39]

With regard to the last, although it is understandable that the two women closest to the reigning Emperor (his mother and wife) should be commemorated on a Claudian coin, Messalina's appearance with Antonia is very unusual. Valeria Messalina, an extremely scandalous woman, was the granddaughter of Antonia Maior, the elder sister of our Antonia (see Family Tree 2). She was killed in shameful circumstances in AD 48, and therefore the coin must predate that year.[40] Since she married Claudius in *c.* AD 39 when she was fourteen, Antonia, who died in AD 37, would hardly have had enough time to develop any special relationship with her (other than that of great-aunt to great-niece). After Messalina's death, when many stories of her sexual profligacy were circulated, this coin from Caesarea(?) would have seemed strikingly ironical: Antonia, universally renowned for her discreetness, depicted together with Messalina who was strongly satirised by Juvenal as follows:

> Then look at the God's rivals, hear what Claudius
> Had to put up with. The minute she heard him snoring,
> His wife – that whore-empress – who dared to prefer the
>   mattress

Of a stews to her couch in the Palace, called for her
   hooded
Night-cloak and hastened forth, alone or with a single
Maid to attend her. Then, her black hair hidden
Under an ash-blonde wig, she would make straight for
   her brothel,
With its odour of stale, warm bedclothes, its empty
   reserved cell.
Here she would strip off, showing her gilded nipples and
The belly that once housed a prince of the blood (= the
   murdered Britannicus, son of Claudius). Her door-sign
Bore a false name, Lycisca, 'The Wolf-girl'. A more than
   willing
Partner, she took on all comers, for cash, without a break.
Too soon, for her, the brothel-keeper dismissed
His girls. She stayed till the end, always the last to go,
Then trailed away sadly, still with a burning desire,
Retiring exhausted, yet still far from satisfied, cheeks
Begrimed with lamp-smoke, filthy, carrying home
To her imperial couch the stink of the whorehouse.[41]

One further type of provincial bronze comes from Panias(?)
(modern Baniyas in northern Israel – F.7) which is dated to the
fifth year of King Agrippa I, that is, September/October AD 40 to
September/October AD 41; but since Caligula was assassinated

Figure 67 A reconstruction of the Paneion at Panias.

on 24 January AD 41, it probably dates to the last few months AD 40.[42] It depicts the effigies of Antonia on the obverse and Drusilla, the daughter of Germanicus, on the reverse. This issue belongs to a series struck by Agrippa I in an effort to compliment Caligula and his family, who not only had freed him from prison but had given him a kingdom to rule. Antonia had been a 'second mother' to Agrippa I throughout his early life, and even as a mature man he relied on her for borrowing money (see p. 28). The ultimate assistance she gave him was when he was thrown into prison by the order of Tiberius. Josephus describes the circumstances in detail:

> (Antonia) gained from Macro (= the successor of Sejanus in the position of the praetorian prefect) the following concessions for him (Agrippa): that the soldiers who were to guard him and that the centurion who would be in charge of them and would also be handcuffed to him should be of humane character, that he should be permitted to bathe every day and receive visits from his freedmen and friends, and that he should have other bodily comforts too. His friend Silas and two of his freedmen, Marsyas and Stoecheus, visited him bringing him his favourite viands and doing whatever service they could. They brought him garments that they pretended to sell, but, when night came, they made him a bed with the connivance of the soldiers, who had Macro's orders to do so. These things went on for six months.[43]

Further, and due to its chronology, the coin minted by Agrippa I may have been meant as a compliment to Caligula for suspending his decision (after the king pleaded with him) to erect his statue in the Temple of Jerusalem. Caligula's outrageous plan had stirred up serious trouble in Judaea at the time.[44]

This coin has been recently debated on the basis of a specimen in the British Museum, reading on the obverse [. . .]ONIA GYNE CEB[. . .]. Burnett claimed that the lady depicted on the obverse must be '[Caes]onia the wife of Aug[ustus]', that is to say of Caligula, while on the reverse 'Drusilla the daughter of Augustus' must be his daughter. But according to Meshorer one copy in the Israel Museum seems to read fully: ANTONIA [. . .] SEBASTOY, while Qedar maintains that a copy in his collection reads: [. .]TONIA. An additional objection to Burnett's theory is

Figure 68 A bronze coin probably minted at Panias under Agrippa I, depicting Antonia on the obverse.

that Caesonia and Drusilla are unknown in art or on coinage, and that Drusilla was only about two when murdered in AD 41 – by no means the young lady depicted on the reverse of this coin.[45] Nevertheless Meshorer and Qedar still have to explain how Antonia could be the wife of one, and Drusilla the daughter of another 'Augustus'. Drusus, the husband of Antonia, never became such, nor did his son Germanicus, the father of Drusilla.

The answer to this would be that the title SEBASTOS in the Greek world was not applied as strictly as AVGVSTVS was in the Latin West. Local Greek authorities may occasionally have assigned titles to members of the Imperial family which had not been officially conferred in Rome. They would do this out of eagerness to please or as a proposal for such a title to be bestowed. For example, an inscription from Paphos and another from Aphrodisias, commemorating Julia the daughter of Augustus, refer to her as SEBASTE, although she had never received this title; likewise Drusilla, on a coin from Lesbos.[46]

If the solution put forward here is plausible, both Drusus and Germanicus were unofficially named *Augusti* in the East. We may compare this to the worship of the Emperor in the eastern provinces, when emperors rejected deification during their lifetime. Also comparable is the conception of the Greek term for 'god' (*theos*) which differs from the Latin *divus* in referring to living persons as well as dead.[47] My solution would offer yet another new approach, by which we may succeed in reidentifying several provincial issues from the Greek East. But this lies beyond the scope of the present book.

A coin of Antonia from Amphipolis in Macedonia reported by

Figure 69 A bronze coin probably minted at Gortyna on Crete under Claudius, depicting Antonia and Drusus on the reverse.

Cohen is probably confused with one of the types from Thessalonica. Cohen further reported coins of Antonia (and Drusus) from Smyrna and Ephesus in Ionia, and perhaps these too are confusions with coins of Claudius and the younger Agrippina from Smyrna and Ephesus.[48] Franke, however, recently mentioned a coin of Antonia from Ephesus, now in Vienna, which seems to be unpublished. He also referred to a specimen of Antonia with the younger Agrippina from Aezanis in Phrygia kept in Munich; perhaps also unpublished.[49] Finally, Cohen reported a coin of Antonia from Carthage in North Africa with the legend 'Perpetual Peace' (PACI PERP.) around a lighted altar in a laurel wreath on the reverse.[50] Its existence cannot be verified today, but it would be interesting to know whether it ever existed, particularly due to the identification of Antonia with Peace (*Pax*), which is in agreement with her representations as Safety (*Salus*) and Justice (*Iustitia*), according to the theory advanced above (cf. the 'Grande Camée' of France – see p. 137).

ROMAN TOKENS

The general term used in classical texts for tokens scattered as largesse was *missilia*. Some of these 'free gifts' thrown to the people by emperors and other officials, especially those that could be redeemed for money, went by the name *tesserae*. But the largest number of extant *tesserae* are private products made by merchants for their own commercial purposes.

Roman *tesserae* served a wide variety of functions in the administration and economy of the Empire. For instance, lead

Figure 70 Pewter portrait-*tesserae* of the 'wreath', the 'liberality' and the 'numeral' types.

tickets regulated the grain distribution (*frumentationes*), the games and the theatre. In Egypt the collection of certain taxes was arranged with tokens, while in Palmyra terracotta examples were concerned with priestly functions in the city temples.[51] In Caesarea Maritima, the superb Herodian port on the coast of Palestine, some of the tokens thrown to spectators were valid for visits to prostitutes. That houses of ill-repute existed here is proved by Josephus, who, in his vivid account of the episode at the time of Agrippa I's death, described how the people dragged the statues of the king's daughters, set them upon the roofs of the brothels and abused them.[52]

Pewter imperial portrait-*tesserae* of the city of Rome were distinct pieces, each made for distribution at a particular event, an initiative that may have been taken by Claudius to advertise his family and the legitimacy of its occupation of the throne.[53]

Two *tesserae* of Antonia were published early this century (G.1,2). The first bore on the obverse her portrait with the inscription [ANTO]NIA DRVSI and on the reverse a laurel

105

wreath. The second also had her portrait on the obverse, but only with ANTONIA, and on the reverse EX LIBERALITATE TI·CLAVDI·CAE·AVG·, which translates: 'from the liberality of Tiberius Claudius Caesar Augustus'.[54] This significant text illustrates the private character of the enactment by which the Emperor circulated the token. Claudius did not hesitate to advertise his 'generosity', since he was actually giving away to individuals the value that it carried. In the opinion of some, right or wrong, by the second century AD 'Generosity' became the spirit (*numen*) of the Emperor's donative, an important power for Roman propaganda.[55]

Two other *tesserae* have been listed as perhaps belonging to Antonia, but their effigies are uninscribed (G.3, 4). On the reverse they bear the numerals III and IIII respectively.[56] In recent years a non-portrait specimen was published (G.5) with CLAV(dius) on the obverse and AN(tonia) D(rusi) on the reverse. Notably, after deification Antonia could now and again still be called '(wife) of Drusus' without the attachment of her official title 'Augusta'. It is difficult to guess the exact events that generated the striking of Antonia's *tesserae*, but they must have been of a religious, theatrical, or athletic nature; or even private dinners or parties.[57]

Finally, two municipal *tesserae*, minted by sacred societies or minor priesthoods (*sodalitates*),[58] one from Velitrae (modern Velletri – G.6) and another from Tusculum (near modern Frascati – G.7), although uninscribed were once considered to bear portraits of Antonia. These may have been struck to promote some religious gathering, followed by a banquet, given to the townspeople in the name of Antonia.

Velitrae, on the southern rim of the Alban Hills in Latium,

Figure 71 A non-portrait *tessera* of Claudius and Antonia.

was distinguished as the place from which the family of Augustus originated. It produced the celebrated sculptural portrait of Octavia Minor, the sister of Augustus and mother of the two Antonias, now in the National Museum at Rome.[59] We may safely assume that Octavia, and indeed her brother, would have possessed property at Velitrae, part of which may have passed to her daughters.

Tusculum, at the north end of the Alban Hills, about fifteen miles from Rome, was famous for its villas. Strabo gives us a brief sketch:

> It is on (the Alban Hills) that Tusculum is situated, a city with no mean equipment of buildings; and it is adorned by the plantings and villas encircling it, and particularly by those that extend below the city in the general direction of the city of Rome; for here Tusculum is a fertile and well-watered hill, which in many places rises gently into crests and admits of magnificently devised royal palaces.[60]

The *tessera* of Antonia from Tusculum is interesting not only in depicting Drusus' portrait on its reverse, but also in having been struck in an area from which at least two sculptural portraits of Antonia have come, and where a villa which probably belonged to her was located (see pp. 121, 125, 156–7).

5

ANTONIA AND SCULPTURE

It is on iconography that most work on Antonia has been concentrated (see p. xx). Given its speculative character conclusions drawn can only be tentative. Nevertheless the accepted repertoire of sculptural-portraits of Antonia does carry some historical probability, as their similarity to her coin-portraits illustrates. This repertoire is classified on the basis of two main criteria: the physiognomic and stylistic interrelations among the portraits, and the establishment of replica series (*Replikenreihen*).

Replica series are formed on the basis of the following axiom: portraits of members of the Imperial family are essentially different from private portraits, since they were regularly copied and distributed throughout the Empire. But though valuable for drawing basic guide-lines, this axiom need not be followed too rigidly.[1] Just because an Imperial portrait belongs to a replica series it does not have to be absolutely identical with the remaining portraits of the same series. Artists in different parts of the Empire working from copies would occasionally have made changes to their model; often by introducing a few personal touches. Consequently a degree of flexibility will always be necessary in interpreting individual effigies.

Unfortunately no originally inscribed sculptural-portrait of Antonia has been found, although the head from Lepcis Magna and the statue from Cemenelum (see below) nearly approached this ideal situation. The initial evidence for the existence of sculptures portraying her in antiquity comes generally from the thirteen 'portrait-inscriptions' already examined (see p. 34). Two of these might have provided us with evidence for what she actually looked like; but, alas, this was not to be the case: the text of Antonia from Marruvium (A.2), found over two hundred years ago, was associated with a statue which was transferred to the Museum of Naples and which, surprisingly, still remains unidentified;[2] the dedication to Antonia from Herculaneum (A.16) is on a base of a statue of which only the feet have been preserved! Otherwise we have seen (p. 39) how the *Tabula Siarensis* testifies to a portrait of Antonia placed on the Arch of Germanicus. Further, we may point to Claudius' well-known letter sent to the Alexandrians and preserved in a papyrus, in which a statue of Antonia erected in Egypt (together with statues of other members of Claudius' family) may be implied:

> And first I permit you to keep my birthday as 'Augusta' (= venerable day) in the way you have yourselves proposed; I allow you to erect statues of myself *and my family* in appropriate places – because I appreciate your anxiety to establish all kinds of memorials of your piety towards my house . . . But I resign from (the idea of) appointing a high priest to me and the building of temples, for I do not wish to be indecent to my contemporaries – I judge that temples and the like have by all ages been granted as privileges to the gods alone.[3]

Although my aim is to give as complete a list of sculptural remains as possible, I make no attempt to include every single piece that has been attributed to Antonia in the past; first because of the large number involved (of which many were assigned to her with no explicit reason), and second because of limitations of space. However, at least fifty items (twenty-six heads, fourteen busts, eight statues and two reliefs) from some twenty-six sites are listed (Registers H, I, J; see fig. 109, p. 167). Of the available classifications, Erhart's will broadly be followed, as being practical, but with rearrangement and many additions.[4] 'Youthful and individualised', 'Youthful and idealised' and 'Mature and individualised' are the three main iconographic categories that may be distinguished.

YOUTHFUL AND INDIVIDUALISED

The nearest approach to an absolute identification of a sculptural portrait of Antonia is in Lepcis Magna in North Africa (H.2). Seven of the portraits discovered here were almost certainly connected with the monumental gate (*porta*) of the

Figure 72 A reconstruction of the harbour of Lepcis Magna.

Temple of Rome and Augustus in the Old Forum.[5] This bore
the Neo-Punic 'group portrait-inscription' (A.7), dated to *c.* AD
18 (see p. 45), which mentioned nine members of the Imperial
family. Three of those found were of females, as against the five
(Livia, the elder Agrippina, Livilla, Antonia Minor and Vipsania
Agrippina) originally referred to in the text. But since the image
of the elder Agrippina would have been removed after her
banishment in AD 29, as, it appears, was that of Livilla whose
memory in AD 32 suffered condemnation (*damnatio memoriae*)
and whose name was erased from the inscription, only Livia,
Antonia and Vipsania could qualify as candidates for the three
portraits in question. Livia was easily recognised by facial features known from her coins. The unknown portrait was presumed to be that of Vipsania, since her commemoration
elsewhere is extremely rare. The identification of the third was
substantiated by its familiarity from coins of Antonia and its long
replica series (see below).[6]

The head at Lepcis Magna portrays Antonia in her late teens
or early twenties, even though by about AD 18 she was fifty-
three. One reason would be to match the youthful portraits of
Drusus who died prematurely (although he was not commemorated at Lepcis). Antonia has a rather triangular face with broad
cheekbones, protruding ears, fairly large, widely set eyes, a
straight nose, soft lips and a small round chin. Her *coiffure* is
characteristic, with the hair parted in the middle and combed to
the sides in three waves. It is pulled back behind the ears, twisted
into a thick roll along the lower hairline and drawn into a round,

braided hairknot at the nape of the neck (cf. Salus coin, E.1; and the Ara Pacis relief below). A row of curls running round the forehead (cf. Alexandria and Corinth coins, F.8, F.6), is an innovation, as regards Roman circles,[7] to the female hairstyle of Late Augustan times.

The 'youthful and individualised' type of Antonia seems to have existed from the time of Augustus until that of Claudius, and to have coexisted with other of her known types. It has a long replica series covering a wide geographical area, and it would have originated in Rome – a head in the National Museum (H.1) may well have served as a model for the many examples. In the Vatican Museum there is a bust (H.8) of the same type, like one previously in the Art Market (H.9) published from an old photograph by Poulsen.

In Italy other possible replica portraits include a head from Spoletium (Spoleto near Perugia – H.3), first mentioned by Felletti-Maj and now in private hands at Rome,[8] and a head from Faesulae (Fiesole near Florence – H.4) found close to the city's theatre. In Sicily a head came from Tyndaris (H.10) in the north of the island, and perhaps another from Centuripae

Figure 73 The bust from the Roman villa in Malta.

111

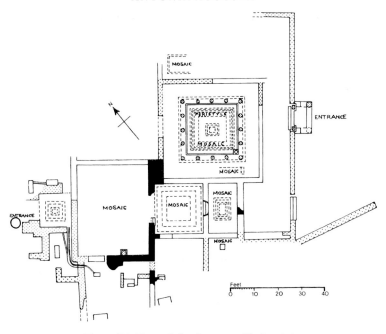

Figure 74 Plan of the Roman villa in Malta.

(H.11) on the mainland. In Malta a bust excavated together
with a portrait of Claudius in a costly Roman villa at Rabat
(H.12), now converted into a museum,[9] probably belonged to
a domestic shrine (*lararium*) in which Antonia and her son
were privately worshipped. In Algiers a wonderful statue discovered at Iol-Caesarea (modern Cherchel – H.13) undoubtedly recalls the same series, and there seems to be an
adequate explanation of why Antonia was commemorated in
the Latin-speaking part of North Africa. This city was the
capital of Mauretania,[10] the kingdom of Juba II, who not only
had been brought up in Rome close to Antonia, marrying her
half-sister Cleopatra Selene, but also sent his children to be
instructed in her remarkable court (see Family Tree 1). In the
Agora of Athens a fragmentary head (H.6) has been correctly
identified by the excavator and an apparent copy, found in an
excellent state of preservation on the island of Samos (H.7)
together with a portrait of Caligula, is now in Berlin. Another
example was recorded by Poulsen as being in Munich
(H.14).[11] Lastly, a small bust in the British Museum (H.5),

rarely commented upon, resembles this series in its facial features, protruding ears and small, sporadic curls round the forehead. It could date from the transitional period (Early to Late Tiberian) when Antonia (if it is she) was gradually abandoning her more usual style with a full row of curls.

YOUTHFUL AND IDEALISED

This category must begin with Antonia in relief on the Ara Pacis, where she appears more classicised than idealised. Her impressive image here seems to have become the prototype that influenced many aspects of her subsequent artistic tradition. It might have been assumed that Antonia's likeness began to be portrayed soon after her marriage to Drusus (c. 18 BC), the first event of consequence in her public life. As yet, however, her appearance in art cannot be dated before the Ara Pacis in 13–9 BC and this is consistent with her earliest 'portrait-inscription' from Ulia (A.1), dated about 12 BC. A few words about the monument as a whole will be useful (cf. fig. 8, p. 14).

As Augustus himself records, this great Altar of Peace (*Ara Pacis Augustae*) was erected by the Senate to celebrate his return from Spain and Gaul and the ensuing peace. As entered in the Roman Calendar, its foundation day was 4 July 13 BC, while its dedication day was 30 January 9 BC.[12] Since Augustus was fifty in 13 BC (*dies natalis* = 23 September 63 BC) the occasion may also have marked his special half-centenary birthday. That this is not specifically stated in our sources should not cause surprise; there were many obvious anniversaries in Rome that have remained unrecorded.[13] The suggestion relates well to the dedication day, which coincided with the half-centenary birthday of Livia (*dies natalis* = 30 January 58 BC). Livia was in fact forty-nine in 9 BC, but again such 'elastic views' (to quote Grant) in keeping celebration dates were commonplace in the Roman world.[14]

On the foundation day of the Ara Pacis, Augustus, accompanied by members of his family, senators, magistrates, priests, Vestal Virgins and other notables, went in procession to the site chosen for the altar in the Campus Martius.[15] His engagement was to consecrate it and offer sacrifice on his safe return (*pro reditu suo*). The monument was to be an almost square enclosure,

113

Figure 75 Close-up of Antonia's heads on the Ara Pacis and Ravenna reliefs.

in the centre of which, on a stepped platform, stood the altar. The marble superstructure, which includes a variety of panels and friezes, was elaborately carved with a skill unsurpassed in the history of Roman sculpture. Antonia and Drusus, aged twenty-three and twenty-five respectively, together with their son Germanicus can be seen on the south frieze (I.1). The boy looks hardly younger than three, but he can have been only two if he was born in 15 BC (see p. 11).[16] Antonia's *coiffure*, surmounted by a laurel wreath (*stephanê*), consists of a simple parting in the middle, with the hair gathered to form a short braided knot at the back. There were as yet no curls. This simple style, recommended by Ovid, continued to be popular into the reign of Tiberius.[17] The image of Antonia on the Ara Pacis can be effectively compared with that on the Salus coin (E.1).

Another comparison can be made with Venus Genetrix, the mother of the Augustan gens (lineage), on the splendid relief from Ravenna (I.4). This represents Antonia 'under the cloak' of the goddess (*sub specie deae*), although here she is wearing a diadem (cf. the Iustitia coin, E.2) and she appears posthumously stylised. The Ravenna relief is part of a frieze from an altar comparable to the Ara Pacis.[18] Bonanno believes it postdates Claudius, since members of the Imperial family commemorated on it are all dead and deified, including the late Emperor himself. Yet he is uncertain whether the figure next to Antonia and Germanicus is really Claudius.[19] A more realistic view is that, as the only figure depicted in military dress, it is the elder Drusus, who died while campaigning, and that the monument should therefore date to the mid-first century AD. It would be Claudius who honoured his father, mother and brother (the *trio*, incidentally, of the Ara Pacis), along with Augustus and Livia (the half-preserved seated figure), all of whom were by then dead and deified. Venus was the goddess associated in popular belief with Antonia, and Claudius would have had no hesitation in identifying her with his mother. During his reign the atmosphere was highly charged with the boosting of Julio-Claudian origins. Renewed interest in Aphrodite, among other Greek cults, became widespread, and existing temples such as those of Venus Genetrix in the Forum of Julius Caesar, Venus Victrix in the Theatre of Pompey and Venus on the Capitoline (*Aedis Capitolina Veneris*, see p. 63) must have flourished anew. Under

115

Figure 76 The Temple of Venus Erucina as depicted on the reverse of a
silver coin from Sicily dated to the Republican period.

Claudius even the Temple of Venus Erucina, on Mount Eryx in
Sicily, was restored at the Emperor's command.[20]

As evidence of the link between Antonia and Aphrodite an
amazing archaeological discovery was recently made in the Gulf of
Pozzuoli. Underwater excavation of the submerged imperial summer palace at Baiae, north of Bauli (modern Bacoli, where the villa
of Antonia was located – see p. 154), revealed a huge dining-salon
(*triclinium*) enriched with monumental fountains dedicated to the
Nymphs (*nymphaeum*), the female spirits of nature.[21] In a niche on
the western wall of the building a marble statue of Antonia was
found in the form of Venus (I.5). Her portrait, crowned with a
marvellous open-work *corona*, has been rightly claimed as one of
the most beautiful portraits Imperial Rome ever created (see
frontispiece). On her left shoulder there perched an Eros or
Cupid, in the style of Arcesilaus' famous Aphrodite in the
Temple of Venus Genetrix in the Forum Iulium.[22]

There is a brief but charming description of the town of Baiae
in Josephus:

> This is a little city in Campania situated at a distance of about
> five furlongs (that is, under a mile; the distance is in fact
> about three miles) from Dicaearchia (= Puteoli). There are
> royal residences there lavishly furnished, for each of

Figure 77 The statue from Baiae.

117

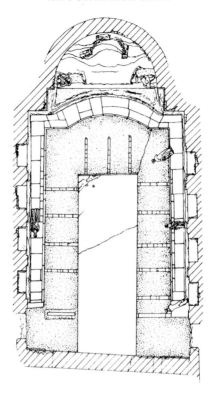

Figure 78 Plan of the underwater Nymphaeum at Baiae.

the emperors was ambitious to outdo his predecessors. The locality also affords hot baths, which spring naturally from the ground and have a curative value for those who use them, not to mention their contribution to easy living in other ways.[23]

The Venus–Antonia of Baiae is good support not only for the proposed interpretation of the Ravenna relief but also for the Aphrodisias inscription (A.18 – see p. 49). Moreover the overwhelming beauty of Antonia, praised by Plutarch and other writers (see p. 28),[24] finds its definitive expression in this portrait. A dedicatory epigram of Crinagoras, composed for one of her days of celebration, reminds us:

> The sweet company of the five lyric poets
> united in this volume
> offer the work of the inimitable Graces.

We come on her festal morning to Antonia,
supreme in beauty and mind.[25]

The most idealised portrait in this category is the posthumous
'Juno Ludovisi' head in the National Museum at Rome (I.6).
This colossal head, measuring almost four feet in height
(1.16 m), is breath-taking. Its hairstyle is clearly Claudian.[26] A
hairloop takes the place of the hairknot of the Ara Pacis, and a
long thick ringlet has been added behind each ear. A diadem
with a beaded wool band (tutulus) in front completes the decoration. The tutulus has been shown by Furtwängler to be the
symbol of priesthood, and Rumpf argued that it was specifically
connected with the 'Priestess of the Divine Augustus' (sacerdos
divi Augusti). Until the time of Claudius only two women were
accorded the title: Livia and Antonia.[27] The features do not
resemble Livia's, and under Claudius the priestess per se was
Antonia. The head can be compared with the idealised Pietas
coin (E.3), though the latter is veiled. Nevertheless two other
coins of Antonia, one from Thessalonica (F.5) and one from
Crete (F. 12), depict her veiled. Antonia as Juno, the Roman
equivalent of the Greek Hera, the wife of Zeus, apparently took
over the top position of divinity previously held by Livia. Juno,
who together with Jupiter and Minerva constituted the sacred
Capitoline Triad, was the queen of the pantheon, with at least
seven major temples to her account in Rome.[28]

The statue to which the 'Antonia–Juno Ludovisi' head belonged would have stood (if it was not seated) over nineteen feet
high. Where was it erected? Statues of the famous, including
Imperial ladies, had filled most public areas of Rome (market-
places, basilicas, colonnades, etc.), but this is a cult image worked
in expensive marble of unusual dimensions, and it has not
weathered. It was probably erected inside a temple,[29] and the
one that immediately suggests itself is Antonia's, possibly
reported by the elder Pliny and apparently built by Claudius.
According to Pliny in this temple was deposited the extraordinary painting of Hercules executed by the legendary Apelles of
Cos (actually he was from Ephesus) who flourished at the end of
the fourth century BC:

The Heracles with Face Averted in the Temple of
Antonia(?) is also believed to be by his hand – so drawn that
the picture more truly displays Heracles' face than merely

119

Figure 79 The 'Juno Ludovisi' head in the Museo Nationale at Rome.

suggests it to the imagination – a very difficult achievement.[30]

An alternative location for this 'megatheriac' statue of Antonia is the Temple of Divus Augustus in the Roman Forum (see p. 96), in which Claudius, we are told, had placed a statue of his grandmother Livia. Or it may even have been the Claudianum, a temple eminently qualified to accept such a statue. This was a grand building on the Caelian Hill dedicated immediately after his death to the Deified Claudius. Its construction was begun by the younger Agrippina. Nero interrupted the work by incorporating it into his Golden House, and Vespasian completed it in a lavish style.[31]

There are many examples of idealised portraits in this category: the Villa Albani head in Rome (I.8), the Venice fragment (from ancient Altinum? – I.12), the Warsaw head from Rome (I.9), and even (though with reservations) the head at St Petersburg (I.10). The latter is said to have originated in Veii, a town famous for its statuary since the Etruscans.[32] In addition, with less idealisation, we may include the head published by Polaschek from an old photograph in the German Institute at Rome (I.7),[33] and also the head discovered at Luni (I.11), a town near the Carrara marble quarries which were used extensively in the Roman period. Finally, we should mention the statue from

Catania in Sicily (I.3), an excellent piece bearing a profile strikingly similar to that of the Iustitia coin (E.2).

MATURE AND INDIVIDUALISED

This category centres principally around the evidence of the Imperial coin-portraits of Antonia struck under Claudius. The mature type lowers the hairline, omitting the curls of the young Antonia, and transforms the hairknot into a hairloop or ponytail. If the provincial coin of Antonia from Clazomenae (F.1) dates from about AD 18 (see p. 98), the mature portrait made its appearance earlier than Erhart anticipates.[34]

A number of groups in this category may be delineated. The plainest and least mature is a head in the New Capitoline Museum at Rome (J.1), compared by Fittschen and Zanker to an unpublished head from Grosseto (J.2 – perhaps from the Etruscan town of Rusellae).[35] There is a simple but more mature head from Baeterrae (Béziers in southern France – J.7), discovered together with eight other Julio-Claudian portraits in 1844, which evidently forms a group linked to the Imperial Cult of the region and is assigned to the Late Tiberian period. It constitutes the only material evidence of Antonia so far retrieved from Roman Gaul. Poulsen compared it with a head at Dresden in East Germany (J.8) and with a statue found at Tusculum (J.9) now to be seen at the Vatican Museum.[36]

Another group (Polaschek's *schlichte*) comprises mature examples with a characteristic fillet in front (*infula*), a mark of status and distinction but not necessarily identical with the beaded wool band (*tutulus*) of the 'Juno Ludovisi' head which directly denoted priesthood. Examples are the busts now in the following places: Erbach in West Germany (J.10); Kurashiki in Japan (J.11), bought with a bust of Augustus in Rome; and Pythagoreion on the Greek island of Samos (J.12), discovered in the German excavation of the Kastro Tigani. We may add the veiled statue in Tripolis Museum (J.14) found at Lepcis Magna and compared by Heintze to a statue in the Torlonia Museum at Rome,[37] and perhaps two other elegant sculptures, one from Cemenelum (Cimiez, north of Nice) and another at Cambridge, Mass. We shall examine both more closely.

The statue from Cemenelum (J.16) in the Roman Maritime Alps, representing a diademed Antonia, was dug up two

Figure 80 The bust in the Ninagawa Museum at Kurashiki, Japan.

decades ago in the cold room (*frigidarium*) of the North Baths.[38] We have already noted (p. 46) the fragmentary inscription (A.3) from another room of these baths. If this text had been found *in situ* attached to the statue, it would have given us the absolute identification of Antonia's portrait we want. At all events the Cemenelum material has added to our view of the great lady. This city guarding the 'Way of the Alps', the long highway which led from Italy to Gaul and Spain, must have been passed by the elder Drusus (sometimes probably with Antonia) on his expeditions. In fact at La Turbie, a town along the same road, a bust of the elder Drusus was unearthed in the middle of the nineteenth century, and although it is difficult to draw clear parallels between it and the statue of Antonia from Cemenelum we can sense the level of popularity enjoyed by the celebrated imperial couple in this part of the Roman Empire.[39]

The marble bust in Cambridge, Mass. (J.17), previously in the Wilton House collection in England, is a fine example and the most mature portrait of Antonia on record (apart from the disputed Nomentum bust – see below). The engraving 'Antonia' on her left shoulder identifies her correctly, but this was perhaps achieved by a comparison with the likeness of Antonia on coins, since the inscription is assumed to date only from the end of the seventeenth century when the bust was purchased by Thomas Herbert, the eighth Earl of Pembroke and

Figure 81 The statue from Cemenelum.

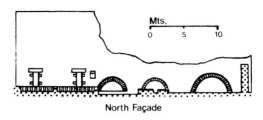

North Façade

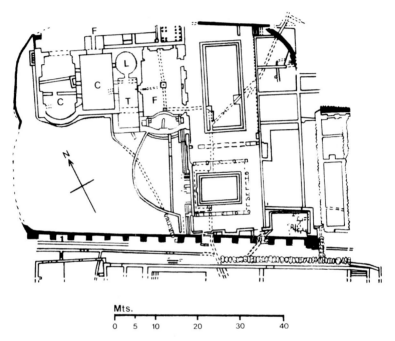

Figure 82 Plan of the North Baths complex at Cemenelum. F = cold room (*frigidarium*); T = warm room (*tepidarium*); L = hot-dry room (*laconicum*); C = hot room (*caldarium*).

Montgomery.[40] No doubt this bust illustrates the 'matriarch' of the Roman people at the time of Claudius. It may even be a copy of the image of her which was borne by a carriage (*carpentum*) in the Circus Maximus at the annual games held on her birthday. After such processions, in which effigies of other members of the Imperial family and of gods would also have been paraded, carried on various stretchers or sedan chairs held by men (*fercula*) and carts drawn by animals (*tensae*), the portrait of Antonia would have been placed on the permanent sacred couch (*pulvinar*) built

Figure 83 The bust in the Fogg Art Museum at Cambridge, Mass.

by Augustus in the officials' box.[41] Although the pompous specimen at Cambridge is said by Erhart not to have any sculptural
parallels, we may tentatively compare it with a bust in Florence
(J.18) once considered to be Antonia.[42]

The last group (Polaschek's *Schläfenlöckchentypus*) retains the
fillet but has in addition two or three small curls by the ear. A
statue from Rome (J.19) and a bust from Tusculum (J.20), both
now in Paris, fall into this group even though their authenticity
has been questioned in the past.[43] The group also includes
heads in Erbach (J.21), Florence (J.22) and the Villa Borghese in
Rome (J.23). There is a further head in Bologna (from ancient

125

Figure 84 A *tensa*, the cart drawn by animals on which the images of the gods were carried at the games, as appears in a scene depicted on a Roman sarcophagus.

Bononia? – J.24) which seems to belong with them. This is diademed and bears a delicately carved *tutulus*, the symbol of Antonia's major priesthood. The only other 'mature and individualised' example wearing a diadem or crown (*corona*), an almost regular feature of the 'youthful and idealised' category, is the statue at Cemenelum (J.16), with which, however, the Bologna head shares certain facial configurations.

Finally, there are three highly disputed portraits of Antonia which I am inclined to accept both on general considerations and for the strong resemblance they bear to Antonia, as known in numismatics and sculpture. First is the bust now in Copenhagen which came from Tralles (Aydin, Turkey – J.3) in north-west Caria, a city renowned for its school of oratory.[44] This portrait, which Poulsen has compared to a head of a statue found in the Roman theatre of Vicetia (Vicenza in northern Italy – J.4) and also to two heads in the Vatican Museum (J.5, 6), would fit the very beginning of the 'mature' category. The profile of the Tralles bust can be successfully compared with: the 'young and individualised' head from the Greek island of Samos (H.7), though without curls; the 'young and idealised' statue from Sicilian Catania (I.3), though without the diadem; and the 'mature' head from Gaulish Baeterrae (J.7), ignoring the age factor.

Second, the so-called 'Clytie' bust in the British Museum (I.2), once the prized possession of Towneley into whose collection it came perhaps from Naples,[45] evidently falls into the 'youthful and idealised' category. This aesthetic portrait was initially

identified with the nymph Clytie, one of the female spirits of
nature highly benevolent to mankind, who pined away for love
of the sun-god Helios and was turned into a flower said to
resemble a violet. However, the petals around the base of the
bust occur on other portraits and have no mythological significance.[46] She may well be Antonia even if, as is argued by
Polaschek, this particular copy is not antique.[47] Selectively, we
may compare 'Clytie' with the fragmentary head from Venice
(I.12), the Kurashiki bust (J.11) and the head in the Villa
Borghese (J.23), besides a number of gems attributable to
Antonia (see pp. 132–40). There is something soft and romantic
about all these specimens which suits Antonia's character as
expressed in her lasting passion for Drusus, but they also reflect
a hidden melancholy which may remind us of her love's tragic
finale. Looking particularly at the 'Clytie' of the British Museum
with Antonia in mind, we may be allowed to create the following
imaginary picture: an idealised young woman of great beauty
and Imperial status, in a sensuous or even erotic pose, who is

Figure 85 The 'Clytie' bust from Naples, now in the British Museum.

127

emotionally involved but whose lover is fated not to be with her physically.

Third is a bust, currently assigned to Antonia, which was unearthed in 1949 at the Forum of Nomentum (Mentana, north-east of Rome – J.13), a town famed for its wine and villas. If the identification is correct and the portrait is not of Livia or another Julio-Claudian matron, this is the most mature likeness of Antonia in existence, even more mature than the Cambridge bust (J.17).[48] It was found together with heads of Germanicus and the younger Drusus. Though it may therefore be Livia, since this trio is known as a group in sculpture elsewhere,[49] it probably dates to the time of Caligula, so that Antonia is a more likely candidate. Antonia's appearance with the two *Caesares*, her son Germanicus and her son-in-law Drusus, would be understood in the context of her avenging of their death, when she adduced evidence first against Piso and then against Sejanus (cf. Honestus' epigram, A.15 – see p. 92). Antonia at Nomentum may be thought of as in her late sixties or early seventies, but her

Figure 86 The bust from Nomentum, now in the Museo Nationale at Rome.

features remain unaltered and authoritative. Her *coiffure* retains the usual middle parting, though the hair is not combed to the sides in large waves but instead twisted in a series of thick rolls, all drawn back to form an aristocratic hairloop. Antonia wearing the priestly *tutulus* could even depict 'Augusta', in the manner in which she was seen publicly for the last time during the ceremony of Caligula's coronation, a few weeks before her death in AD 37.

Vermeule tentatively named three sculptural pieces as Antonia, two of which, a head in Istanbul and a fragment of a veiled and diademed head of enormous proportions from Cos, seem to be of the elder Agrippina.[50] The third piece, however, a *ptotomê* or marble mask from the portico-frieze in the Agora of Aphrodisias, is worth considering. The Ionic-style portico in the Forum of this city was dedicated to the Emperor Tiberius, and it was enriched by a masterly decorated frieze featuring an array of handsome masks joined by garlands.[51] Faces imitated mythological and religious beings as well as members of the Imperial family. Though stylised, Antonia may be recognised in this example from a facial resemblance but also from the hairstyle. This identification would be consistent with the fact that inscriptions of her (A.12, 18) were found in Aphrodisias (see p. 49).

That Antonia ought to have been represented in the large

Figure 87 A marble mask (thought to represent Antonia) from the portico-frieze at Aphrodisias.

129

collection of sculpture at Aphrodisias, the city of Venus/
Aphrodite and also a centre of the Imperial Cult in Asia Minor
(with both of which Antonia was linked), is an assumption hardly
escapable. In fact if we look closer at individual pieces from this
collection, we may make another identification. On a relief-
panel from the portico of the Sebasteion there is a headless
imperial woman performing a kind of sacrifice. She wears a
long, sleeved, woollen garment, the Greek *chiton*, belted under
the breasts with a knotted fillet, and an outer garment, the
Greek *himation*, over the left shoulder and under the right.
Smith, after examining the separated fragmentary head, tentatively identified the figure as Livia, while he ruled out the
younger Agrippina on 'portrait grounds'. Antonia, he thought,
without giving any reasons, was 'the least likely'. Yet, as he
admitted, the hairstyle does not match that of any defined
portrait-type of an imperial woman; it is basically classicised.
Further, it has a possible diagnostic element, the distinct 'single'
row of tiny curls around the forehead, which, if at all compatible
with the hairstyle of one of the three women mentioned, has to
be with that of Antonia (see the 'young and individualized' series
above and also coins from Corinth and Alexandria, F.6, 8). A
few examples attested by Smith in favour of Livia have
elongated locks without the curled ends, which are difficult to
compare with the Aphrodisias head.[52] In the case of Antonia
this type of curl is almost a standard feature.

Nevertheless, since Smith's pioneering publication demands
more study, and since some ambiguity remains in the attribution
of the relief under scrutiny to either Livia or Antonia, I have not
included it in the registers of this book. Nor have I included the
mask from the frieze of the Forum of Tiberius discussed above.
Both, for the moment, must be regarded only as possible additions to our collection of Antonia's portraits.

6

ANTONIA
AND MINOR ARTS

As noted, the iconography of Antonia examined through sculpture, even with numismatic help, is speculative. With minor arts our evidence becomes increasingly conjectural. But a careful comparison of the sculptural- and numismatic-portrait features of Antonia with glyptic-portrait (as well as context considerations), can often lead to acceptable identifications. Intaglio (incised) and cameo (relief) gems are by far the richest source, but other luxury objects will also be investigated.

Nowhere is the genius of the Augustan and Julio-Claudian age more manifest than in the art of the gem-engraver and the cameo-cutter. The artists were overwhelmingly Greek, as inscriptions prove, but their artistic conception was Imperial Roman. They continued and developed Hellenic methods, without mere imitation. Engraved gems served as seals, amulets and ornaments, while cameos were purely for decoration. By the time of Augustus gems were cut in various stones such as sard, cornelian and onyx. Rarer stones (amethyst, garnet, aquamarine and sapphire) were also used, and imported from as far as India.[1] The subjects vary considerably and give an excellent idea of Roman art in general: from scenes of daily life to deities and copies of Greek art, from mythological motifs to portraits. It was regarded as an honour to have the image of a distinguished ancestor on your seal. Naturally there were both official and private seals. One with the head of Augustus was used by later emperors as the Imperial seal of Rome, and another with the head of Claudius to gain admittance to the Imperial presence. Claudius was exceedingly fond of gems.[2] During his reign a great number of gems, together with sculpture, coins and

Figure 88 The signature of Saturninus.

tesserae, were produced to glorify individual members of his family and to propagate the established Empire.

ENGRAVED GEMS

As with sculpture, a complete account of gems assigned and reassigned to Antonia in modern times will not be the aim. I shall try rather to analyse current and relatively plausible ascriptions, especially those that conform with Antonia's iconographic categories (see Registers K, L, M).

In the 'youthful and individualised' category we should place an agate-onyx cameo in Paris inscribed with the engraver's name: Saturninus (K.1). It presents a frontal bust of Antonia looking to her right, wearing a *décolletée* garment and having a *coiffure* similar to that of the sculptured head in the National Museum at Rome (H.1). The curls running round the forehead are sparse, and this may be why Erhart has claimed it as 'mature'.[3] To this cameo we may variously compare two other engraved gems: a topaz intaglio in Florence (K.2), thought to be Livia, which omits the curls but retains the same hairstyle and in facial characteristics more closely resembles Antonia; and a black opaque glass-cameo with white finish in Munich (K.3) which may just qualify for the present classification.

The 'youthful and idealised' category may include a sardonyx intaglio ring-stone in New York (L.1) which employs a three-quarter view and depicts a quite ethereal image. The hair is parted in the middle and pulled to the sides in rich waves and her general physiognomy is reminiscent of the Ara Pacis, although on the gem she is veiled. A white-brown glass-cameo in Brussels (L.3), comparable in some features to the head at the Villa Borghese (J.23), and a cornelian intaglio in Paris (L.2) with the provenance of Berytus (Beirut, Lebanon) should also be included.

Because of their nature and size engraved gems were eminently transportable in ancient times, as indeed they were a few
centuries ago when the large collections of antiquities began to
be formed in Europe. Most gems in such collections have
changed hands several times before settling in their present
location, thus making their classification (not to mention their
authentication) a difficult task. Often it is impossible to say
where a gem originated. In the case of the Berytus intaglio the
available information is of real interest for context considerations, even though we cannot be certain whether it was locally
manufactured or was imported or lost there. In Claudian times a
number of cities in Phoenicia and Syria came under the growing
influence of Agrippa I, king of Judaea, whose protectress, as we
saw, had been Antonia. As I have suggested earlier, the great
lady herself may have visited the region. Agrippa I (and later his
children) contributed to the colony of Berytus in the most mega-
lomaniac way, if this is how we are to understand Josephus:

> he conferred special favours on the people of Berytus. He
> built them a theatre surpassing many others in its costly
> beauty; he also built an amphitheatre at great expense,
> besides baths and porticoes; and in none of these works did
> he allow either the beauty or the size to suffer by stinting
> on the expenses. He was also magnificently lavish in his
> provision at the dedication of them; in the theatre he
> exhibited spectacles, introducing every kind of music and
> all that made for a varied entertainment, while in the
> amphitheatre he showed his noble generosity by the num-
> ber of gladiators provided. On the latter occasion also,
> wishing to gratify the spectators by ranging a number of
> combatants against each other, he sent in seven hundred
> men to fight another seven hundred.[4]

Agrippa I, who struck the Panias(?) coin depicting Antonia (F.7),
seems also to have been fond of engraved gems. Such objects of
considerable value and beauty dated by some scholars approximately to his time were discovered in excavations at Jerusalem in
Israel and Machaerus in Jordan.[5] It is possible that the Berytus
specimen of Antonia was made during the time of Agrippa's
patronage of the Roman colony.

A more idealised portrait is seen on the amethyst intaglio in

Paris (L.4) depicting Antonia as the goddess Ceres holding the cornucopia of prosperity and happiness (cf. Constantia coin, E.7, 8). She is half-veiled, wearing a wreath on her head and a *bijou* around her neck: in other words a kind of *collier* or necklace with a hanging row of precious stones. Her features are analogous to the sculptured bust in Kurashiki (J.11), though the latter is more 'mature'. An almost perfect copy of the Ceres–Antonia intaglio in Paris, also of amethyst, is the intaglio in St Petersburg (L.5) with the important addition of the engraver's name: Hyllos. As another gem proves, he was the son of Dioskourides, the creator of Augustus' signet, whose skill was frequently praised in antiquity.[6] This fact provides us with some chronological parameters (perhaps within the later part of the reign of Augustus) for the engraving of Antonia's gem. Dioskourides' family was of eastern Greek origin and probably came from Aigiae in Cilicia. Hyllos may not have spent his entire working life in the Latin West, but at some point he may have found employment in Cyprus; an intaglio from Salamis bears his name.[7]

Figure 89 An impression from the amethyst intaglio of 'Ceres' in Paris.

134

Figure 90 The signature of Hyllos.

Figure 91 The signature of Epitynchanos.

Of the Ceres–Antonia amethyst intaglio there is a post-classical copy in the British Museum inscribed: Epitynchanos. The engraver's choice of this name is curious, since the real Epitynchanos signed an authentic gem-portrait of Germanicus, son of Antonia.[8] Was the post-classical copy executed by an ingenious specialist, or was it actually based on a lost original?

Further, there is a high-relief sardonyx cameo of a different type of Ceres (L.6) which was reported early this century in the collection of Francis Cook in London and said to bear a likeness to the 'Clytie' bust (I.2). This portrait, however, wears a wreath with a thin veil thrown over the back of the head.[9] Although it has sometimes been attributed to Livia, it is much more in line with the Ceres–Antonia artistic tradition. The folds draping her shoulders are kept in place by the left hand just below the shoulder. Both the face and the semi-transparent drapery are delicately modelled but, as was once observed, the bust gives the overall impression of having been copied from a full-length statue, since the introduction of the hand lopped off at the wrist is peculiarly ugly in an oval bust.

At a higher level of idealisation, Antonia appears on two precious stones: a sardonyx cameo in Vienna (L.8) depicting a youthful portrait which, though uncrowned, may be juxtaposed to the 'Juno Ludovisi' head (I.6), and a chalcedony head broken

Figure 92 The sardonyx cameo of the Cook collection.

off a statuette formerly in England but now in the Paul Getty Museum in Malibu (L.9). The last presents Antonia diademed and veiled. Most unusually the centre of the diadem is decorated by a medallion in intaglio with the portrait of Augustus.[10] Evidently she is the priestess of the divine Augustus (*sacerdos divi Augusti*), and hence a clue that the statuette should date to Claudian times.

Additionally, despite Erhart's objections,[11] Antonia appears classicised and stylised on the largest ancient cameo to survive (31 × 26.5 cm). The sardonyx 'Grande Camée' of France (L.7), according to my understanding, illustrates Tiberius' reception of Germanicus on his return from Germany in AD 17, and features Antonia as the personification of Peace (*Pax*) welcoming her son.[12] She is embracing Germanicus to kiss him, resting one of her hands on his shield and the other behind his helmet. As in the heroic age of Sparta, when a mother would courageously insist on her son's departure for battle that either he must return carrying his shield or his dead body be carried back on it, so the victorious Germanicus brought his shield back to his mother and to Rome.[13]

Supporting evidence for this is the depiction in the sky above him of his 'consecrated' father Drusus, equally heroic in military dress but lying on his shield: the manner in which he returned, lifeless, from an earlier German war to his mother Livia. The latter is now portrayed sitting next to her other son, the Emperor Tiberius. Behind Germanicus is his wife Agrippina holding in her left hand the scroll in which her husband's brave acts were recorded. In her right she holds her young son Caligula (five years old in AD 17; he was born on 31 August AD

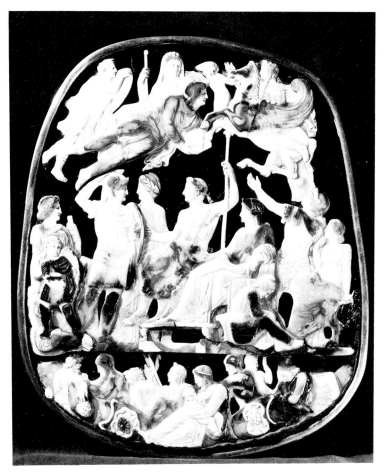

Figure 93 The sardonyx *Grande Camée* in Paris.

137

Figure 94 Antonia as represented on the Great Cameo.

12)[14] in diminutive military dress and 'little boots' (*caliga* = the half-boot worn by soldiers), which verifies Suetonius' testimony:

> His surname Caligula he derived from a joke of the troops, because he was brought up in their midst in the dress of a common soldier.[15]

Antonia does not seem to appear in the scene of the other famous sardonyx cameo known as *Gemma Augustea* in Vienna. The young lady, sometimes identified with her, seated with two children holding a cornucopia, should be the elder Agrippina, who in AD 12 (the date of the scene) had two sons aged five and six.[16]

The 'mature and individualised' category includes the black jasper intaglio in New York (M.1) and another intaglio in Hanover in Germany (M.2). Schlüter unconvincingly compares the latter with a terracotta head in Berlin.[17] Both should rather be compared with the sculptured head of Antonia in the New Capitoline Museum at Rome (J.1), though its hairstyle has a ponytail instead of a knot. The ponytail can be seen on a sardonyx cameo in the British Museum (M.3), dated on the basis of its curls not later than the middle of Tiberius' reign, when Antonia seems to have abandoned this type of hairstyle. These gems together with a cornelian intaglio (M.4), once said to be in the collection of Devonshire House in England,[18] and with two portrait-gems in Vienna (M.5, 6) are to be associated with the coin-portraits of Antonia.

A cornelian intaglio in Hanover (M.7) depicts Antonia facing

Figure 95 An impression from the black jasper intaglio in the Metropolitan Museum of Art at New York.

Figure 96 The cornelian intaglio in the Kestner Museum at Hanover.

her husband Drusus, very much like the provincial coin from Crete (F.12), and bears the inscription PHO[E]BE·IVVE·VITA, which could be understood as a presentation for life to a young lady called Phoebe. Alternatively, the name may be that of the Titaness, in Greek mythology the daughter of Heaven and Earth, who in Roman poetry often denoted the Moon but also the goddess Diana, the equivalent of the Greek Artemis.[19] In such a case the anonymous female owner of the gem may have meant to transform it into an amulet, by inscribing on it the name of her divine protector, who would have kept her young and beautiful in life. Moreover, since Diana was largely a goddess of women and childbirth, she appropriated the portrait of Antonia.[20] The latter is seen next to Drusus, constituting the 'ideal' couple, which would have reflected the aspiration of young and aristocratic Roman women for a marriage like theirs.

139

Finally, three post-classical examples in this category have also been recorded.[21] The most interesting, from the point of view of tracing the engraver's mistakes, is a lapis-lazuli cameo in the Ashmolean Museum at Oxford.

DECORATED SILVER PLATE

The late Republic and early Empire produced many master-pieces in the department of 'minor arts'. Apart from engraved gems, some of which were of incredible workmanship and lux-urious quality, metalworking flourished in Italy and in some of the provinces. Silver vessels were ardently amassed, and some fine craftsmen were producing for the Roman market. Cups of immense value, decorated with artistic and symbolic ornamen-tation as well as with mythological and even historical scenes, are known to us today.[22]

A silver tankard (*kantharus*), with a scene from the Orestes cycle in embossed (*repoussé*) work, needs to be examined here. This exquisite cup, made perhaps in Ephesus, is now in the British Museum. The scene was recognised as the legend be-lieved to have been the subject of Sophocles' lost play *Chryses*.[23] It is known from a Latin handbook of mythology of the second century AD, called *Genealogiae*, but usually known as *Fabulae* and attributed to one Hyginus. The story runs thus: Chryseis (daughter of the priest of Apollo at Sminthe) became a concu-bine of Agamemnon, the legendary king of Mycenae, and had by him a son named Chryses. When Orestes, the son of Aga-memnon and Clytemnestra, together with his sister Iphigeneia and his childhood friend (and future brother-in-law) Pylades escaped from the country of the Tauri (in the Crimea), snatch-ing away the image of Artemis, they sought sanctuary at Sminthe where Chryses lived. Chryses tried to surrender the company to the pursuing king of the Tauri, but his mother Chryseis intervened, telling him that he was a half-brother of Orestes and Iphigeneia. Chryses and Orestes then joined forces and killed the king.

The portraits of Orestes and Pylades on the cup are of Julio-Claudian princes, and the scene has therefore been thought to bear Imperial political symbolism and propaganda. Several com-binations are possible, when it is allowed that the family relation-ships in the legend cannot be exactly paralleled. For example, it has been suggested that Chryseis–Livia is interceding with Chryses–Augustus on behalf of her grandsons Orestes–Germanicus and Pylades–the younger Drusus; hence Iphigeneia is Agrippina, the wife of Germanicus. Or, to take another example, Chryseis–Livia is advancing the fortunes of her own children Orestes–Tiberius and Pylades–the elder Drusus, and the seated Iphigeneia covering her head, holding under her right arm the image of Artemis, is Antonia the wife of Pylades–the elder Drusus.[24] Such an equation of Iphigeneia with Antonia would give rise to a number of further possible identifications: for example, on two Pompeiian paintings, sometimes considered in a study of Antonia but only on stylistic grounds.[25]

Identifications which take such liberties are not convincing, however. We could propose a new interpretation by stating at first that Orestes is indeed Germanicus. His classicised image on

Figure 97 The silver *cantharus* from Ephesus, now in the British Museum.

141

Figure 98 The entire scene on the *cantharus*.

Figure 99 Chryseis–Antonia from the scene on the *cantharus*.

the cup can be effectively compared with that on the Ravenna relief; with the relief on the commemorative breastplate of a headless statue of Caligula from Iol-Caesarea; and, to some extent, with the relief at Aphrodisias (fig. 7, p. 12).[26] The simple, Greek, half-naked manner in which he is dressed is related by Tacitus:

> (Germanicus) adopted many practices popular with the multitude, walking without his guards, his feet in sandals and his dress identical with that of the Greeks . . . Tiberius passed a leniently worded criticism on his dress and bearing.[27]

Suetonius briefly adds to our picture of Germanicus' stature:

> His legs were too slender for the rest of his figure, but he gradually brought them to proper proportions by constant horseback riding after meals.[28]

In the scene on the cup Orestes' sister Iphigeneia has to be

Livilla, as she is the sister of Germanicus, while Orestes' brotherly friend Pylades is Claudius, the brother of Germanicus. Chryseis can now be seen as Antonia, the mother of the three, who promotes her orphans' interests to Chryses–Tiberius, reminding him that they are the children of his natural brother, the elder Drusus. In fact in this interpretation the story of Antonia comes so close to the Orestes legend that the metal-worker at Ephesus is unlikely not to have noticed or intentionally used it. He may have been active around AD 18, when Asia Minor was visited by Germanicus' family. The image of Chryseis–Antonia is stylised; she is veiled and wearing the Greek *chitôn*.

OTHER OBJECTS

The commonest military decorations in the Roman army were small discs or badges of metal, glass, or paste called *phalerae* and usually awarded in sets of nine. But the term also applies to horse-trappings, which are not always readily distinguishable from the badges of rank, since both are ornate and designed to be attached to leather straps.[29] The soldier who was honoured with *phalerae* wore them like medals on the chest. A glass *phalera* from the time of Tiberius depicting Antonia and presumably belonging to a special Imperial set of nine (seven have survived – but unfortunately not Antonia's) has been postulated by Toynbee and Richmond.[30] One of these with the portrait of the elder Agrippina discovered in a well at Luguvallium(?) (Carlisle in England)[31] was once argued forcefully, although incorrectly, by King to show Antonia. The point was omitted by all the published accounts of this *phalera*.[32] Of course such fine objects will have had a long life, and the Tiberian example from northern Britain could not have been lost at least until the Flavian period (when the Roman conquest expanded).

In the British Museum there is a small bust broken off a silver libation dish (*patera*) and tentatively attributed to Antonia.[33] It came from Boscoreale, the buried township between Vesuvius and Pompeii, famed as the place in which ninety-four marvellous pieces of silver plate were excavated at the end of the last century, and are now displayed in the Louvre. These objects, however, need not have originated at Boscoreale, but may have been transferred from a wealthier place in Campania and hidden

Figure 100 The lamp from Puteoli now in the British Museum.

there.[34] If the small silver bust is of Antonia, we may ask whether the *patera* had been used for libations in private sacrifices connected with the cult of her 'guardian spirit' (*iuno*) during her lifetime, or with her personal posthumous cult (*Diva Augusta*) some time in the reign of Claudius.[35] We have seen that a possible shrine was built to Antonia in the Naples area by two of her slaves or freedmen (see p. 58).

Finally, there is another related object in the British Museum, once thought to depict Antonia: an attractive terracotta lamp from Puteoli (modern Pozzuoli) near Naples.[36] On the flat top of the lamp, within a circle, a small bust can be seen in profile. The features are those of an Imperial matron and the hairstyle resembles Antonia's, particularly the hairknot and the long ringlet behind the ear. But the depiction is very stylised and absolute certainty is not possible.

As the major harbour of Rome, Puteoli was a vital commercial entrepôt. By 125 BC it had become second only to Delos in the whole Mediterranean. All Rome's eastern imports and exports, including the crucial transport of grain, passed through it.[37] In its heyday the harbour was fashionable for its villas, one of which may have been lit by the British Museum lamp said to be Antonia's. Among its famous visitors we should note the following three characters who have often appeared in this book: the Herodian Agrippa I, who arrived at Puteoli from Alexandria in AD 36, on his way to pay court to Tiberius; the Apostle Paul, who reached the port around AD 59 (on board the Alexandrian ship *Castor and Pollux*) and met with fellow-Christians; and the Jewish historian Josephus, who disembarked here from a Cyrenian ship in AD 63, after a shipwreck as terrifying as the one suffered earlier by Paul.[38]

7

ANTONIA
AND ARCHITECTURE

With architectural remains, our archaeological search for
Antonia Augusta approaches its end. Many public and private
buildings associated with her have already been mentioned,
though next to nothing remains of them. Our evidence is mostly
documentary. Thus the following have already been noted: in
Rome, a temple of Antonia (possibly reported by Pliny), a basilica dedicated to her and her homonymous sister (B.2), the Ara
Pacis depicting Antonia on its south frieze (I.1), the Arch of
Germanicus (A.9) and the Arch of Claudius (A.19) bearing
statues of her, and at least one *columbarium* (of Marcella Minor's
family) which has produced a number of funerary inscriptions
belonging to members of her household; in Baiae, the underwater *nymphaeum tricliniare* (I.5) where a statue of Antonia once
stood; in Ravenna, another Ara (?) depicting her in relief (I.4);
in Naples and Athens, among other places, possible shrines
dedicated to her (B.15, 36, 38; H.6; I.2); in Cemenelum, the
North Baths in which her statue and a few fragments of an
inscription were found; in Aphrodisias, the portico of the
Sebasteion with an architrave-inscription (A.18) probably mentioning Antonia, as well as a statue of her with a dedication on its
base (A.12); at Lepcis Magna, a monumental *porta* attached to
the Temple of Rome and Augustus that bore her portrait (A.7;
H.2; J.14); and in Egypt, in various villages of the Arsinoite
nome, the farmsteads on the rural estates belonging to Antonia.

Beyond these, of course, in her association with the Imperial
Cult, Antonia can be assumed to have been associated with many
temples, *arae* and private sanctuaries (*lararia*) in wealthy houses
throughout the Empire: for example, Baeterrae (J.7), Samos
(H.7; J.12) or the villa at Melita (Malta – H.12). Naturally the

146

buildings most closely related to our great matron would have been her own town-house (*domus*) and country-houses (*villae*), the architectural remains of which will now be examined.

THE HOUSE OF ANTONIA

Although it is an important question where precisely Antonia resided for the great part of her life, no answer has yet been attempted. As argued earlier in this book, Antonia was conceived in Athens but born in Rome (see pp. 6, 36). Even this straightforward fact (not to mention her chronology, often misstated) has rarely been discussed, and then only to be misunderstood. The fact that she died in Rome (see pp. 28, 36) has also been misinterpreted.[1]

Octavia Minor gave birth to Antonia on 31 January 36 BC in the house of Mark Antony which she then occupied.[2] Dio refers to a house of Antony on the Palatine, which Tamm thinks would have been that of Fulvia, his third wife (not counting Cytheris whom he did not marry but only lived with – see Family Tree 1), passing to him after her death in 40 BC; Fulvia would have inherited this property from her first husband, Publius Clodius.[3] According to Tamm, Antony could have had no family home, because his father left him penniless. But Octavia and her children do not seem to have been living on the Palatine in 36 BC. Augustus insisted that Octavia should leave Antony's house and come to 'her own home', which may imply a location for the former further away from, rather than on, the Palatine, where Augustus himself resided.[4] At all events we know that Antony did take possession of the house of Pompey on the Esquiline, in the district Carinae, perhaps known as *domus rostrata* due to its external decoration with prows of ships, and it is here that we may suppose Antonia was born and lived her first four years.[5]

Where Octavia and her children turned after her expulsion from these premises in 32 BC is hard to determine with any certainty.[6] If she inherited the house of her first husband Gaius Marcellus, she may have gone there – of unknown location but perhaps on the Aventine. Alternatively, she may have moved into the family house of the Octavii, if any such existed at that time, possibly near the Colosseum valley, or she may even have headed towards 'her own home', namely Augustus' house on the

Figure 101 Laurel branches and oak crown fixed by the door of Augustus' house, as shown on the reverse of a gold aureus minted in Rome.

Palatine which was now rebuilt and expanded as a new palace, the *domus Augusti*.[7] That Octavia resided at her brother's after 32 BC is the most attractive solution, for Antonia would then have been raised with the elder Drusus, who married her some four-teen years later. Crinagoras' epigrams dedicated to Antonia before and after her wedding would fit this theory, since the poet was employed by the Imperial court (see p. 11). Further, it is clear that after Antonia married Drusus she stayed in the house of her mother-in-law, Livia. This was Augustus' original palace which was left to Livia after the creation of the south-western extensions (*domus Augusti*), with which it must not be confused.[8] Antonia lived here continuously (except for holidays in the countryside or the occasional voyage overseas) until her death in AD 37.

The first palace of Augustus and Livia on the Palatine was a house previously owned by Quintus Hortensius the orator.[9] It is now generally known as the House of Livia ('Casa di Livia'), largely because of an inscription on a lead water-pipe (*fistula plumbea*) found in the excavation of the site. First excavated in 1869, it is the most complete and best-preserved private dwell-ing of the Augustan period, though of modest dimensions (770 sq. m). Apparently it was retained unaltered down the centuries, as if an object of veneration.[10]

148

Its construction is of tufa-concrete with refined *opus reticulatum*: that is to say, a brick facing, consisting of a network of small squared blocks laid in diagonal lines. The lower storey is set in a sort of hollow area against the side of a low rocky ridge, so that the upper storey behind is level with the road which runs along the higher ridge. A flight of travertine (silvery-grey calcareous stone) stairs with a vaulted roof leads down to the *atrium*. This principal hall, though usually with a rectangular opening in the roof (*compluvium*), was probably here a *testudinatum*: that is to say, it was covered by a roof. On two sides (south-west and south-east) of the *atrium* various public rooms open out. On the south-western side, in the centre opposite the entrance, is a kind of parlour (*tablinum*) with side-rooms (*alae*). On the walls are fine examples of Augustan wall-painting. The best is that of Io, the mythological priestess of Hera, watched by the monster Argos, while Hermes on the orders of Zeus approaches stealthily round a large rock, preparing to kill Argos and liberate Io. On the south-eastern side of the *atrium* is the dining-room (*triclinium*), which is paved with white mosaic, studded with irregularly shaped pieces of coloured oriental marble and alabaster, brilliantly contrasted with the white background.[11]

Next to the *triclinium* a dark vaulted room may perhaps be identified as the kitchen (*culina*). The private apartments and bedrooms (*cubicula*), mostly very small rooms, are all behind, at the higher level of the hill. Remains exist of a staircase which once led to a still higher storey, now destroyed. A door opposite leads into a long underground vaulted corridor (*crypta* or *crypto-porticus*) which branched in three directions. Another such corridor began from near the top of the stairs leading down to the *atrium* and communicated with the long corridor which ran into the palace of Caligula.

This connection makes it possible that the mysterious 'House of Germanicus', into which the assassins of Caligula escaped after stabbing him inside the passage, was actually a part of Livia's house.[12] This is mentioned only by Josephus:

> once they had settled their business with Gaius, [they] saw that there was no chance of escape if they followed the route by which they had come . . . the passage-ways along which they had done the deed were narrow and blocked by a great crowd of his attendants . . . so they took another

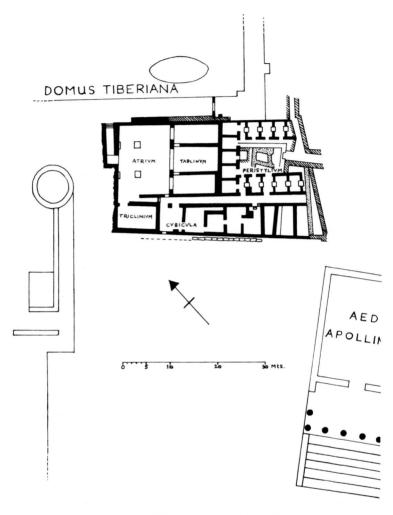

Figure 102 Plan of the 'Casa di Livia' on the Palatine.

route and came to the house of Germanicus . . . which was
contiguous with the palace of Gaius.[13]

Epigraphical evidence already adduced (see p. 67), concerning
the interconnections between members of Antonia's personal
staff and the staff of Germanicus and his wife Agrippina (as
well as of Marcella Minor, half-sister of Antonia), suggests, at
this point, the identification of the households of Antonia and

Figure 103 The central painting on the south-west wall of the *tablinum*, showing Io guarded by Argos below the statue of Juno, with Mercury hurrying to the rescue.

Figure 104 The excavated back rooms of the House of Livia.

Germanicus. Further, these can now be located within the House of Livia, of which they were parts. The apparent contradiction in Suetonius can also be explained: why Caligula on the one hand is said to have lived with, and been looked after by, Livia until AD 29, whereas on the other hand he was caught while a 'minor' violating his sister Drusilla in the house of Antonia, where they were both brought up.[14] Antonia's dwelling formed a part of Livia's household. Claudius, too, was placed under the control of Antonia in AD 29, but until then he had lived in the palace of Tiberius which was clearly separated from the house of Livia.[15] The house of Hortensius–Augustus–Livia–Antonia–Germanicus passed, after Antonia's death, to Claudius (perhaps via Caligula) and then on to the younger Agrippina, the mother of Nero.[16]

In this beautiful home (as described), we can briefly reflect on some of the sad or happy moments in the life of Antonia: her early years in the precious company of her husband Drusus, and later bringing up her children on her own. We picture her carefully dressed by Pamphila for a dinner given to her wealthy friends in which Liarus the cupbearer served the cold drinks, while Quintia and Tertius sang heavenly melodies. When she fell ill in an unusually bad winter, we visualise her principal doctor Celadus attending at her bedside with the many medicines he had skilfully prepared. It was here, in the drama of AD 31, that she dictated to Caenis the crucial letter in which Sejanus was fatally accused.

The small size of the house would have enabled only a few of her personal staff to live at home and hardly any of the foreign princes and princesses supervised by her. Separate accommodation was required for all these persons. Nevertheless close members of her family did live here together and the greatest intimacy must have been created. This, in a way, would have contributed not only to the tight relationship between them, but also to some of the complicated intrigues developed in the house's history.

THE VILLAS OF ANTONIA

Hortensius, who had owned the House of Livia, had also owned a villa by the sea (*villa maritima*) at ancient Bauli in the Baiae district. This too became the property of Antonia. It was in this Campanian villa, a couple of days' journey south of Rome, that according to Pliny Antonia kept in a fishpond (*piscina*) her favourite lamprey adorned with earrings. The spectacle was so unusual, says Pliny, that crowds of sightseers continued to flock to the area.[17]

The location of ancient Bauli has been debated for two hundred years. Maiuri finally settled the argument by identifying it with modern Bacoli, which faces the coast about two miles south of Baiae in the Gulf of Pozzuoli. He pointed to the ruins of an enormous villa of the Republican period, the 'Cento Camerelle', which seem to be the remains of the villa of Hortensius–Antonia.[18] D'Arms clinched the identification by showing that among the proposed locations this is the only one from which Pompeii can be seen, as Cicero testifies.[19]

The 'Cento Camerelle', or 'building with the hundred chambers', was excavated in 1910/11 and again in 1927. The results are inadequately reported and we can draw only tentative conclusions. The structure is formed by two superimposed edifices of different periods and, as is clear from their different orientations, quite independent of each other. The upper building is a water cistern with four parallel corridors intercommunicating by means of great archways. These are roofed with barrel-vaulting and faced with a single layer of *opus signinum*: that is to say, concrete varied by irregular splinters of brick, stone and marble. On the lower floor, reached by a wooden stairway, a series of parallel galleries, intersected at right angles by low narrow passages and opening towards the sea, points to a large earlier villa. These galleries later became the substructure and the reservoir of the upper complex.[20]

It would have been here that Antonia patronised the two cultivated Greeks, the poets Thallus and Honestus, who may have enjoyed her hospitality at Bauli[21] – perhaps under the procuratorship of her freedman Diadumenus Antonianus (B.39–41; see p. 64). Here too the younger Agrippina was

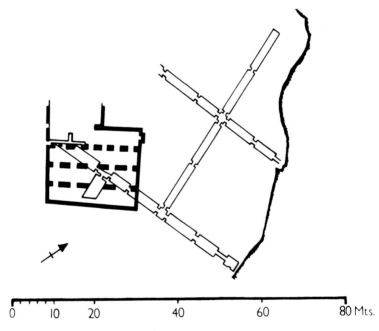

Figure 105 Plan of Antonia's villa at Bauli.

murdered, after she had escaped from drowning in the shipwreck devised by her son Nero. Nero had previously given her
Antonia's villa, besides Antonia's house in Rome, as we have
seen.[22] Further, according to Dio it was at Bauli that Caligula
conceived one of his maddest schemes, deciding to bridge the
waters of the gulf, which was about 3.5 miles wide, so that his
chariot could be driven across the sea, from Bauli to Puteoli.[23]
Antonia did not live to see this absurd show, which was realised
by bringing together a huge number of ships and anchoring
them in a double line. A mound of earth was then heaped on top
of them and fashioned in the manner of the Appian Way. Dio
says that the undertaking did not provide merely for a bridge.
Resting-places and lodging-rooms were also built along its
course which even had running water suitable for drinking!
Suetonius is the only writer who tried to find a rational explanation for this incredible project:

> I know that many have supposed that Gaius devised this
> kind of bridge in rivalry of Xerxes, who excited no little
> admiration by bridging the much narrower Hellespont;
> others, that it was to inspire fear in Germany and Britain,
> on which he had designs, by the fame of some stupendous
> work. But when I was a boy, I used to hear my grandfather
> say that the reason for the work, as revealed by the
> Emperor's confidential courtiers, was that Thrasyllus the
> astrologer had declared to Tiberius, when he was worried
> about his successor and inclined towards his natural grand-
> son (= Tiberius Gemellus), that Gaius had no more chance
> of becoming emperor than of riding about over the Gulf of
> Baiae with horses.[24]

Confiscation of the vast wealth of the Hortensii brought into
the hands of Augustus and Mark Antony many houses and
villas, some of which, like Bauli, may eventually have passed to
Antonia. Other known Hortensian property, such as at
Laurentum and Tusculum, may have also been inherited by
Antonia, though for Laurentum there is admittedly no associated evidence and for Tusculum it is circumstantial. At
Laurentum, on the coast not far from Ostia below the mouth of
the Tiber, where the celebrated villa of the younger Pliny was
situated, Hortensius possessed an estate that had as its main
attraction a fascinating deer park.[25] At Tusculum (see p. 107),

155

Figure 106 Cento Camerelle.

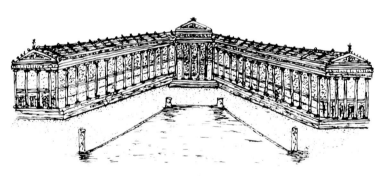

Figure 107 A fresco from Pompeii showing a villa by the sea.

whence came a *tessera* of Antonia (G.7) as well as a statue (J.9) and a bust (J.20), Hortensius owned a large country-house.[26]

Antonia's presence at Tusculum, evidently during a summer vacation, is shown by Josephus' account of the events which led to the arrest of Agrippa I:

156

In time, when Tiberius moved from Capri to Tusculum (=
summer AD 36), a distance of a hundred furlongs (= about
15 miles) from Rome, Agrippa besought Antonia to take
steps to secure a hearing on the charges which Eutychus
(= a freedman of Agrippa) had brought against him . . .
Antonia seized her opportunity . . . Tiberius was once
reclining as he travelled in a litter; Gaius, her grandson,
and Agrippa were in front, having just had lunch. Antonia,
who was walking beside the litter, entreated him to sum-
mon Eutychus and to examine him.[27]

The charge, an injudicious remark to Caligula, overheard by
Eutychus and reported to the Emperor, to the effect that
Agrippa hoped that Tiberius would soon die and leave him the
throne, was proved, and the Jewish prince languished in prison
for the last six months of Tiberius' reign (see p. 102).[28]

Where exactly Antonia resided at Tusculum at the time of this
episode is not easy to discern from the text of Josephus. Tiberius
seems to have occupied an Imperial summer-palace here, perhaps in the direction of Rome, which had a hippodrome
nearby.[29] But Antonia need not have stayed with Tiberius. She
may have spent the nights in her own private villa, possibly that
of Hortensius, if indeed, again, she had the good fortune to
inherit it. This villa, if identical with the one passed on later to
the younger Agrippina, possessed the most wonderful
gardens.[30]

Finally, it is conceivable that there were other villas belonging
to Antonia in the regions surrounding Rome (Latium,
Campania, Samnium, Umbria and Etruria), where we have
noted materials connected with her, such as at Velitrae (G.6 –
see p. 106), Marruvium (A.2), Nomentum (J.13), Veii (I.10),
Spoletium (H.3) and Rusellae (J.2). Even the Imperial estate
near Herculaneum may once have been her property. This
building, like so much else, fell to the anger of Caligula, who
ordered it to be immediately razed to the ground because it was
there that his mother, the elder Agrippina, had once been
confined under Tiberius.[31]

CONCLUSION

A general feature of the history of Antonia Augusta is its division into four main phases. This need not be due to any pattern in her personal circumstances but may only reflect the nature of the evidence available to us. Peaks of popularity in her lifetime would have readily influenced the historians of the time, and may have caused a substantial amount of materials to enter the archaeological record.

The first phase of her life, under Augustus, is the short period she was married to the elder Drusus (18–9 BC), in which her youth, beauty and prudence made her the idol of Rome. The second, under Tiberius, is the time she followed Germanicus' political career and his mission in the East (AD 14–19), during which she was seen as a mature goddess and the real 'mother' of the Imperial family. The third phase, after the death of Livia in the closing stage of Tiberius' reign (AD 29–37), is when, old but still firm and alert, she reached the zenith of her public life: directing a remarkable court, surpassing even the authority which Livia had enjoyed, saving the Empire from self-destruction and being venerated worldwide. The fourth, wholly posthumous, began under Caligula but became intense at the beginning of Claudius' reign (AD 41–4). Reconfirmations of her titles and restatements of her virtues were now spread as an essential part of wider Imperial propaganda.

In examining the relevant evidence together (literary, non-literary and archaeological), I have put forward many new points, as well as reassessing old ones. Antonia was conceived in Athens early in May 37 BC, but born in the House of Antony at Rome on 31 January 36 BC. She grew up in the newly built palace of Augustus, and after her marriage she settled in the

158

house of her mother-in-law Livia, situated within the same
building-complex on the Palatine. This dwelling eventually
became her own household, which, as inscriptions show, provided employment to a great number of slaves, slave-girls, freedmen and freedwomen. In its political aspects her household was
famous as the place where future emperors and kings were
supervised.

Antonia may have followed her husband Drusus in some of
his missions: possibly in Spain (given that he might have been
there), certainly in Gaul. She also seems to have accompanied
her son Germanicus in Asia Minor and perhaps in Syria-
Palestine (though apparently not in Egypt). These deductions
based principally on epigraphic evidence are not supported by
Tacitus, but the historian often fails to convince us that he had
adequate knowledge of Antonia, whom he even occasionally
confused with her sister of the same name. The recently discovered *Tabula Siarensis* indicates that Tacitus' research on the
activity of Antonia in Rome at the time of Germanicus' funeral
was not as careful as it might have been.

The eastern journey of the Antonian-Claudian family became
highly symbolic, as was inevitable in view of the memory of Mark
Antony in this part of the world, and the warm welcome reserved by the Greek communities there for his descendants.
When Tiberius decided to send Germanicus to the East, he
could hardly have expected such an atmosphere to be created,
especially half a century after the death of Antony. But although
the Emperor's attention was almost certainly attracted to the
local response, there is no reason to believe (despite some of our
sources) that he let it trouble him to the extent of initiating a plot
against his adopted son and his family.

Antonia helped to avenge the death of Germanicus, evidently
by adducing evidence against Piso, from events she would have
witnessed during her participation in her son's mission. In any
case her main political involvement was in uncovering the conspiracy of Sejanus, and we cannot help wondering how Roman
Imperial history would have turned out if Sejanus had succeeded in putting Tiberius and Caligula out of the way, and
usurping the position of *princeps*! Reinterpretations of the
inscription of Honestus, the coins of Salus, Pietas, Iustitia and
Nikê/Victoria (and perhaps the earliest papyrus mentioning
land in Egypt belonging to Pallas), amplify the testimony of

Josephus that Antonia clearly testified against Sejanus.

Among other assets Antonia's wealth included many Italian country villas, the most important being that at Bauli (Bacoli) on the Bay of Baiae. From all the clues we have gleaned from the papyri, her property in Egypt was enormous. Judging from these documents, which constitute only a tiny sample, Antonia must have been the wealthiest woman of the Imperial house – certainly after the death of Livia, perhaps even during the latter's lifetime. A number of questions are raised. How did she come to possess this property? The logical assumption is that most of it once belonged to Mark Antony, though there is no record of his landholdings. Could Antonia have administered such vast wealth through the medium of procurators (notably Alexander the Alabarch), without giving it her personal attention? The extent of her Egyptian estates and their profits should have required at least one journey to the land of the Nile. Did she ever visit this country? The speech of Germanicus in Alexandria found on a papyrus does not give much ground for arguing that Antonia went to Egypt in AD 19, the natural opportunity we would have expected her to take. But it is always possible that she went there on an unrecorded occasion.

Antonia's extraordinary independence as a woman must have developed along with the direct handling of her economic power. Of course the minor changes in the legal status of women effected by Augustus, her personal reputation, and the honours and respect she earned through her 'political' acts, played a significant role in this development. Nevertheless her wealth would have enabled her to control and manipulate certain situations, which may eventually have become significant factors in her elevation to such unprecedented heights for a woman.

Antonia died on 1 May AD 37, at the advanced age of seventy-two, only six weeks after her grandson Caligula assumed the purple, and perhaps after only two weeks under his direct rule. She seems to have taken her own life because of the rapidly changing attitude of the young Emperor, who had at first bestowed several titles upon her, including that of priestess of the Divine Augustus (as seen on the chalcedony statuette) and 'Augusta'. Caligula viewed her cremation with indifference, almost as if she had committed suicide without asking his permission!

According to Suetonius Antonia refused the title of 'Augusta' during her lifetime. The surviving documentary evidence shows that it was used while she was alive at the beginning of Caligula's reign, at least in Greece. Was it simply that her decision had been ignored in the eastern provinces? Or did she reject the title at some earlier point in her life? Tiberius had special respect for his sister-in-law, particularly after she saved his throne in AD 31. It is not impossible that he then considered offering her the vacant rank of 'Augusta', previously held by his mother Livia, but that Antonia refused to accept it.

A more general and important question has been raised. How far precisely was the Greek 'Sebastos' or 'Sebaste' equivalent to the Latin 'Augustus' or 'Augusta'? Numismatic and epigraphic evidence suggests that the former was used casually in the East, as opposed to the strictly official application of the latter in the West. Eastern authorities seem to have named members of the Imperial family 'Sebastoi', even though no formal grant of the title 'Augusti' had been made to them by the Senate in Rome. If so, many Greek coins and inscriptions may stand in need of reidentification or reinterpretation, including some connected with Antonia.

Antonia's consecration in the East during her lifetime was also unofficial in terms of the rules of the Roman Senate, though it was a usual procedure observed by the local authorities. A cult of Antonia and her husband was established in Athens from an early period, probably while the elder Drusus was alive. The individual worship of Antonia (as *Thea*) in Athens came later, when a temple or shrine was built for her, since she possessed a priestess and (at another time) even a high priest. Other shrines of her cult can be presumed to have existed at Aphrodisias (where another of her priests is on record), Ilium (inscription), Clazomenae (coin) and perhaps Egypt (papyrus). The exact relationship of her personal cult to the wider Imperial Cult, in which she also took part, as sculptural and epigraphic evidence prove (for example, at Corinth and Samos in the East, or Lepcis Magna in North Africa and Baeterrae in the West), is not clear. But some association between the two is more than likely.

In Rome and the Latin-speaking West, Antonia may have been formally consecrated (as *Diva*) only after her death (Ravenna relief), though such a deification is not related explicitly by the sources. The supposed temple built for her by Claudius in Rome would be direct support for such a theory, as would her shrine in Naples (implied by an inscription). The gatherings in her name undertaken by minor priesthoods at Velitrae and Tusculum (as shown by *tesserae*), the sacrificial libations to her spirit at Boscoreale or some other Campanian town (as might be guessed from the *patera*), and the private *lararium* of the villa in Malta (in view of the bust found therein), would probably reflect a cult of Antonia's *iuno* during her lifetime, rather than the posthumous cult of her as *Diva* (equivalent to the Greek *Thea*). One way or another, it is difficult to be certain.

Antonia personified various goddesses, notably Venus/ Aphrodite (as in the statue from Baiae and perhaps the inscription of her slave looking after the Temple of Venus on the Capitoline) because of her unusual physical beauty. She was specifically linked to Venus Genetrix (as in the Ravenna relief and the inscription from Aphrodisias), which would reflect her popular capacity as 'the mother of the Imperial gens', and presumably metaphorically 'the mother of Rome'. She seems also to have been identified with Vesta/Hestia, the protector of Roman houses (as in coins of Caligula). Further, her family and childbearing role, readily praised by Roman women, may have associated her with Diana/Artemis (if the 'Phoebe' gem from Hanover has been accurately interpreted).

After the death of Livia, Antonia was upgraded to the personifications of the goddess Ceres/Demeter (as in coins of Claudius and on the amethyst intaglio in Paris) and the ultimate Juno/ Hera (as in the 'Juno Ludovisi' head). In her representations of major state virtues, she may have been identified with the Salus, Iustitia and Pietas (as on Tiberian coins); she certainly represented Constantia (on Claudian coins) and most probably Pax (on the 'Grande Camée' of France). In the East, she was seen as an equal to the great goddess Cybele/Magna Mater at Clazomenae (coin), and to Nikê/Victoria at Thessalonica (coin). Myths and legends were searched by ancient artists for any metaphorical accommodation of Antonia's story. In sculpture she may be depicted as Clytie (British Museum bust), the highly benevolent female spirit of nature, while in decorated silver plate she is presented as Chryseis (British Museum *cantharus*) promoting the interests of her children Orestes–Germanicus, Iphigeneia–Livilla and Pylades–Claudius.

Finally, since I claimed in the introduction that Antonia

equalled Livia in significance, and in fact in some aspects exceeded her, a brief comparison of the two ladies may be of some profit. The sheer amount of documentary evidence available for Livia (several times as much as for Antonia) tends to blur the picture. But much of the prestige that generated this formidable corpus of material, seems to have resulted from flattery towards Augustus: Livia was hailed as Juno, because Augustus was seen as Jupiter.[1]

Dio's overall assessment of Livia is the closest we can get even to a surface understanding of her authority. She had the right to erect her statues; she could administer her own affairs without a guardian, and she possessed the same security and inviolability as was enjoyed by the tribunes. Also, she could hold banquets with Augustus in the Temple of Concord.[2] But all these privileges she shared with Octavia Minor and no doubt subsequently with Antonia, Octavia's daughter (cf. chapter 1, n. 34).

Further, although an arch was voted in Livia's honour Tiberius never built it.[3] While no arch was ever voted to Antonia personally, we noted her direct association with the arches of Germanicus and Claudius. The dedications of *arae* with which Livia was apparently connected (such as the Ara Pacis or the Ara Numinis Augusti) were made only in conjunction with Augustus, and the portico with which Livia was honoured by her husband had precedents.[4] A far greater portico had been dedicated to Octavia Minor, and it was perhaps she who undertook to honour her daughters, the two Antonias, with a whole basilica (tentatively located here in the area of the Circus Flaminius).

Livia is said to have saved the lives of not a few, to have reared the children of many, and to have helped others pay their daughters' dowries, for which she was called by some 'Mother of her Country'.[5] Antonia's social contribution was certainly equally substantial, not to mention that she saved the life of the Emperor himself and safeguarded his principate. Livia was renowned for her influence on Augustus on account of her chastity, by doing whatever pleased him, not meddling with his affairs and pretending not to notice his favourites.[6] But no serious comparison can be made with the proverbial chastity and principles of Antonia, who even dared, in an affluent and corrupt society, to become a *univira*! In reality, Livia's chastity should not have been so lauded, if only because she was taken from her first husband by Augustus under scandalous circumstances.

163

At the time she was pregnant with Drusus, to whom she gave birth only three months after her marriage to Augustus. Suetonius immortalised the satirical comment which was then current: 'In three months' time come children to the great'![7]

When Augustus died, Livia was adopted into the Julian gens, received the title 'Augusta' and became the first priestess of the new Cult of the Divine Augustus. For a while she seems to have tried to dominate her son, the new Emperor Tiberius, by becoming involved in state affairs, though Tiberius removed her entirely from the public scene and restricted her to the home. She was consecrated only by Claudius.[8] There is not much here that Antonia would envy. She received all these titles after Livia's death, though it is not clear whether she was actually deified. On the other hand, she avoided all the difficulties of getting in the way of the Emperor, or intriguing and arguing with him. Tiberius therefore respected her more than his mother.

In the final analysis Antonia made more constructive use of her powers than Livia, particularly of her economic wealth, which may have been greater than Livia's. Her adoration by the populace and high regard in the state were real and sincere, and her 'political' influence was thus far-reaching. Antonia Augusta was not only the most chaste of the Imperial women but also the most dynamic, and the one who should rightly be seen as the Roman matron *par excellence.*

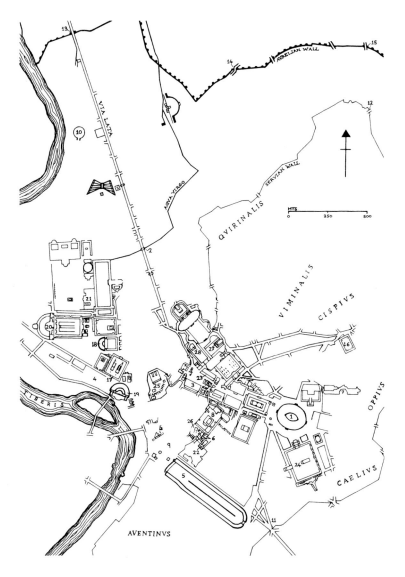

Figure 108 Rome in the Julio-Claudian period, with some later buildings relevant to this book.

166

Key for Figure 108

1. Amphitheatrum Flavium
2. Arcus Claudii
3. Basilica Iulia
4. Circus Flaminius
5. Circus Maximus
6. Domus Augusti and Liviae
7. Domus Aurea
8. Domus Tiberiana
9. Forum Boarium
10. Mausoleum Augusti
11. Porta Capena
12. Porta Collina
13. Porta Flaminia
14. Porta Pinciana
15. Porta Salaria
16. Porticus Liviae
17. Porticus Octaviae
18. Theatrum Balbi
19. Theatrum Marcelli
20. Theatrum Pompei
21. Thermae Agrippae
22. Templum Apollonis
23. Templum Concordiae
24. Templum Divi Claudii
25. Templum Iovis Optimi Maximi
26. Templum Magnae Matri
27. Templum Martis Ultoris
28. Templum Veneris Genitricis

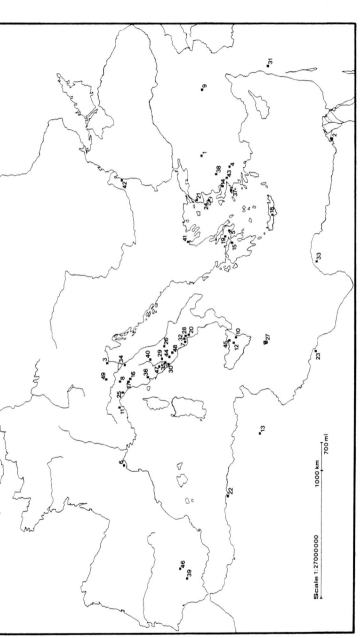

Figure 109 Known sites in which inscriptions, coins and *tesserae*, and sculpture of (or relevant to) Antonia were made or found.

Key-table for Figure 109

	SITES	INSCR.	C & T	SCULPT.
1.	AEZANIS	-	1	-
2.	ALEXANDRIA	-	1	-
3.	ALTINUM?	-	-	1
4.	APHRODISIAS	2	-	-
5.	ATHENS	3	-	1
6.	BAETERRAE	-	-	1
7.	BAIAE	-	-	1
8.	BONONIA?	-	-	1
9.	CAESARIA?	-	1	-
10.	CATANIA	-	-	1
11.	CEMENELUM	1	-	1
12.	CENTURIPAE	-	-	1
13.	CIRTA	1	-	-
14.	CLAZOMENAE	-	1	-
15.	CORINTH	1	1	1*
16.	FAESULAE	-	-	1
17.	FLORENTIA?	-	-	2
18.	GORTYNA?	-	1	-
19.	HELICÔN	1	-	1*
20.	HERCULANEUM	1	-	1*
21.	ILIUM	1	1	1*
22.	IOL-CAESAREA	-	-	1
23.	LEPCIS MAGNA	1	-	2
24.	LESBOS	1	-	1*
25.	LUNI	-	-	1*
26.	MARRUVIUM	1	-	1*
27.	MELITA	-	-	1
28.	NEAPOLIS	1	-	1
29.	NOMENTUM	-	-	1
30.	OSTIA	1	-	-
31.	PANIAS?	-	1	-
32.	PAUSILYPON	3	-	-
33.	PTOLEMAIS	1	-	1*
34.	RAVENNA	-	-	1
35.	ROME	38	8+5T	15+1*
36.	RUSELLAE	-	-	1
37.	SAMOS	-	-	2
38.	SARDIS	1	-	1*
39.	SIARUM	1	-	-
40.	SPOLETIUM	-	-	1
41.	THESSALONICA	-	4	-
42.	TOMIS	-	1	-
43.	TRALLES	-	-	1
44.	TUSCULUM	-	1T	2
45.	TYNDARIS	-	-	1
46.	ULIA	1	-	1*
47.	VEII	-	-	1
48.	VELITRAE	-	1T	-
49.	VICETIA	-	-	1
		61	21+7T	44+10*

* = Assumed to have existed from the 'portrait-inscription' of the same site. The total
number for sculpture could have been raised, if the sites of origin of six more items were to
be known (see Registers H to J, listing 50 items); not to mention the case of Aphrodisias (pp.
128–30). On the other hand, however, the number may actually be lowered if a few of the
above items have been wrongly attributed to Antonia.

169

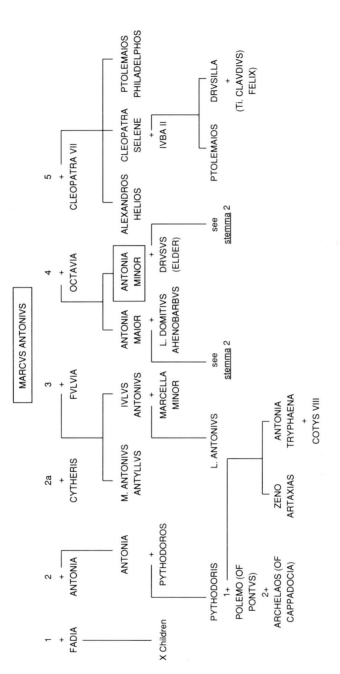

Figure 110 Family Tree 1: Mark Antony.

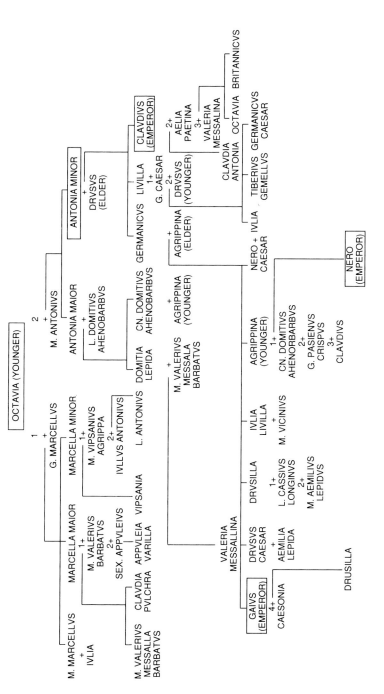

Figure 111 Family Tree 2: Octavia (Younger).

REGISTERS OF MATERIAL

REGISTER A

	Direct Inscr.	Locat.	Type*	Lan.	Epithets & titles	Date
1	CIL 2.1543	ULIA	GPI	L	ANTONIAE M·F·	c. 12 BC
2	CIL 9.3663	MARRUV.	GPI	L	ANTONIA . . . [DRVSI] . . .	AD 14–37
3	Laguerre 1975, 21–2, no. 10	CEMEN.	PI	L	M·F·CL[AV· . . . DRVSI . . . UXOR] . . .	AD 14–37
4	IG 12:2.207	LESBOS	PI	G	. . . ANTΩNIAN . . . ΓYNAIKA . . . EYEPΓETIN . . .	c. AD 18
5	IK 3, no. 88	ILIUM	PI	G	ANTΩNIAN . . . AΔEΛΦIΔHN . . . ΓYNAIKA . . . MHTEPA . . . ΘEAN . . . EYEPΓETIN . . .	c. AD 18
6	IGRR 1.1025	PTOLEM.	PI?	G	ANTΩNIA . . . [ΓYNAIKI] . . .	c. AD 18
7	Tripol. 28	L.MAGNA	GPI	N-P	ⲡⲣⲣⲝⲧⲗⲡ ⲭ[ⲁ ⲧⲗ]ⲩⲡⲧⲗⲧⲁ	c. AD 18
8	CIL 6.911a = 31199a	ROME	CONS	L	. . . ANTONIA MATRIS . . .	AD 19
9	TS Frag.1	SIARUM	CONS	L	. . . MATER GERMANICI . . .	AD 20
10	Corin. 8:2.17	CORINTH	GPI	L	. . . ANT[ONIAE] AVGV[STAE] . . .	AD 37
11	CIL 14.4535	OSTIA	FAST	L	. . . ANTONIA . . .	AD 37
12	Reynolds 1980, 322, no. 5	APHROD.	PI	G	ANTΩNIAN ΣEBAΣ{Σ}THN . . .	AD 37–54
13	CIL 6.2028c	ROME	ACTA	L	. . . ANTONIAE AVGVSTAE . . .	AD 38
14	CIL 6.32346e	ROME	ACTA	L	. . . [ANTONIAE AVGVSTAE] . . .	AD 39
15	Jamot 1902, 153–5, no. 4	HELICON	PI	G	. . . ΣEBAΣTH . . .	AD 41 (or 37?)
16	CIL 10.1417	HERCUL.	PI	L	ANTONIAE AVGVSTAE MATRI . . .	AD 41–54
17	Sard. 7:1.37	SARDIS	GPI?	G	ANTΩ[NIAN] . . . [MHTEPA]	AD 41–54
18	Reynolds 1980, 317–18, no. 1	APHROD.	DED	G	AΦPOΔITHI ΘE[A]I ΣEBAΣT[HI] . . .	AD 41–54
19	CIL 6.921	ROME	GPI	L	ANTONIAI AVGVSTAI DRVSI SACERDOTI DIVI AVGVSTI MATRI	AD 51–2

* CONS = CONSULTA; DED = DEDICATION; FAST = FASTI; GPI = GROUP PORTRAIT-INSCRIPTION; PI = PORTRAIT-INSCRIPTION

REGISTER B

	Indirect inscr.	Locat.	Type*	Lan.	Epithets & titles	Date
1	CIL 6.33368	ROME	EPIT	L	... ANTONIAES MINORIS ...	25–18 BC?
2	CIL 6.5536	ROME	EPIT	L	... ANTONIARVM DVARVM	25 BC–AD 37?
3	CIL 6.4100	ROME	EPIT	L	... ANTO[NIAE] ...	9 BC–AD 37?
4	CIL 6.4332	ROME	EPIT	L	... ANTONIAE ...	9 BC–AD 37?
5	CIL 6.4365	ROME	EPIT	L	... ANTONIAE ...	9 BC–AD 37?
6	CIL 6.4383	ROME	EPIT	L	... ANTONIAE ...	9 BC–AD 37?
7	CIL 6.5216	ROME	EPIT	L	... ANTONIAE ...	9 BC–AD 37?
8	CIL 6.33370a	ROME	EPIT	L	... ANTONIAES ...	9 BC–AD 37?
9	CIL 6.4434	ROME	EPIT	L	... ANTONIAE ...	AD 10–37
10	CIL 6.4451	ROME	EPIT	L	... ANTONIAE ...	AD 10–37
11	CIL 6.4537	ROME	EPIT	L	... ANTONIAE ...	AD 10–37
12	CIL 6.4562	ROME	EPIT	L	... ANTON[IAE] ...	AD 10–37
13	CIL 6.4609	ROME	EPIT	L	... ANTONIAES ...	AD 10–37
14	CIL 6.4689	ROME	EPIT	L	... ANTO ...	AD 10–37
15	IG 2/3².5095	ATHENS	CONS	G	... ΘΕΑΣ ΑΝ[Τ]ΩΝΙΑΣ	AD 18–37
16	CIL 6.4693	ROME	EPIT	L	... ANTONIAE... DRVSI	AD 29–37?
17	CIL 6.4148	ROME	EPIT	L	... ANTONIAE DRVSI ...	AD 29–37?
18	CIL 6.4327	ROME	EPIT	L	... ANTONIAES DRVSI ...	AD 29–37?
19	CIL 6.4350	ROME	EPIT	L	... ANTON·DRVSI ...	AD 29–37?
20	CIL 6.4387	ROME	EPIT	L	... ANTONIAE DRVSI ...	AD 29–37?
21	CIL 6.4402	ROME	EPIT	L	... ANTONIAE DRVSI ...	AD 29–37?
22	CIL 6.4563	ROME	EPIT	L	... ANTONIAES DRVSI ...	AD 29–37?
23	CIL 6.8817	ROME	EPIT	L	... ANTONIAE DRVSI ...	AD 29–37?
24	CIL 6.9065	ROME	EPIT	L	... ANTONIA[E] DRVSI ...	AD 29–37?
25	CIL 6.9097	ROME	EPIT	L	... ANTONIAE DRVSI ...	AD 29–37?
26	CIL 6.19475	ROME	EPIT	L	... ANTONIAE DRVSI ...	AD 29–37?
27	CIL 6.22868	ROME	EPIT	L	... ANTONIAE DRVSI ...	AD 29–37?
28	CIL 6.22895	ROME	EPIT	L	... ANTÓNIAE DRVSI ...	AD 29–37?
29	CIL 6.29624a,b	ROME	EPIT	L	... ANTONIAE DRVSI ...	AD 29–37?
30	CIL 6.33762	ROME	EPIT	L	... ANTONIAE DRVSI ...	AD 29–37?
31	CIL 6.33774	ROME	EPIT	L	... ANTONIAE DRVSI ...	AD 29–37?
32	CIL 6.33974	ROME	EPIT	L	... ANTONIAE DRVSI ...	AD 29–37?
33	CIL 6.37451	ROME	EPIT	L	... ANTONIAE DRVSI ...	AD 29–37?
34	IG 2/3².7091	ATHENS	EPIT	L + G	... ANTONIAE DRVSI ...	AD 29–37?
35	CIL 6.4487	ROME	EPIT	L	... AVGVSTAE ...	AD 37–54
36	IG 14.734	NEAP.	DED	G	... ΑΝΤΩΝΙΑC CΕΒΑCΤΗC ...	AD 37–54
37	CIL 8.7075	CIRTA	EPIT	L	... AVG ...	AD 37–54
38	IG 2/3².3535	ATHENS	PI	G	... ΑΝΤΩΝΙΑΣ ΣΕΒΑΣΤΗΣ ...	AD 47–54
39	Eph.Epigr.8.335	PAUS.	GRAF	L	... AVG ...	AD 65
40	Eph.Epigr.8.336	PAUS.	GRAF	L	... AVG ...	AD 65
41	Eph.Epigr.8.337	PAUS.	GRAF	L	... AVG ...	AD 65
42	CIL 6.12037	ROME	EPIT	L	... ANTONIAE AVG ...	AD 73–4

* CONS = CONSULTA; DED = DEDICATION; EPIT = EPITAPH; GRAF = GRAFFITI; PI = PORTRAIT-INSCRIPTION

REGISTER C

Def. & Prob.* Pap.	Land Loc.	Typ.Doc.	Epithets & Titles	Date
1 P.Tebt. 401*	ARS:TEBT.	ACCOUNT	... Ἀντωνίας ...	AD 14–37
2 P.Oxy. 2435*	OXY:OXY.	ACTA?	... μητρός ...	c. AD 20?
3 P.Oslo 123	ARS: ?	PETITION	... Ἀ[ν]τωνίας Δρού[σου] ...	AD 22
4 P.Oxy. 244 = P.Lond. 791	OXY: ? KYN: ?	TRANSFER	... Ἀντωνίας Δρούσου ... *Antoniae Drusi* ...	AD 23
5 P.Princ. 11*	ARS:PHIL. ARS:PTOL.	REGISTER	... Ἀντωνίας ... (Par.)	AD 35
6 P.Ryl. 140	ARS:EUH.	PETITION	... Ἀντωνίας Δρούσου ...	AD 36
7 P.Ryl. 141	ARS:EUH.	PETITION	... Ἀντωνίας Δρούσου ...	AD 37
8 P.Ros.Georg. 2:12 = P.Rainer 178	ARS: ?	REGISTER	... [Ἀν]τωνίας Σεβαστῆς ...	AD 48
9 P.Vindob. Tandem 10	ARS:EUH.?	LEASE	... Ἀντωνίας Σεβαστῆς ...	AD 54
10 P.Ryl. 171	ARS:HER.	LEASE	... Ἀντωςνία[ς Σεβαστῆς] ...	AD 56–7
11 P.Stras. 267*	ARS:PSEN.	LEASE	... Ἀντωνίας ... (Par.)	AD 126–8
12 P.Oxy. 2105*	OXY:OXY	EDICT	... θεῶν Λιβίας κα[ί Ἀντωνίας] ...	AD 147–8
13 BGU 280*	ARS:KAR.	RECEIPT	... Ἀντωνίας ...	AD 158–9

REGISTER D

	Pos. & Impr.* Pap.	Land Loc.	Description	Date
1	P.Princ. 14*	ARS:BOUB.	. . . Ἀντω(νίας)θυγατρός . . .	AD 23–40
2	P.Phil. 19	ARS:PHILA.		AD 90–120
3	P.Lond. 900?	ARS:THEAD.		AD 94–5 or AD 110–11
4	P.Berl.Leihg. 31	ARS:THEAD.		AD 100–30
5	BGU 277	ARS:SOK.N.		AD 100–200
6	SB 5670	ARS:BOUK.		AD 100–200
7	SB 11011	ARS:PATS.		AD 100–200
8	P.Mil.Vogl. 52?	ARS:TEBT.		AD 138
9	P.Col. 1, ver.4	ARS:THEAD.	(in all 'possible'	AD 138–61
		ARS:POLYD.	papyri of Antonia,	
10	P.Mil.Vogl. 75?	ARS:TEBT.	nos 2–25, the	AD 144–5
11	P.Fay. 60	ARS:PHILO.	description is	AD 145
12	BGU 1893	ARS:B.AIG.	that of Ἀντωνιανή)	AD 149
13	P.Stras. 551?	ARS:THEAD.		AD 150–80
14	BGU 1894	ARS:THEAD.		AD 157
15	BGU 212	ARS:SOK.N.		AD 158
16	P.Chic. 7	ARS:KARAN.		AD 158–9
17	P.Col. 1, ver.1a	ARS:THEAD.		AD 160
18	P.Berl.Leihg. 1 ver.	ARS:THEAD.		AD 164–5
19	P.Mich. 224	ARS:KARAN.		AD 172–3
20	BGU 2064 = SB 10761	ARS:THEAD.		AD 173
21	P.Mich. 225	ARS:KARAN.		AD 173–4
22	BGU 199 ver.	ARS:SOK.N.		AD 180–220
23	P.Aberd. 24	ARS:SOK.N.		AD 194
24	BGU 653	ARS:SOK.N.		AD 207
25	P.Giss.Univ. 52	ARS:TEBT.		AD 222–3

REGISTER E

	Coin Issues of Rome	Met.	Legends	Date
1	*BMCRE* 1, Tib., nos 81–4, pl. 24:2 (dupondius)	AE	S·C, TI·CAESAR·DIVI·AVG· F·AVG·P·M·TR·POT·XXIIII; SALVS·AVGVSTA	AD 22–3 or AD 31–2?
2	*BMCRE* 1, Tib., nos 79–80, pl. 24:1 (dupondius)	AE	S·C, TI·CAESAR·DIVI·AVG· F·AVG·P·M·TR·POT·XXIIII; IVSTITIA	AD 22–3 or AD 32–3?
3	*BMCRE* 1, Tib., no. 98, pl. 24:7 (dupondius)	AE	S·C, DRVSVS·CAESAR·TI· AVGVSTI·F·TR·POT·ITER·; PIETAS	AD 22–3 or AD 33–4?
4	*BMCRE* 1, Cal., nos 41–3, pl. 28:6 (sestertius)	AE	C·CAESAR·AVG·GERMANICVS· P·M·TR·POT, PIETAS; DIVO AVG S C	AD 37–8
5	*BMCRE* 1, Cal., nos 45–8, pl. 29:2 (as)	AE	C·CAESAR·AVG·GERMANICVS· PON·M·TR·POT·; VESTA S C·	AD 37–8
6	*BMCRE* 1, Cl., nos 166– a, pl. 35.8 (dupondius)	AE	ANTONIA AVGVSTA; TI· CLAVDIVS·CAESAR·AVG·P·M· TR·P·IMP·S C	AD 41
7	*BMCRE* 1, Cl., nos 109–10, pl. 33:19 (aureus)	AV	ANTONIA AVGVSTA; CONSTANTIAE AVGVSTI	AD 41–5
8	*BMCRE* 1, Cl., no. 111, pl. 33:20 (denarius)	AR	ANTONIA AVGVSTA; CONSTANTIAE AVGVSTI	AD 41–5
9	*BMCRE* 1, Cl., nos 112–13, pl. 33:21 (aureus)	AV	ANTONIA AVGVSTA; SACERDOS DIVI AVGVSTI	AD 41–5
10	*BMCRE* 1, Cl., no. 114, pl. 33:22 (denarius)	AR	ANTONIA AVGVSTA; SACERDOS DIVI AVGVSTI	AD 41–5
11	Kubitschek 1921, 151, pl. 7:5 (mint uncertain)	AR	ANTONIA AVGVSTA DIVI AVGVSTI; SACERDOS	AD 41–5 (or 37?)

REGISTER F

	Provinc. Coin Issues	Mint	Types	Titles	Date
1	*McCleanColl.* 3, no. 8045, pl. 277:3	IONIA: CLAZ.	CYBELE	ΘΕΑΝ ΑΝΤΩΝΙΑΝ	c. AD 18?
2	Gaebler 1935, 126, no. 49, pl. 24:10	MACED: THESS.	WREATH	ΑΝΤΩΝΙΑ	AD 32–7?
3	*BMCGC*, Maced., 117, no. 80	MACED: THESS.	HORSE	ΑΝΤΩΝΙΑ	AD 32–7?
4	Mionnet 1822, 496–7, no. 359	MACED: THESS.	NIKE	ΑΝΤΩΝΙΑ	AD 32–7?
5	*McCleanColl.* 2, no. 3784, pl. 141:18	MACED: THESS.	CALIG./ ANTON.	ΑΝΤΩΝΙΑ CEBACTH	AD 37–41
6	*SNGDen.*, Corin. pl. 5, no. 229	ACHAEA: CORIN.	HORNS	ANTONIA AVGVS	AD 37–41
7	Meshorer 1982, pl. 9, nos 3–31M	PALEST: ?PANI.	ANTON./ DRUSIL.	?ΑΝΤΩΝΙΑ ΓΥΝΗ CEBACTOY	AD 40–1
8	*BMCGC*, Alex., 9, nos 65–7	EGYPT: ALEX.	CLAUD./ ANTON.	ΑΝΤΩΝΙΑ CEBACTH	AD 41–2
9	*BMCGC*, Troas, 62, no. 39	TROAS: ILIUM	CLAUD./ ANTON.	ΑΝΤΩΝΙΑ CEBACTH	AD 41–54
10	Pick & Regling 1910, 676, pl. 21:13	MOESIA: TOMIS	CORN	ΑΝΤΩΝΙΑ CEBACTH	AD 41–54?
11	*HunterColl.* 2, 164, no. 5	CAPPAD: ?CAES.	MESSA./ ANTON.	ΑΝΤΩΝΙΑ CEBACTH	AD 45–6?
12	*BMCGC*, Crete, 2, no. 7, pl. 1:5 ´	CRETE: ?GORT.	CLAUD./ DR.-AN.	ΑΝΤΩΝΙΑ	AD 52–4?

REGISTER G

	Tesserae	Mint	Legends	Date
1	*Sylloge*, 2, no. 9, pl. 1:6	ROME	[ANTO]NIA DRVSI	AD 41–54
2	*Sylloge*, 2, no. 10, pl. 1:7	ROME	ANTONIA; EX·LIBERALITATE· TI·CLAVDI·CAE·AVG	AD 41–54
3	Cohen 1930, 8, 260, no. 1	ROME	III	AD 41–54
4	Cohen 1930, 8, 260, no. 2	ROME	IIII	AD 41–54
5	Mitchiner 1984, 103, no. 2, pl. 25:2	ROME	CLAV; AN D	AD 41–54
6	*CPABN*, 80, no. 2	VELITR.	SODALI·VELITER·FEL·; CERANO· CVRA·FELI·	AD 41–54
7	*CPABN*, 83, no. 13	TUSCUL.	SODAL·; TUSC·	AD 41–54

REGISTER H

	Youthful & Individualised	Type	Origin	Date
1	Museo Nazionale Romano, inv. 620, Rome; Picciotti-Giornetti 1979, 338–40, no. 202	HEAD	ROME	LATE AUGUSTAN?
2	Tripolis Museum, Tripolis; Aurigemma 1940, 88–90, figs 65–6	HEAD	L. MAGNA	EARLY TIBERIAN
3	Private Collection, Rome; Sensi 1984/5, 240–3, no. 7, pls 5 & 23	HEAD	SPOLETIUM	LATE TIBERIAN?
4	Museo Civico, Fiesole; Galli 1919, 131, no. 346, fig. 121b	HEAD	FAESULAE	LATE TIBERIAN?
5	British Museum, inv. 1875, London; BMCS 3, 149, no. 1875, pl. 6	BUST	?	LATE TIBERIAN?
6	Agora Museum, inv. 5220, Athens; AAPS, 24, no. 12, pl. 8:12	HEAD	ATHENS	CALIGULAN?
7	Staatliche Museum, inv. 1802, Berlin; KSAS, 11, R23, pl. 16	HEAD	SAMOS	CALIGULAN
8	Museo Vaticano (Ingresso), inv. 103, Vatican; LipSVM, 4–5, no. 5, pl. 4	BUST	ROME	CLAUDIAN
9	Art Market (?), Rome; V.H. Poulsen 1946, 25, fig. 19	BUST	ROME	CLAUDIAN
10	Museo Nazionale, inv. 705, Palermo; RGRS, 60–1, no. 74, pl. 34:3–4	HEAD	TYNDARIS	CLAUDIAN
11	Museo Nazionale, inv. 35829, Syracuse; RGRS, 60, no. 73, pl. 34:1–2	HEAD	CENTURIPAE	CLAUDIAN
12	Rabat Villa Museum, Malta; Ashby 1915, 39–40, fig. 10	BUST	MELITA	CLAUDIAN
13	Musée Nationale des Antiquités, Algiers; SAMSG, 34–7	STATUE	IOL-CAES.	CLAUDIAN
14	Residenz, Munich; EA 4, 16, no. 1006	HEAD	?	CLAUDIAN?

REGISTER I

	Youthful & Idealised	Type	Origin	Date
1	Ara Pacis (S. frieze), Rome; Bonanno 1976, 27–8, pls 65–7	RELIEF	ROME	AUGUSTAN
2	British Museum, inv. 1874, London; BMCS 3, 147–9, no. 1874, pl. 14	BUST	NEAPOLIS	AUGUSTAN/ CLAUDIAN
3	Museo Comunale, inv. 361, Catania; RGRS, 63, no. 77, pls 36:1–2; 90:3	STATUE	CATANIA	AUGUSTAN/ CLAUDIAN
4	Ravenna Museo, Ravenna; Bonanno 1976, 42, pls 89; 92	RELIEF	RAVENNA	CLAUDIAN
5	Baia Museo, Baia; Andreae 1983, 54–6, pls 122–41	STATUE	BAIAE	CLAUDIAN
6	Museo Nazionale Romano, inv. 8631, Rome; Lachenal 1983, 133–7, no. 58	HEAD	ROME	CLAUDIAN
7	Art Market, Rome; German Institute neg. 27.384; 69.2069	HEAD	ROME	CLAUDIAN
8	Villa Albani, inv. 711, Rome; EA 4, 34, nos 1121–2; 14, 53, no. 4335	HEAD	ROME	CLAUDIAN
9	Museum Narodowe, inv. 198714, Warsaw; CSIRPol, 22–3, no. 13, pl. 11	HEAD	ROME	CLAUDIAN
10	Hermitage, inv. A383, St Petersburg; ASE, 40–2, no. 283, pls 31–2	HEAD	VEII	CLAUDIAN
11	Museo Civico, inv. 512, Genoa (Pegli); EA 5, 67, nos 1368–9	HEAD	LUNI	CLAUDIAN
12	Museo Archeologico, inv. 140, Venice; MAVR, 32–3, no. 15, pl. 15a–b	HEAD	ALTINUM?	CLAUDIAN

REGISTER J

Mature & Individualised	Type	Origin	Date
1 Museo Nuovo Capitolino (Sala 7.12), inv. 922, Rome; *KRPCM*, 45, no. 54, pls 68–9	HEAD	ROME	EARLY TIBERIAN?
2 Museo Archeologico, inv. 97774, Grosseto; *KRPCM*, 45, no. 54, n. 2	HEAD	RUSELLAE	EARLY TIBERIAN?
3 Ny Carlsberg Glyptothek, inv. 743, Copenhagen; *PRCarl.*, 77–9, no. 42, pls 70–1	BUST	TRALLES	EARLY TIBERIAN?
4 Museo Civico, inv. EI21, Vicenza; *SGRMCV*, 113–16, no. 30	STATUE	VICETIA	EARLY TIBERIAN?
5 Museo Vaticano (Chiaramonti), Vatican; *AmelSVM*, 789, no. 701, pl. 85	HEAD	ROME	EARLY TIBERIAN?
6 Museo Vaticano (Magazzino), Vatican; *SMMV*, 264, no. 616, pl. 97	HEAD	ROME	EARLY TIBERIAN?
7 Musée St Raymond, inv. 30 006, Toulouse; Clavel 1970, 472, 493, figs 58–60	HEAD	BAETERRAE	LATE TIBERIAN
8 Staatliche Kunstsammlungen, Albertinum inv. 347, Dresden; West 1933, 100, pl. 24.95	HEAD	?	LATE TIBERIAN
9 Museo Vaticano (Braccio Nuovo) inv. 2194, Vatican; *AmelSVM*, 94–5, no. 77, pl. 13	STATUE	TUSCULUM	LATE TIBERIAN
10 Schloss no. 8, Erbach; *KASSE*, 58–61, no. 18, pls 20:1–4; 32:1	BUST	?	LATE TIB./ CLAUDIAN
11 Ninagawa Museum, Kurashiki; Simon 1982b, 236–43, no. 167	BUST	ROME	LATE TIB./ CLAUDIAN

REGISTER J

Mature & Individualised	Type	Origin	Date
12 Tigani Museum no. 53, Samos; Tölle-Kastenbein 1974, 174, pl. 337	BUST	SAMOS	LATE TIB./ CLAUDIAN
13 Museo Nazionale Romano, inv. 125713, Rome; Pala 1976, 31, I.38, no. 3	BUST	NOMENTUM	CALIGULAN
14 Tripolis Museum, Tripolis; Aurigemma 1940, 74–5, figs 51–2	STATUE	L. MAGNA	CLAUDIAN
15 Museo Torlonia, Rome; CMT, 300, pl. 143, no. 554	BUST	ROME	CLAUDIAN
16 Musée Archéologique, Cimiez; Benoit 1962b, 711, pl. 40	STATUE	CEMENELUM	CLAUDIAN
17 Fogg Art Museum, inv. 1972.306, Cambridge, Mass.; Erhart 1978, figs 1–3	BUST	?	CLAUDIAN
18 Galleria Uffizi, inv. 1914.99, Florence; GUS, 58–9, no. 45, pl. 45a–b	BUST	FLORENTIA?	CLAUDIAN
19 Louvre, inv. 1228, Paris; SGRML, 153, no. 1228	STATUE	ROME	CLAUDIAN
20 Louvre, inv. 1229, Paris; SGRML, 152–3, no. 1229	BUST	TUSCULUM	CLAUDIAN
21 Schloss no. 7, Erbach; KASSE, 61–2, no. 19, pl. 21:1–4; 32:2	HEAD	?	CLAUDIAN
22 Galleria Uffizi, inv. 1914.546, Florence; GUS, 65, no. 56, pl. 56a–b	HEAD	FLORENTIA?	CLAUDIAN
23 Villa Borghese, inv. 62, Rome; GBR, 8, no. 62	HEAD	ROME	CLAUDIAN
24 Museo Civico Archeologico, inv. 4435, Bologna; F. Poulsen 1928, 21	HEAD	BONONIA?	CLAUDIAN

REGISTER K

Youthful & Individualised	Type	Stone	Date & Insc.
1 Bibliothèque Nationale, Paris; *CCPGBI*, 34, no. 206	CAMEO 37 × 26 mm	AGATE-ONYX	LATE AUGUSTAN – 'CATOPNEINOC'
2 Museo Archeologico, inv. 211, Florence; Vollenweider 1966, 117, pl. 75:2, 4	INTAGLIO 22 × 18 mm	TOPAZ	EARLY TIBERIAN?
3 Staatliche Münzsammlung, inv. A2927, Munich; *AGDSMun*, 214, no. 3530, pl. 332	CAMEO 15 × 13 mm	GLASS-PASTE (black opaque; white finish)	EARLY TIBERIAN?

REGISTER L

Youthful & Idealised	Type	Stone	Date & Insc.
1 Metropolitan Museum of Art, inv. 48.12.3, New York; *CEGMM*, 105, no. 480, pl. 58	INTAGLIO 11 × 8 mm	SARDONYX	LATE AUGUSTAN?
2 De Clercq Collection, Paris, *CCPG*, 695, no. 3183, pl. 25	INTAGLIO 22 × 17 mm	CORNELIAN	LATE AUGUSTAN?
3 Musée du Cinquantenaire, Ravestein Collection no. 1649, Brussels; Vollenweider 1966, 114, pl. 67:2–3	CAMEO 20 × 12 mm	GLASS-PASTE (white-brown)	LATE AUGUSTAN?
4 Bibliothèque Nationale, Paris; *CCPGBI*, 269–70, no. 2080	INTAGLIO 30 × 20 mm	AMETHYST	LATE AUGUSTAN?
5 Hermitage, inv. G1259, St Petersburg; Richter 1971, 151, no. 710, pl. 710	INTAGLIO 19 × 15 mm	AMETHYST	LATE AUGUSTAN – 'ΥΛΛ (OC)'
6 Private Collection?, London?, *CACFC* 2, 69, no. 297, pl. 13	CAMEO 50 × 28 mm	SARDONYX	LATE AUGUSTAN?
7 Bibliothèque Nationale, Paris, *CCPGBI*, 28–31, no. 188	CAMEO 310 × 265 mm	SARDONYX	EARLY TIBERIAN
8 Kunsthistorisches Museum, inv. IXa34, Vienna; *KKHM*, 64, no. 23, pl. 5	CAMEO 48 × 55 mm	SARDONYX	CLAUDIAN?
9 J. Paul Getty Museum, Malibu; Henig 1988, pl. 25:b	STATUETTE (head)	CHALCEDONY	CLAUDIAN

REGISTER M

Mature & Individualised	Type	Stone	Date & Insc.
1 Metropolitan Museum of Art, inv. O7.286.124, New York; *CEGMM* 481, no. 479, pl. 58	INTAGLIO 25 × 34 mm	BLACK JASPER	LATE TIBERIAN?
2 Kestner-Museum, inv. K751, Hanover; *AGDSHan*, 217, no. 1094, pl. 148	INTAGLIO 10 × 8 mm	BLACK JASPER	LATE TIBERIAN?
3 British Museum, London; *BMCG*, 338, no. 3591, pl. 39	CAMEO 12 × 10 mm	SARDONYX	LATE TIBERIAN?
4 Devonshire House Collection, England; Furtwängler 1900, 2, 244, no. 38; 1, pl. 50:38	INTAGLIO 12 × 10 mm	CORNELIAN	CLAUDIAN?
5 Kunsthistorisches Museum, inv. XII.919, Vienna; *AGKHMW*, 68, no. 819, pl. 38	INTAGLIO 13 × 10 mm	GLASS-PASTE (light-blue)	CLAUDIAN?
6 Kunsthistorisches Museum, inv. XII.919, Vienna; *AGKHMW*, 68, no. 820, pl. 38	INTAGLIO 12 × 9 mm	GLASS-PASTE (white)	CLAUDIAN?
7 Kestner-Museum, inv. K1752, Hanover; *AGDSHan*, 217, no. 1095, pl. 148	INTAGLIO 10 × 12 mm	CORNELIAN	CLAUDIAN? – 'PHO[E]BE· IVVE·VITA'

NOTES

See Bibliography A for details of primary sources which are cited in the notes in abbreviated form; when two or more successive citations refer to the same primary source, the author's name is cited in the first only. See Bibliography B for details of secondary sources, cited in the notes by author's surname and date of publication.

PREFACE

1 See the selection under Kokkinos in the bibliography.
2 *PIR*² A 885; *PFOS* 90, no. 73; cf. *RE* 1, 2640, no. 114.
3 E.g. Julio-Claudians (Esser 1958; Meise 1969); Tiberius (Seager 1972; Levick 1976); Germanicus (Akveld 1961; Galotta 1987); Caligula (Balsdon 1934; Nony 1986); Claudius (Momigliano 1934; Scramuzza 1940); Roman women (Ferrero 1925; Balsdon 1962; Dixon 1988); other themes (Syme 1939; Syme 1986).
4 Gaggero 1927; in connection with Sejanus, e.g. Nicols 1975.
5 Treggiari 1973; for 'portrait-inscriptions' see Hanson and Johnson 1946.
6 Parassoglou 1978.
7 Trillmich 1978; Mitchiner 1984.
8 Bernoulli 1886; Rumpf 1941; Poulsen 1946.
9 Polaschek 1973; Erhart 1978.
10 Benoit 1966; Clavel 1970; Simon 1982a; Andreae 1983.

INTRODUCTION

1 Pembroke 1967.
2 Herod., 1.184; Diod., 2.4–20; J. Turner 1983.
3 Plut., *Mor.* 245, 257.
4 Arist., *Polit.* 2.6.6; Tac., *Germ.* 18; Bard., *Laws of Countries*, 23.9 (ed. Cureton).
5 Tac., *Ann.* 14.30.1; *Hist.* 3.45; Dio, 62.2.2–12.6.
6 Lefkowitz 1983, 57; cf. Macurdy 1932.
7 Dixon 1983, 91.

8 The first known example of the bestowal of divine honours upon a
Roman woman is Fulvia, third wife of Mark Antony, who was
depicted as the winged goddess Nikê or Victory in 43/42 BC (see
Toynbee 1978, 46–8). The second example is Octavia Minor, sister
of Augustus, assuming that her temple at Corinth, mentioned by
Pausanias (2.3.1), was built when she became the fourth wife of
Mark Antony (and of course cf. her deification in Athens –
Raubitschek 1946).
9 Livy, 34.2.11–34.3.2
10 Pomeroy 1975, 126; cf. Bremen 1983, 226, 237.
11 Finley 1968, 129, 139.
12 *Mt.* 19.4–6; *Mk.* 10.6–8.
13 Rich and poor (*Lk.* 8.1–3); strong (*Mt.* 9.18–19; *Mk.* 5.21–4; *Lk.*
8.40–2); weak (*Lk.* 13.11–13); adulteress (*Jn.* 8.3–11).
14 Judaean (*Mt.* 26.7–10; *Mk.* 14.3–9; *Lk.* 7.37–50); Samaritan (*Jn.*
4.7–27); Galilaean (*Mt.* 9.20–2; *Mk.* 5.25–34; *Lk.* 8.43–8); Greek-
Phoenician (*Mt.* 15.22–8; *Mk.* 7.25–30).
15 See Bruce 1988.
16 *Gal.* 3.28; it is unfortunate that when Christianity took root in the
pagan world, it developed into a patriarchal and misogynist religion, despite the line of diversion on this point from Judaism drawn
by Jesus himself.

1 ANTONIA IN HISTORY

1 App., *Civ.* 5.93–5; Dio, 68.54.3; cf. Tarn 1934, 54; Singer 1948;
Bengtson 1977, 182.
2 Plutarch (*Anton.* 35.1) was in error that Octavia had already had
their two daughters (followed by Huzar 1986, 143). First, he is
contradicted by historians (App., *Civ.* 5.95; Dio, 68.54.4) who testify
that Antony had then only one daughter by Octavia; second, their
other daughter was not born until the beginning of the following
year (*CIL* 6.2028c; cf. Crin., *Anth.* 6.345; see also p. 36).
3 App., *Civ.* 5.76.
4 Dio, 68.54.4; Plut., *Anton.* 35.5; cf. Syme 1939, 226.
5 Cf. Sen., *Epist. mor.* 83.25; on Mark Antony in general see Bengtson
1977; on Cleopatra see Lindsay 1971; Grant 1972.
6 Plut., *Anton.* 54.2; 57.3; Livy, 132.
7 Clark 1981, 198; cf. the Roman bride who carries a spindle and
distaff (Plut., *Mor.* 271).
8 Ovid, *Ars Amat.* ch. 3; cf. Balsdon 1969, 92–106.
9 Strabo, 14.5.14; some wealthy daughters had teachers for Greek
(Plut., *Mor.* 737b).
10 Dio, 51.15.7; e.g. *P.Oslo* 123; cf. Jos., *Ant.* 19.276.
11 Dixon 1985, 148; see Gardner 1986.
12 Tac., *Ann.* 3.29; Dio, 54.10.4; Suet., *Cl.* 11.3; *Inscr.It.* 13:2, 158–9, pl.
55; Sumner 1967, 424–5, n. 1.
13 Hopkins 1964/5, 319; cf. Shaw 1987, 33. Two of Antonia's grand-
daughters were married at the age of fifteen and seventeen, when

they were already at 'an advanced age' (Tac., *Ann.* 6.15); Antonia may have waited (Plut., *Anton.* 87. 3; cf. Anonym., *Gens Caes.* 92b). She would have had the opportunity to further her education, which, however, need not have stopped with marriage. The younger Pliny and his friend Pompeius Saturninus continued the literary education of their wives – the latter's could verse excellent Latin poems (Pliny, *Ep.* 4.19; 1.16; cf. Plut., *Pomp.* 55.1). As regards the Imperial family, although we know of no work left by Antonia, her granddaughter, the younger Agrippina, is said to have written an autobiography (Tac., *Ann.* 4.53).

14 Crin., *Anth.* 6.345; cf. 9.239.

15 ibid. 6.244.

16 Suet., *Cl.* 1.6; cf. Plut., *Anton.* 77.3; Anonym., *Gens Caes.* 94b; *IGRR* 4.206; *CIL* 6.921; 10.1417.

17 Tac., *Ann.* 2.43; Suet., *Cal.* 1.1; *CIL* 6.2028b; Sumner 1967, 427; cf. Angeli-Bertinelli 1987, 28–9.

18 Dio, 54.19.5–6.

19 ibid. 54.22.3.

20 ibid. 54.23.7; *CIL* 2.1543.

21 Dio, 54.25.1; Flor., 2.30.

22 Livy, 138; *CIL* 13.1668; Dio, 54.32.1; see Fishwick 1987, 97–9 .

23 Suet., *Cl.* 1.2; Dio, 54.32.3.

24 For the confusion of her first marriage see, for example, the family tree of *CAH* 10; for date see Dio, 65.10.18; for marriageable age see *Dig.* 23.1.9; cf. Shaw 1987, 42.

25 *CIL* 6.2298; Suet., *Cl.* 2.1.

26 Dio, 54.35.4; Livy, 140.

27 Suet., *Cl.* 1.3; Dio, 55.1.1.

28 Riding accident (Livy, 140; cf. Strabo, 7.1.3; V. Max., 5.5.3); disease (Dio, 55.1.4); poisoning (Suet., *Cl.* 1.4).

29 Pliny, *N.H.* 7.84; Livy, 142; Dio, 55.2.3; cf. Hill 1909, 160–2.

30 Ovid, *Cons. ad Liv.* 299–342.

31 See Suet., *Aug.* 34.1; cf. *Dig.* 23.2.23, 44; *EDRL*, 553–4; Raditsa 1980; V. Max., 4.3.3; Jos., *Ant.* 18.180.

32 V. Max., 4.3.3.

33 Cf. Parker 1946; Suetonius (*Cal.* 3.1–2) speaks highly of Germanicus' Greek and Roman oratory and learning, as well as of Greek comedies left among other fruits of his studies (cf. Pliny, *N.H.* 8.42; Ovid, *Fast.* 1.23–4; *Pont.* 4.8.67). A version of the *Aratea*, the Latin poems translated from the Greek astronomical work of Aratus, is usually ascribed to him (cf. Gain 1976, 20; Baldwin 1981). Incidentally, we know the name of a preceptor of Germanicus, Cassius Silanus, no doubt employed in this post by Antonia (Pliny, *N.H.* 33.156). As we shall see below, Claudius, also, excelled in Roman history and Greek studies. He even dared to introduce three new letters into the Latin alphabet (Suet., *Cl.* 41.3). Although Claudius complained that his instructor (*paedagogus*) was a barbarian and a former chief of muleteers (Suet., *Cl.* 2.2), he had been taught by people such as Livy and Sulpicius Flavus (Suet., *Cl.* 41.1),

no doubt, again, at the recommendation of Antonia.

34 Cf. Crook 1986, 67; Gai, *Inst.* 1.145, 194; there is a possibility that Antonia could have become a free agent even without the use of the *ius liberorum*. She could have inherited this right from her mother Octavia Minor, to whom it had been granted by Augustus, together with 'the same security and inviolability as the tribunes enjoyed' (Dio, 49.38.1). Incidentally, another right that could have passed from Octavia to Antonia is to hold banquets with her family in the ancient Temple of Concord beside the Roman Forum (Dio, 49.18.6). This temple of the personification of 'Agreement' (the Greek Homonoia), was rededicated in the name of Tiberius and his brother Drusus, in AD 10 (Dio, 56.25.1). It is almost certain that Antonia would have participated in the ceremony on this occasion, representing her dead husband.

35 Tac., *Ann.* 1.3, 14; 2.43; Suet., *Tib.* 15.2; *Cal.* 1.1; Jos., *Ant.* 18.54.

36 Mommsen 1878; Charlesworth 1934, 619–22; Magie 1950, 497–9; Köstermann 1958; Akveld 1961, 71–104; Vermeule 1968, 187–90; Sidari 1979/80; Pani 1987; Gallotta 1987.

37 Tac., *Ann.* 2.53.

38 For Patrae (*AE* 1979, 567; 1981, 755; Moretti 1980, 453–4; cf. Touratsoglou 1978); for Lesbos (Tac., *Ann.* 2.54).

39 Suet., *Cal.* 7; 8.3; cf. Humphrey 1979; Tac., *Ann.* 3.1; but 2.70 perhaps *contra*.

40 Suet., *Cal.* 10.1; *IGRR* 4.251; Tac., *Ann.* 3.2; Magie 1950, 497; *IGRR* 4.74, 75; cf. *Sard.* 7:1, no. 35; see Raepsaet-Charlier 1982, for how common it was for provincial governors to travel to their posts *en famille*, as it were.

41 *IGRR* 3.94; Tac., *Ann.* 2.55.

42 Magie 1950, 1356–8.

43 Cf. Tac., *Ann.* 2.42, 56; it seems that Zeno's mother Pythodoris, the queen of Pontus (Strabo, 12.3.29), was the daughter of a half-sister of Antonia with the same name (*IGRR* 4.1407; cf. Magie 1950, 1130, n. 60; Forrer 1969, 64–5; Sullivan 1980, 920, n. 28); see Family Tree 1.

44 *OGIS* 629; see Matthews 1984, 164; Cantineau 1931, 139–41, no. 18; Tac., *Ann.* 2.59.

45 Jos. *Ant.* 17.220; 18.165; *War* 2.15; cf. Strabo, 16.2.46; Josephus in *Ant.* 18.143 may be inaccurate to say that Agrippa was taken to Rome shortly before the death of Herod the Great in 4 BC – the most appropriate time was after the death of Herod in the company of his mother and grandmother (ibid.); for the excursion to 'various provinces' cf. Tac., *Ann.* 2.62.

46 For Drouseion tower (Jos., *War* 1.412; *Ant.* 15.336); for Antonia fortress (Jos., *War* 1.401; *Ant.* 15.409).

47 Suet., *Aug.* 93; Dio, 65.10.18.

48 Tac., *Ann.* 2.57; cf. Dio, 51.6.5; 49.32.5; see Family Tree 1.

49 Tac., *Ann.* 2.59; cf. Suet., *Tib.* 52.2; Jos., *Apion* 2.63; but cf. *Sel. Pap.* 211, 212; Oliver 1971.

50 Suet., *Cal.* 3.2; *Aug.* 17.5; Flor., 2.21.10; Dio, 51.15.1; Plut., *Anton.*

86; cf. Vell., 2.87.1.

51 *W.Chr.* 413; Tac., *Ann.* 2.61.

52 Milne 1916; cf. Hennig 1972.

53 Tac., *Ann.* 2.60; for the validity of the absolute dates in Old World history and archaeology, see now James *et al.* 1987 and 1991, which includes contributions by the author.

54 *Inscr.It.* 13:1, 329, pl. 94; cf. 13:2, 519; see also pp. 127, 159; Tac., *Ann.* 2.69; Suet., *Cal.* 2.1; Dio, 57.18.9; cf. Jos., *Ant.* 18.54.

55 Tac., *Ann.* 2.43.

56 Cf. Rogers 1932; Cramer 1954, 99–104; Smallwood 1956; Moehring 1959; cf. Aune 1980, 1516–23.

57 For the date cf. Rogers 1931; for Piso's mildness see Dio, 57.15.9; *contra* Marsh 1931, 281, who discounted the event; see Cramer 1951, 21–9; Rapke 1982, 63–4.

58 Tac., *Ann.* 2.69; cf. Tupet 1980; for Germanicus' great interest in astronomy, see the *Aratea* ascribed to him (Gain 1976).

59 Suet., *Cal.* 6.1; Jos., *Ant.* 18.209; Tac., *Ann.* 2.82–3.

60 Suet., *Cal.* 5.

61 *P.Oxy.* 2435; cf. Tac., *Ann.* 2.71; 3.2.

62 Tac., *Ann.* 3.3; cf. 3.18.

63 Tac., *Ann.* 4.44; 12.64; cf. Scheid 1975, 354–5; Syme 1986, 309.

64 Judaea (Jos., *Ant.* 18.143, 164–7); Commagene (Dio, 59.24.1; cf. 59.8.2); Thrace (*IGRR* 4.145); Armenia (Jos., *Ant.* 18.139; Tac., *Ann.* 6.40; cf. certainly *Res Gest.* 27.2); Mauretania (Suet., *Cal.* 26.1; cf. Dio, 51.15.6; Sen., *De Tranq.* 11.12); other (cf. Braund 1984, 9–21; 165–80); Parthia (Jos., *Ant.* 18.103; cf. Suet., *Cal.* 19.2).

65 Cf. Moscovich 1983.

66 Suet., *Cal.* 10.1; *contra* 24.1, see also p. 152; Dio, 60.2.5.

67 Tac., *Ann.* 11.3.

68 Jos., *Ant.* 18.181–2; cf. Dio, 65.14.1.

69 *Contra* Vell., 2.127.3–4; see Tac., *Ann.* 4.2; Dio, 57.19.1–8; Hennig 1975.

70 Sen., *Cons. ad Marc.* 22.4–7; cf. Philo, *Flac.* 1.

71 Dio, 58.4.3; 58.7.4; 58.9.2; Suet., *Tib.* 65.

72 Suet., *Tib.* 65.1; cf. *ILS* 6044; see Bird 1969, 88–9; Tac., *Ann.* 6.3; Jos., *Ant.* 18.18; cf. Philo, *Leg.* 37, 159.

73 *Inscr.It.* 13:1, 329, pl. 96; 13:2, 510; Tac., *Ann.* 4.3, 8, 11; Dio, 57.22.2; 58.11.6.

74 *Inscr.It.* 13:1, 186–7, pl. 68:5; *ILS* 158; one of her informants must have been Satrius Secundus, 'a client of Sejanus' according to Tacitus (*Ann.* 4.34), who is said to have been involved with the disclosure of the plot (Tac., *Ann.* 6.47).

75 Juv., *Sat.* 10.61–9; cf. Arnaud-Lindet 1980; see Tac., *Ann.* 3.14; *TDAR*, 466; Dio, 58.11.5.

76 Suet., *Cal.* 15.2; Dio, 59.3.4.

77 Suet., *Cl.* 11.2; e.g. *CIL* 6.2028c; *McCleanColl.* II, no. 3784.

78 Jos., *Ant.* 18.236; Suet., *Cal.* 23.2; 24.1; 29.1.

79 *CIL* 14.4535; Dio, 59.3.6; Suet., *Cal.* 23.2, 3.

80 Suet., *Cal.* 15; cf. Kubitschek 1921, 151; see p. 37.

81 Crin., *Anth.* 6.345, 9.239; Ovid, *Cons. ad Liv.* 300; *IGRR* 4.206; Jos., *Ant.* 18.180; Plut., *Anton.* 87.3; V. Max., 4.3.3.

82 Pliny, *N.H.* 7.80; Jos., *Ant.* 18.164–7, 202–3.

83 Suet., *Cl.* 41.1–2; Suetonius mentions not only Claudius' 'mother' but also his 'grandmother' as preventing him from relating the early events of the Empire. This has been taken by Rolfe, the translator of *De Vita Caesarum* (*LCL*, vol. 2, 76, n. a), to mean 'Octavia' the mother of Antonia. Also, Feldman (1962, 331) approved of Rolfe's assumption. However, they are both mistaken and, no matter how strange it may sound, Suetonius must clearly have meant 'Livia', mother of the elder Drusus the father of Claudius. Octavia, as we saw (p. 13), died a year before Claudius was born!

84 Suet., *Cl.* 3.2; cf. Sen., *Apocol.* 1; see Suet., *Cl.* 4.4. Claudius' physical disability may have been the reason why Antonia abstained from his upbringing, and even Livia who nurtured him (see above note 66) may have left him largely under the care of notable ladies of the court. Perhaps these included the Herodian Salome I (and later her daughter Berenice I), thus explaining not only how Claudius was brought up together with his friend Agrippa I, but also how he came to be accused by the Alexandrian Isidorus of being a 'cast-off son' of Salome the Jewess (*BGU* 511; *CPJ* 156; Jones and Milns 1984, no. 93; Braund 1985, no. 575; cf. Kokkinos 1986b, 41 and Kokkinos forthcoming 2).

85 Dio, 58.11.7; this kind of punishment reminds one of that inflicted upon Vestal Virgins for unchastity (Plut., *Num.* 10.4–7; *Fab. Max.* 18; Livy, 4.44; 8.15; 22.57; Suet., *Dom.* 8; Dio, 67.3; 77.16); for the privileges of the Virgins accorded to Antonia see p. 96; for Livilla and Sejanus see Dio, 58.11.7; Tac., *Ann.* 4.3.

86 Suet., *Cl.* 11.2; Dio, 60.5.1.

87 Naples (*IG* 14.734) – though this need not necessarily be connected with the posthumous cult of *Diva*, but only that of her *iuno* (guardian spirit) while she was alive; Athens (*IG* 2/3².3535, 5095) – cults of living members of the Imperial family were perfectly acceptable in the East; Graindor 1927, 157–8; cf. Raubitschek 1946.

88 *CIL* 6.5536.

89 Tac., *Ann.* 12.53; 14.65; Dio, 62.14.3; cf. Oost 1958.

90 Virg., *Aen.* 8.51; 9.104.

91 Pliny, *Ep.* 7.29; see 8.6.

92 Jos., *Ant.* 18.182; Suet., *Vesp.* 3.1.

93 Dio 65.14.1.

94 Kokkinos 1990.

95 Jos., *Ant.* 18.156; 19.276; *PIR²* A 837; Protos would have administered some land around Ptolemais left to Antonia by Berenice I.

96 *CIL* 6.4350, 4451, 4689.

97 Galen, *De Comp. Med.* 4.8 [445].

98 Scrib. Largus, *Compos.* 271.

99 Cichorius 1922, 356–8, 363–5; Pliny, *N.H.* 9.172; Tac., *Ann.* 14.5.7; 13.18; see p. 154.

2 THE INSCRIPTIONS OF ANTONIA

1 See Millar 1983, 136; Jones and Milns 1984.
2 With the exception of A.9 – which seemed to fit this category best, because, among other reasons, it implies that an inscription referring to Antonia in a more direct way would have accompanied her statue set upon the arch.
3 Cf. Hanson and Johnson 1946, 394 for some of them.
4 *DGCN* 3; Hoffman-Lewis 1955, 144–50; Henzen 1868.
5 Pellegrini 1865; cf. Burn 1871, 440–1.
6 Henzen 1874, XLIII; cf. *Inscr.It.* 13:2, 405; Crin., *Anth.* 6.345; *ADLI* no. 83, pl. 37b.
7 Vidman 1982, 11, 42–3, 70, pl. IV:ch; *Inscr.It.* 13:1, 188–91, pl. 69:10.
8 *CIL* 6.2028; 32344; it was further decreed that this day be called Parilia, as a token that the city had been founded a second time (Suet., *Cal.* 16.4). For some unknown reason it was supposed by Cicero's time (*Div.* 2.98; Varro, *Rust.* 2.1.9) that the festival to the god and goddess Pales (that is, Parilia) held on 21 April, marked the foundation-day of Rome (*natalis urbis*).
9 *CIL* 14.4535; Balsdon 1934, 25–6; Suet., *Cal.* 15.1; cf. Dio, 59.3.5.
10 Suet., *Cal.* 29.1.
11 Dio, 58.27.4.
12 For Siarum see Pliny, *N.H.* 3.11, but not in *PECS*; for the *tabula* see Conzàlez and Fernàndez 1981; Conzàlez 1984; *AE* 1984, 508; Lebek 1986 and 1987; Sherk 1988, 63–7, no. 36; cf. Reynolds *et al.* 1986, 128–9, 138–9; Millar 1988.
13 Tac., *Ann.* 2.83; the surviving part in the Vatican (*CIL* 6.31199c) does not mention Antonia, but she was named in one of the two lost fragments (*CIL* 6.911a = 31199a); cf. further the 'Tabula Hebana' (Javier Lomas 1978).
14 Tac., *Ann.* 3.2, 3; cf. Potter 1987, 270.
15 Strabo, 12.2.2; Suet., *Cl.* 1.3; Dio, 55.2.3; cf. *CIL* 6.911.
16 Tac., *Ann.* 2.64; cf. Ward-Perkins 1981, 28–32, 45.
17 See Castagnoli 1984.
18 Cf. *ADLI* no. 13, pl. 45a; see Castagnoli 1942, 58–73.
19 Front., *De Aquis* 1.10; cf. Ashby 1935, 177–80; *TDAR*, 35–6; *PDAR* 1, 102, figs. 104–7; *CIL* 6.920, 31203.
20 Dio, 60.22.1; cf. Claudius' proposal to admit into the Senate Gaulish citizens, *CIL* 13.1668; cf. Wellesley 1954; Griffin 1982.
21 Suet., *Cl.* 1.3; cf. Dio, 55.2.3; *PDAR* 1, 79–80.
22 *BMCRE* 1, Cl., no. 2, pl. 31:2; nos 95–103, pls 33:11–4; Dio, 60.5.1; cf. Suet., *Cl.* 11.2–3; see examples in brass (*orichalcum*) of AD 41 and 42, *BMCRE* 1, Cl., nos 121–3, 187–91, pls 34:10; 36:2; Dio, 60.8.7; *contra TDAR*, 36, *s.v.* 'Arcus Claudii (3)'.
23 *BMCRE* 1, Cl., nos 29, 32–6, 49–50, pls 31:20, 23–5; 32:5–6.
24 Cf. Gow and Page 1968, 269–79; Strabo, 9.2.5, 25; Cic., *Verr.* 2.4.135.
25 Cichorius 1922.

26 Nicols 1975, 53, 54. His argument is based on a common misunderstanding of the chronology of Agrippa I before he was king of Judaea. Agrippa returned to Palestine only in AD 32/3 after the fall of Sejanus (see Kokkinos forthcoming 1 and 2).

27 Hanson and Johnson 1946, 390; Dio, 54.23.7.

28 Pottier and Hauvette-Besnault 1880, 432, no. 18; Schliemann 1884, 258, no. 15; cf. Bailie 1846, 196–8, no. CCVI:a; Tac., *Ann.* 2.54.

29 *IGRR* 4.206; Frisch (*IK* 3, no. 88) takes '*pleistas kai megistas archas tou theiotatou genous paraschousan*' to mean that she provided money for the holding of the most offices (*archai*) in Ilium. But in view of the reference to 'the most divine *genos*', such an understanding does not come naturally to me. Thus for the moment, I would take *archai* to mean the moral 'principles' of the Imperial family, which Antonia (renowned for hers) had introduced. I admit, however, that it is not very clear to whom her 'provision' (whether of principles or offices) was made: to the Imperial family itself, the world in general, Philo the beneficiary, or the people of Ilium?

30 Ptolemais (Kraeling 1962); Lepcis Magna (Bianchi-Bandinelli *et al.* 1966).

31 For A.6 cf. *CIL* 5186; for A.7 cf. Reynolds and Ward-Perkins 1959, 252.

32 Cf. Aurigemma 1940, 20–4, 'AD 14–19'; *contra* V.H. Poulsen 1946, 44–5, 'AD 20–23'.

33 See e.g. for Tiberius: *ILS* 157 from Interamna in Umbria; *ILS* 158 from Gortyna in Crete.

34 For Marruvium see Strabo, 5.4.2; cf. Letta and D'Amato 1975, 89–92; for Cemenelum see Benoit 1966, 375–6, fig. 5; Benoit 1977, 17–18.

35 *CIL* 6.892; cf. Grant 1950a, 101–3; Suet., *Cal.* 15.3; 23.3; Dio, 59.1.3; for this title and some difficulties derived from its application in the eastern world, see p. 103.

36 Tac., *Ann.* 12.9; for A.16 cf. *ILS* 150. During his career at Herculaneum, L. Mammius Maximus also set up statues to Livia (Orelli 1856, no. 5365) and to Augustus (*AE* 1979, 172).

37 Hanfmann 1983, 144; Tac., *Ann.* 2.54.

38 Tac., *Ann.* 2.47; see Magie 1950, 1358–9, n. 23 for collected evidence; cf. Sutherland 1987, 47–9, no. 18.

39 Reynolds 1980; Reynolds 1981.

40 Reynolds 1981, 322; for the Sebasteion see Erim 1986, 106–23; Smith 1987.

41 Reynolds 1981, 317; for the date of the architrave see Smith 1987, 90.

42 No such qualities for Livia despite the *en passant* compliment in Vell., 2.75.3; cf. the more sound assessment of Livia in Dio, 58.2.3–6; for Hera or Demeter see Reynolds 1980, 79, 82; cf. Mullens 1942, 62; Grether 1946, 224; for Julia see *IGRR* 4.9, 114; for Livilla see again the Ilium text; cf. *SEG* 11.922 from Gytheion, where she is described as 'the Venus of younger Drusus' although this fact has not been previously recognised; see Tac., *Ann.* 4.3.

43 Tac., *Ann.* 2.54; cf. Strabo, 14.1.27; see Parke 1985, 125–41; for Germanicus and religious centres see Gagé 1968, 35.
44 Amm. Marc., 22.14.8; cf. Pliny, *N.H.* 8.184–6; Sol., *Coil.* 32.19.
45 Magie 1950, 498.
46 Probably associated with Columbarium III in the vineyard Codini – see Braun 1852, 81–3.
47 Dio, 50.13.7.
48 Cf. *ILS* 5220; Professor Millar comments that although it is possible for *nugari* to mean 'jester', it sounds odd. Instead it might mean 'seller of small trifles', i.e. 'pedlar' or something like that.
49 Pliny, *N.H.* 36.42–3; Suet., *Aug.* 29.5; Shipley 1931, 50; Olinder 1974, 94, 102.
50 Suet., *De Gram.* 21; Plut., *Marc.* 30; Pliny, *N.H.* 36.28; 35.114; 36.22.
51 *PDAR* 1, 232–3, figs 266–8; cf. Carettoni *et al.* 1960; Rodriguez-Almeida 1981.
52 McClees 1920, 9–10.
53 Graindor 1927, 157–8.
54 Cf. Bodnar 1960, 171–2.
55 *IG* 2/3² 1990; Gerkan 1941, 174–7; Koumanoudes 1885, 207, no. 1; *IG* 3.457; Dio, 60.23.4–5; *contra* date in *SEG* 21.742.
56 If Antonia was consecrated by Claudius (see p. 115), then no doubt personal priests dedicated to her service would have existed – Caligula had demanded twenty priests and priestesses for his sister Drusilla when he ordered the building of her shrine (Dio, 59.11.3).
57 Dio 65.14.1; Suet., *Vesp.* 3; Perowne 1974, 102–3; cf. Millar 1977, 79.
58 Friggeri 1977/8.
59 Treggiari 1973, 243, n. 10.
60 For a freedman of Augustus with the same name see Jos., *Ant.* 17.332; for B.31 cf. *ILS* 1663.
61 Weaver 1972, 26, n. 1; cf. *ILAlg.* 2, 783; for Cirta see MacKendrick 1980, 201–5.
62 Cf. Duff 1928, 90.
63 Treggiari 1973, 244, n. 19; for B.32 cf. *ILS* 1696; for B.30 cf. *ILS* 1695.
64 Cf. Treggiari 1976.
65 Cf. Urdahl 1959, 110.
66 Dio, 60.22.2.
67 *TDAR*, 551; Suet., *Cal.* 7; 8.2; *Galba* 18.
68 Cf. *DGCN* 178; Günther 1913, 213, no. 10:1–3; the name of this estate is given in the graffiti as 'The Meadow' (Limon – in Greek *leimôn*) the same way Statius (*Silv.* 2.2) refers to it.
69 Hirschfeld 1902, 47, n. 6.
70 Lewis 1983, 54; cf. Hopkins 1966; Hopkins 1983, 72.
71 Henzen 1847, 49–51; cf. *PDAR* 2, 333–9, figs 1103–10; Lanciani 1897, 331; Toynbee 1971, 113–16.

3 THE PAPYRI OF ANTONIA

1 See E.G. Turner 1968; Metzger 1968; Finegan 1975; Aland and Aland 1987.
2 *P.Köln* 249; Koenen 1970; cf. Reinhold 1972; Bowman 1976, 153–4; Haslam 1979/80; Badian 1980/1; *RGE* 99.
3 Parassoglou 1978, 11.
4 Millar 1977, 177; cf. D.J. Crawford 1976, 40.
5 *CIL* 12.5842; 10.7489; Fraccaro 1940.
6 Jos., *Ant.* 19.276; *War* 5.205; incidentally, the work may have been undertaken by the Alexandrian artist Nicanor, whose inscribed ossuary (that is, stone burial chest) referring to 'the gates' was discovered on the Mount of Olives, see *CIJ* 1256.
7 Dio, 51.15.7; Cic., *Phil.* 2.41; Rostowzew, 1910, 290–1; but *contra* Broughton 1934, 213–17; on property owned generally by women in Egypt, see now Pomeroy 1981; Hobson 1983.
8 For Cleopatra's confiscations see Eitrem and Holst 1928, 223; but cf. *P. Oslo* 33; for purchase of estates see Parassoglou 1978, 21.
9 D.J. Crawford 1976, 41; Rostovtzeff 1957, 295; MacMullen 1976, 20–6; cf. the Ptolemaic gifts, '*dôreai*', equated with '*ousiai*' – Rostovtzeff 1922, 145.
10 D.J. Crawford 1976, 42–3; Suet., *Aug.* 101.3; cf. Rogers 1947.
11 For Livia see lists in Lewis 1974, 52–4; D.J. Crawford 1976, 174, n. 16; Parassoglou 1978, 72, no. 10; for Germanicus see D.J. Crawford 1976, 174, n. 18; Parassoglou 1978, 71–2, no. 8.
12 For Berenice I's will see Jos., *Ant.* 18.156, and cf. the possible land administered by Protos in Ptolemais (above, ch. 1, note 95); for Julia Berenice see *P.Hamb.* 8; for Herodian journeys to Egypt see Jos. index – a colossal head found in Egypt was attributed to Herod by Ingholt (1963); for Salome I's will see Jos., *Ant.* 18.31.
13 *P.Ryl.* 148.
14 Cf. ibid. 126, where another estate is mentioned as being left to Livia perhaps by the same person; for date of death see ibid. 166.
15 Rostovtzeff 1957, 672, n. 45:VI; *CPJ* 420; Jos., *Ant.* 16.394; Parassoglou 1978, 17, n. 12; cf. Jos., *Ant.* 276.
16 *P.Ryl.* 166.
17 Kokkinos 1987.
18 See Jones 1971, 298, 312; Lewis 1983, 36.
19 For this village see Husselman 1979; Gazda 1983.
20 Cf. Wallace 1938, 85–6; *ChLA*, no. 206; Braund 1985, no. 756.
21 Cf. Braund 1985, no. 757.
22 *P.Ryl.* 134.
23 Cf. Lindsay 1963, 139; Braund 1985, no. 758.
24 In theory the Arsinoite nome could have received the news from Rome in much less than forty days, if only for the fact that a reasonably fast sea-voyage from the Roman capital to Alexandria took about ten to thirteen days (Casson 1951, 146; Rathbone 1986, 103). But there are certain complications. Between 10 March and 26 May the sea was considered dangerous for navigation (Veget., *Epit.*

Rei Milit. 4.39; Pliny, *N.H.* 2.47, 125; cf. Casson 1971, 270–99; Sperber 1986, 99–101). A trip overland (a distance of about 3200 miles) using the most efficient Imperial post would have required over sixty days (Eliot 1955, 80). Further, in terms of the closest parallel, the accession of the Emperor Pertinax on 1 January AD 193, was celebrated in Alexandria after only sixty-three days (Ramsay 1925, 69). It must be presumed, therefore, that because of the urgency of the news specifically about Caligula, a sea journey was undertaken in the second half of March. Besides, other journeys made during the so-called 'dangerous' periods are on record. For example, Philo, the Jewish philosopher, left Alexandria for Rome in the midwinter (*Leg.* 190). From an entirely different point of view, the distance over a straight line between Rome and Alexandria (*c.* 1300 miles) could be covered in windless conditions in about two days by trained carrier pigeons. However, the present writer is ignorant as to whether a pigeon post ever functioned between Rome and Alexandria. Of course pigeons were used by the Greeks for sending messages over shorter distances (Pollard 1977, 91). I thank Mr P. James for reminding me of this possibility.

25 Cf. Braund 1985, no. 764.
26 Suet., *Nero* 29; Dio, 61.5; Tac., *Ann.* 14.65.
27 Dio, 60.2.3; Suet., *Cl.* 37.2; *Vit.* 2.5.
28 Parassoglou 1978, 28.
29 Cf. Lindsay 1963, 163.
30 Dio, 60.5.1–2; see pp. 31, 124.
31 See McLennan 1935.
32 Petrie *et al.* 1925, 14–16.
33 Cf. Censor., *De Die Natali* 17.9; Lewis and Reinhold 1955, 55, no. 13, n. 158; cf. Fowler 1920, 111–26.
34 Cf. *DAT* 379; Braund 1985, no. 557; E.G. Turner 1987, 96–7, no. 57.
35 Weingärtner 1969, 73–4.
36 E.G. Turner 1959, 103.
37 Rostovtzeff 1957, 670, no. 8; 671, no. 19; cf. Dio, 51.15.7 = both Antonias; also inscription B.2 = *Antoniarum Duarum.*
38 Parassoglou 1978, 20; for Nero's holdings, e.g. *P.Lond.* 280; *BGU* 181.
39 For this village see Boak 1935.
40 Hauben 1979, 168.
41 See lists in D.J. Crawford 1976, 175, n. 25; Parassoglou 1978, 81, no. 21.
42 As slave see Jos., *Ant.* 18.182; cf. pp. 31–2; for his property in the reign of Tiberius see *P.Lond.* 195; cf. Oost 1958, 116.
43 Parassoglou 1978, 21, n. 43; *P.Fay.* 40; *P.Bour.* 42.

4 THE COINS AND TOKENS OF ANTONIA

1 See M. Crawford 1983.
2 See Hill 1909; Sydenham 1917; Grant 1968; Sutherland 1951; Sutherland 1976; Sutherland 1987.

NOTES TO PAGES 87–97

3 Suet., *Cl.* 11.2; on corn see Tac., *Ann.* 11.4.
4 Bonniec 1958, 277–311; cf. *PDAR* 1, 227–9; but now see Coarelli 1988, 18, 67–8; for Augustus' initiation see Suet., *Aug.* 93; Dio, 51.4.1; cf. Millar 1977, 450; for Tiberius' dedication see Dio, 50.10; Tac., *Ann.* 2.49; *CIL* 6.9969; cf. *TDAR*, 109–10.
5 Cic., *Leg.* 2.21; for Claudius and Ceres see Suet., *Cl.* 25.5
6 Dio, 59.3.4.
7 Cf. Grant 1956, 107; see Trillmich 1978, 175–7, no. 9b, pl. 16:25.
8 *BMCRE* 1, Cl., no. 213, pl. 36:9; *DGCN* 13.
9 *BMCRE* 1, Cl., no. 172; nos 167–71; 188, n.; *BMCRE* 2, XXIII, no. 7.
10 *BMCRE* 1, CXXXV.
11 Gross 1962; on Salus in general see Marwood 1988.
12 *BMCRE* 4, XVII-XVIII, n. 2.
13 Cf. Grant 1950b, 33–4.
14 For Livia see Tac., *Ann.* 5.1; Dio, 58.2.1; *BMCRE* 1, Tib., nos 76–8, pl. 23:18–9; for Agrippina see *ibid.*, Cal., nos 81–7, pl. 30:4–6.
15 Cichorius 1922.
16 See Jos., *Ant.* 18.180–2; despite the fact that Tiberius declared that the honours of women must be kept within bounds (Tac., *Ann.* 1.14), probably frustrated with his mother Livia.
17 For vague statement see Suet., *Cl.* 11.2; for decree of the Senate see Suet., *Cal.* 15.2; Dio, 59.3.4; see p. 27.
18 Cohen 1930, 1.172, no. 12; 1.247, no. 1.
19 Dio, 59.23.7.
20 Grant 1950b, 38.
21 Hes., *Theog.* 901; *Op. et Dies* 256; Eur., *Chil. of Herc.* 941.
22 *Acts* 28.3–5; *Mt.* 5.9.
23 *BMCRR* 2, nos 65–72, pl. CIV:2–8; Mattingly 1928, 67; Wagenvoort 1980, 15; it appears that the name of Pietas was adopted by Antony's brother as his *cognomen* – from then on he was known as L. Antonius Pietas (Dio, 48.5.4; *Inscr.It.*, 13:1, 568); M. Crawford (1975, 1, 524, no. 516; 2, 742) believes that these coins celebrate the consulship of L. Antonius (41 BC), thus the complete inscription PIETAS COS.
24 Antony's brother (Dio, 48.5); Titus' coins (*BMCRE* 2, Tit., nos 289–91, pl. 55:5–7).
25 Cohen 1930, 1.174, no. 28; 1.61, no. 5; 1.173, no. 18; for Crete cf. Sallet 1879, 61.
26 *BMCRE* 1, Cal., 156 (= Hall Coll. C10, pl. 28:9); no. 69, pl. 29:14; no. 59, pl. 29:7; nos 72–3, pl. 30:1.
27 ibid., CXLVI; Dio, 59.3.4.
28 For Temple of Divus Augustus, however, cf. Ward-Perkins 1981, 46; for its position see Dio, 56.46.3; 57.10.2; Tac., *Ann.* 6.45; Suet., *Tib.* 47; cf. *TDAR*, 62–5; *PDAR* 1, 164.
29 For Antonia see Dio, 59.3.4; for Vestals see Suet., *Aug.* 31.3.
30 See Lanciani 1888, 138–42.
31 For Hestia see Farnell 1909, 345–65; for the fire see Ovid, *Fast.* 6.295–7; for Hadrian see Vermeule 1986, VII.28; cf. *PDAR* 2, 505–10; for *penus* cf. Livy, 26.27.14.

32 Plut., *Num.* 10; cf. Beard 1980.
33 Strabo 14.1.36; Pliny, *N.H.* 5.117.
34 Graillot 1912, 320–32; Wiseman 1984; V. Max., 1.8.2; cf. *TDAR*,
   324–5; *PDAR* 2, 27–31; Ward-Perkins 1981, 37; Vermeule 1986,
   VII.3; cf. *DRC, s.v.* 'Tympanum'.
35 Cf. Trillmich 1978, 160–1, no. 5, pl. 15:18.
36 Ovid, *Trist.* 4.10.99.
37 Bellinger 1961, pl. 6:T.122.
38 Trillmich 1978, 162–7, no. 6, pl. 16:1–7.
39 Magie 1950, 1353, n. 9. It appears that the coin, from Cappadocia,
   had been attributed to Crete by Svoronos (1890, 339, no. 29, pl.
   32:24).
40 Tac., *Ann.* 11.37.
41 Juv., *Sat.* 6.116–32.
42 Suet., *Cal.* 56, 58; Jos., *Ant.* 19.105–13.
43 Jos., *Ant.* 18.203–4.
44 Philo, *Leg.* 276–329; cf. Jos., *Ant.* 18.289–300; see Smallwood 1957;
   Bilde 1978.
45 Burnett 1987, no. 6; Meshorer 1982, 247, no. 3IM; Qedar *per litt.*
   and *com.*; for Drusilla see Suet., *Cal.* 25.4; 42; 59; cf. Dio, 59.28.7.
46 For the title Sebastos cf. Rösch 1978, 34–5; for Paphos see *IGRR*
   3.940; for Aphrodisias see the puzzled remark in Reynolds 1980,
   no. 17; for Lesbos see Mionnet 1808, 49, no. 125 – provided that it
   was struck before her death, because she seems to have briefly
   received this title posthumously (Dio, 59.11.2); see ch. 5, n. 27.
47 Dio, 58.8.4; Price 1984a.
48 Cohen 1930, 1.223; *BMCGC,* Ion.: Smyr., 270, nos 281–2, pl. 28:10;
   Eph., 73, nos 203–8, pl. 13:3.
49 Franke *et al.* 1981, Prägetab. nos 3 and 5; the Aezanis specimen in
   Munich has now been confirmed to me (1991), and although it is not
   included in Register F, I do plot the site and list the coin in figure
   109.
50 Cohen 1930, 1.222, no. 3; cf. Grant 1950a, 83, n. 325.
51 For grain see *CPABN*, 65–78; for games and theatre see Friedländer
   1968, 1–130; for Egypt see *CPABN*, 150–3; for Palmyra see Ingholt
   et al. 1955.
52 Hamburger 1986, 189; Jos., *Ant.* 19.357.
53 Mitchiner 1984, 101.
54 See Rostowzew 1905, pl. 1:2; *DGCN* no. 429.
55 E.g. Ferguson 1970, 72.
56 Cf. Belfort 1889, pl. 4:2.
57 Suet., *Cl.* 11.2.
58 Cf. Pliny, *N.H.* 36.116.
59 Suet., *Aug.* 1; Toynbee 1978, 49.
60 Strabo, 5.3.12.

5 ANTONIA AND SCULPTURE

1 Polaschek 1973; cf. Stuart 1939; see Kleiner and Kleiner 1974, 444; cf. Erhart 1978, 196.
2 Cf. *ILS* 149; Hanson and Johnson 1946, 394; McDermott 1948, 421; Letta and D'Amato 1975, 89–92.
3 *P.Lond.* 1912.
4 Erhart 1978.
5 See Bianchi-Bandinelli *et al.* 1966.
6 Erhart 1978, 204; *contra* Polaschek 1973, 38–45.
7 For there may be Late Hellenistic precedents, see Smith 1987, 127, n. 118.
8 *MNRR*, 54; Felletti-Maj 1958, 441; but cf. Sensi (in Register H.3).
9 Trump 1972, 108–9, fig. 20.
10 See MacKendrick 1980, 206–9.
11 V.H. Poulsen 1946, 26, no. 4.
12 *Res Gest.* 12; *CIL* 1:2.244, 247, 320; 212, 232.
13 Suet., *Aug.* 5; naturally every birthday of Augustus was celebrated in the Empire (see *ARS*, 119), but his fiftieth was a special one. For the celebration of Augustus' sixty-fourth in AD 2, see his letter to his adopted son Gaius Caesar in the East, quoted by Gellius (*Noc. Att.* 15.7.3); for unrecorded centenaries see list in Snyder 1940, 234, n. 21.
14 *CIL* 6.2028c; cf. Hanell 1935/6, 9; Grant 1950b, 10.
15 Cf. Toynbee 1953, 72.
16 Cf. Bonanno 1976, 28; Kleiner 1978, 759; it should be pointed out that Levick (1966, 240) has suggested that Germanicus was born in 16 BC, which at this juncture would agree better with his portrait on the Ara Pacis. However, serious objections were raised against her by Sumner (1967, 427). The attempt of Holloway (1984) to reidentify the Ara Pacis portraits has been totally unconvincing. According to Holloway (1984, 627), the young Germanicus must be Lucius Caesar, and therefore instead of Antonia he puts Julia (the daughter of Augustus) in her place. This view ignores, to say the least, the established iconography of Antonia. Lastly, it must be stressed that most studies of the Ara Pacis portraiture take for granted that people are depicted as they looked precisely on 4 July 13 BC. But it is almost certain that the artist executed his work some time after 13 BC and before 9 BC, and therefore it is logical that he would have used (in the absence of photography!) more contemporary images. The possibility of sketches taken by the artist on the day of the procession is extremely far-fetched (he had probably not been selected yet) and even if this was the case, rough sketches could hardly have been adequately detailed. Once this aspect is realised the problem of the age of Germanicus resolves itself.
17 Ovid, *Ars Amat.* 3.137–40; Furnée-van Zwet 1956, 7, 10–11.
18 Cf. Hafner 1955, 164–70, figs 62–3; Ryberg 1955, 92.
19 Bonanno 1976, 42.
20 Cf. *TDAR*, 551–5; Suet., *Cl.* 25.5.

21 Zevi and Andreae 1982; cf. Frost 1983.
22 Andreae 1983, 54–6; for Eros or Cupid, however, see objections of Gigante 1984; Pliny, *N.H.* 35.156; Dio, 47.18.4; cf. Vermeule 1986, VI.7; VII.26.
23 Jos., *Ant.* 18.249.
24 Plut., *Anton.* 87.3.
25 Crin., *Anth.* 9.239.
26 Rumpf 1941, 21.
27 Furtwängler 1895, 326–8; Rumpf 1941, 31; cf. Sensi 1980/1, 61–4; a case may also be made for Drusilla the sister of Caligula, even though this has not been widely recognised. Dio (59.11.2) says that upon her death in AD 38 she received all honours that Livia (and evidently Antonia) had enjoyed. However, the circumstances of Caligula's reign were peculiar and his proclamations did not last. At all events, one should compare this point with the 'Sebaste' coin of Drusilla (p. 103), her shrine (ch. 2, n. 56) and her massive statue (see below, note 29).
28 Farnell 1896, 179–204; Vermeule 1986, VII.14.
29 Cf. Drusilla's gigantic statue erected by Caligula in the Temple of Venus at the Forum Iulium (Dio, 59.11.3).
30 Pliny, *N.H.* 35.94; see Bailie 1846, 407; *DGRBM* 1, 209; Ian 1970, 37: '*Antoniae templum*, 25.94 [read 35.94]'; the name of the temple in the MSS tradition is corrupted, *Dianae* is usually preferred (e.g. Loeb edn), but *Annae* and *Antoniae* have also been assumed as representing the correct reading – cf. Jex-Blake and Sellars 1896, 131, n. 94:9.
31 For Temple of Divus Augustus see Dio, 60.5.2; for Claudianum see Ward-Perkins 1981, 63–6.
32 For Leningrad cf. *MEPR*; for Veii see Pliny, *N.H.* 35.157.
33 Polaschek 1973, 31, n. 45, pl. 16:1–2.
34 Erhart 1978, 209, 211, no. 11.
35 *KRPCM*, 45, n. 2.
36 V.H. Poulsen 1946, 25.
37 Heintze 1964, 319. From the Torlonia catalogue I have not been able to identify the statue that Heintze had in mind, but in the process I have noticed a bust which should almost certainly represent Antonia, despite its being labelled 'Faustina'. Under the circumstances this bust is listed here as J.15, although, not having studied it carefully, I realise that it may belong to another category.
38 Benoit 1966, 370; Benoit 1977, 14–19.
39 Espérandieu 1910, no. 2450; cf. Benoit 1962a, 210.
40 Erhart 1978, 194.
41 Suet., *Cl.* 11.2; Dio, 60.5.1; *Res Gest.* 19; cf. Humphrey 1986, 78–83.
42 Erhart 1978, 207; Ferrero 1925, 202; cf. F. Poulsen 1928, 37, no. 5, figs 81–3.
43 V.H. Poulsen 1946, 31.
44 Strabo, 14.1.42.
45 Hinks 1976, 55, no. 39.
46 Ovid, *Met.* 4.268; cf. Cook 1976, 181, no. 144.

47 Jucker 1961, 64–7, pls 20–1; Polaschek 1973, 38–9; it is always possible that the legend of Clytie was used metaphorically for Antonia and that this bust was meant to identify the two.

48 Sensi 1987, pl. I:2–3; cf. V.H. Poulsen 1960, 14; Kiss 1975, 99–100, 119.

49 Garcia y Bellido 1966.

50 Vermeule 1968, 54, 186, 193; cf. Anti 1928.

51 Cf. Jacopi 1939, col. 133, no. 76, pl. 23.76; Chaisemartin 1987.

52 Smith 1987, 125–7, no. 10, pls 22–3.

6 ANTONIA AND MINOR ARTS

1 For Greek artists see Richter 1971, 131–5; for use of gems see King 1872, 16; for India see Henig 1983, 153.

2 Pliny, *N.H.* 33.12; 37.23.

3 Erhart 1978, 211, no. 8.

4 Jos., *Ant.* 19.335–7.

5 For what appears to be Agrippa's private seal, see Philo, *Leg.* 330; for Jerusalem see Mazar 1971, 17, pl. 25:3; Avigad 1983, 204, nos 253–4; for Machaerus, Vardaman *per litt.* and *com.*

6 Richter 1971, no. 709; Pliny, *N.H.* 33.8; Suet., *Aug.* 50; Dio, 51.3.6–7.

7 Richter 1971, 129; Henig 1983, 154, ill. 122.

8 For Ceres–Antonia see *BMCPCG*, 150, no. 1045, pl. 34; for Germanicus see Richter 1971, no. 674.

9 Cf. *MarGems*, no. 401.

10 Cf. *CGJM*, 30, no. 164, frontispiece; this head was recently in a Swiss private collection (Simon 1982a, 342, pls 25–7), before being acquired by the Getty Museum in 1981 (Henig 1988, 97; 105, n. 21).

11 Erhart 1978, 197–8, n. 18.

12 Cf. Balsdon 1936; see table in Jucker 1976, 248–9 where the majority of scholars identify Antonia.

13 On Spartan women in general see Redfield 1977/8; Cartledge 1981.

14 Suet., *Cal.* 8.1.

15 ibid. 9.1.

16 *KKHM*, 52–6, no. 7, pl. 4.

17 Schlüter *et al.* see *AGDSHan*, 217, no. 1094; Bruns 1946, 50, no. 33.

18 Cf. A. Strong 1907, pl. 30:2.

19 For the Titaness see Hes., *Theog.* 136; as moon see Stat., *Theb.* 1.105; cf. the son of Antonia, Germanicus, referring to Phoebe in the *Aratea* ascribed to him (frag. ii – see Gain 1976, 44–5); as Diana see Stat., *Silv.* 1.3.76.

20 Cf. Ovid, *Fast.* 3.268–9.

21 Richter 1971, 163–4, nos 769, 769 bis, 770.

22 D. Strong 1976, 89–94.

23 Corbett and Strong 1961, 68–86; cf. Henig 1983, 142; for the legend see conveniently Graves 1955, sect. 116.

24 Vermeule 1968, 132.

25 Reinach 1922, 169:5; 170:4; Rumpf 1941, 25–8, pl. 4a,b.

26 Vermeule 1968, 127, fig. 60; Fittschen 1975, 183, pl. 6 = 'Divus Iulius'; Smith 1987, 110–12, pl. 10, no. 4.

27 Tac., *Ann.* 2.59.

28 Suet., *Cal.* 3.2; for his iconography see Curtius 1948; Kiss 1975, 111–30; Fittschen 1987.

29 Maxfield 1981, 91–5.

30 Toynbee and Richmond 1953, 47.

31 Cf. Henig 1974, 97, no. 747, pl. 48 = 'Stanwix'.

32 King 1873, 275–85; Toynbee and Richmond 1953, 41; Toynbee 1955/8; Henig 1974.

33 *BMCSP* 7, no. 26, pl. 7.

34 Villefosse 1899.

35 Cf. public offerings to her shade (*inferiae*) after her death (Suet., *Cl.* 11.2); for sacrifices in general within the Imperial Cult, see Price 1984b, 207–33.

36 *BMCGRL* 88, no. 577, fig. 112; cf. *BMCL* 2.143, no. Q807, pl. 5:47.

37 Strabo, 3.2.6; 17.1.7; Pliny, *N.H.* 36.70; for Puteoli in general see Frederiksen 1984, 319–58.

38 Jos., *Ant.* 18.161; *Vita* 13–16; *Acts* 28.11–13.

7 ANTONIA AND ARCHITECTURE

1 For wrong dates, see Benoit 1977, 14; for wrong place of birth, see Huzar 1986, 143; for wrong place of death, see D'Arms 1970, 85.

2 Plut., *Anton.* 54.2.

3 Dio 53.27.5; for Antony on the Palatine cf. Mann 1926, 128; Tamm 1963, 47, n. 23; for Clodius cf. Babcock 1965.

4 Plut., *Anton.* 54.1.

5 Dio, 48.38; cf. Suet., *De Gram.* 15; see *S.H.A.*: *Vit. Gord.* 3.

6 Plut., *Anton.* 57.3.

7 For the house of Marcellus see Jer., *Ep.* 48.96; for that of the Octavii see Suet., *Aug.* 5; Tamm 1963, 32, n. 15; for the *domus Augusti* see Vell., 2.81.3; Dio, 49.15.5.

8 V. Max., 4.3.3 (see p. 16); for recent excavations of this area, see Carettoni 1983a; Carettoni 1983b.

9 Suet., *Aug.* 72; cf. Richmond 1914, 194.

10 For inscription see *CIL* 15.7264; for excavation see Tamm 1963, 64, n. 6; for veneration cf. *TDAR*, 157.

11 For *testudinatum* see Lanciani 1897, 148; for *alae* see *PDAR* 1, 310–15; for Io painting see Lugli 1970, 170, no. 109; for mosaic see Middleton 1892, 181.

12 Cf. Lanciani 1897, 147–50.

13 Jos., *Ant.* 19.117; cf. Wiseman 1980, 232 = Wiseman 1987, 168.

14 Suet., *Cal.* 10.1; 24.1.

15 Dio, 60.2.5; Stat., *Silv.* 3.3.67; Tamm 1963, 64, n. 6.

16 Tac., *Ann.* 13.18.

17 Cic., *Acad.* 2.9; Pliny, *N.H.* 9.172.

18 Katzoff 1973; Maiuri 1941, 249–60; cf. Caro and Greco 1981, 64–5.

19 D'Arms 1970, 181; Cic., *Acad.* 2.80.

20 Cf. Maiuri 1934, 87.
21 Cichorius 1922, 356–8; 363–5.
22 Tac., *Ann.* 14.8; 14.5.7; cf. Bicknell 1963.
23 Dio 59.17.1–11; cf. Jos., *Ant.* 19.5–6; Sen., *De Brev. Vitae* 18.5–6.
24 Suet., *Cal.* 19.3.
25 Pliny, *Ep.* 2.17; see the ingenious Clifford Pember's model in the Ashmolean Museum at Oxford; Varro, *Rust.* 3.13.2.
26 Pliny, *N.H.* 35.130; cf. 14.96; another bust of Antonia from Tusculum (Ashby 1910, 365 – not registered in the present book) was reported in Edinburgh over a century ago by Coventry (1853), later to become a part of Colonel Maitland Crichton's collection in London (Michaelis 1882, 431); the whereabouts of this piece today is not known to me.
27 Jos., *Ant.* 18.179–204; cf. Dio, 58.24; Rogers 1945/6.
28 Smallwood 1976, 190.
29 For Imperial palace see Jos., *Ant.* 18.195; cf. *CIL* 14. 2671; Hirschfeld 1902, 536–7; for direction towards Rome see Strabo, 5.3.12; cf. p. 107; for hippodrome see Jos., *Ant.* 18.190; cf. Ashby 1910, 330–67.
30 Tac., *Ann.* 14.3.
31 Sen., *De Ira* 3.21.5.

CONCLUSION

1 Ovid, *Pont.* 3.1.117–18; *Fast.* 1.640–1; for Livia see particularly Willrich 1911; Grether 1946; Gross 1962; Purcell 1986; and entries in *RE* and *PIR*^{2}.
2 Dio, 49.38.1; 49.18.6.
3 ibid. 58.2.6.
4 For *arae* see Grether 1946, 226–7; for portico see Dio, 54.23.
5 Dio, 58.2.3.
6 ibid. 58.2.5.
7 Suet., *Cl.* 1.1.
8 Priestess (Dio, 56.46.1); restriction (57.12.1–6); consecration (60.5.2).

BIBLIOGRAPHY

(A) ABBREVIATIONS AND PRIMARY SOURCES

AA = *Archäologischer Anzeiger.*

AAPS = *The Athenian Agora 1: Portrait Sculpture* (ed. E.B. Harrison). Princeton, NJ: The American School of Classical Studies at Athens, 1953.

AClass = *Acta Classica* (Cape Town).

ActaA = *Acta Archeologica.*

Acts = *The Acts of the Apostles*, in *Novum Testamentum Graece* (26th edn, Nestle-Aland). Stuttgart: Deutsche Bibelstiftung, 1981, 320–408.

AdI = *Annali dell' Istituto di Corrispondenza Archeologica.*

ADLI = *Album of Dated Latin Inscriptions: Rome and the Neighborhood, Augustus to Nerva*, vol. 1 (ed. A.E. Gordon). Berkeley, Cal.: University of California Press, 1958.

AE = *L'Année Épigraphique.*

AFLPer = *Annali della Facoltà di Lettere e Filosofia. Università di Perugia.*

AfrIt = *Africa Italiana.*

AGDS = *Antike Gemmen in Deutschen Sammlungen.*

AGDSHan = *AGDS 4: Hannover, Kestner-Museum; Hamburg, Museum für Kunst und Gewerbe* (ed. M. Schlüter *et al.*). Wiesbaden: F. Steiner, 1975.

AGDSMun = *AGDS 1.3: Staatliche Münzsammlung München, Gemmen und Glaspasten der Römischen Kaiserzeit sowie Nachträge* (ed. E. Brandt *et al.*). Munich: Prestel, 1972.

AGKHMW = *Die Antiken Gemmen des Kunsthistorischen Museums in Wien*, vol. 2 (ed. E. Zwierlein-Diehl). Munich: Prestel, 1979.

AHR = *American Historical Review.*

AIV = *Atti dell'Istituto Veneto di Scienze, Lettere ed Arti, Classe di Scienze Morali e Lettere.*

207

AJA = *American Journal of Archaeology.*
AJAH = *American Journal of Ancient History.*
AJP = *American Journal of Philology.*
ALGRM = *Ausführliches Lexicon der Griechischen und Römischen Mythologie*, vol. 1 (ed. W.H. Roscher). Leipzig: Druck and B.G. Teubner, 1884.
AmelSVM = *Die Sculpturen des Vaticanischen Museums*, vol. 1 (ed. W. Amelung). Berlin: G. Reimer, 1903.
Amm. Marc. = Ammianus Marcellinus. *Roman History*, vols 1–3, in *LCL* (Eng. tr. J.C. Rolfe), 1935–40.
AncSoc = *Ancient Society.*
AnnNum = *Annuaire de Numismatique.*
Anonym. = Anonymous. *Gens Caesaris* (ed. S.P. Lambros), in *Neos Ellenomnemon* 1 (1904), 129–55 (Greek).
ANRW = *Aufstieg und Niedergang der Römischen Welt.*
App. = Appian. *The Civil Wars*, vols 3–4, in *LCL* (Eng. tr. H. White), 1913.
ArchClass = *Archeologia Classica.*
ArchEph = *Archaiologike Ephemeris* (Greek).
ArchPhilol = *Archivum Philologicum* (Egyetemes Philologiai Közlöny-Budapesti).
Arist. = Aristotle. *Politics*, vol. 21, in *LCL* (Eng. tr. H. Rackham), 1932.
ARS = *Ancient Roman Statutes* (ed. A.C. Johnson, P.R. Coleman-Norton and F.C. Bourne). Austin, Tex.: University of Texas Press, 1961.
ASE = *Die Antiken skulpturen der Ermitage* (Archäol. Mit. aus Russischen Samml., no. 5), vol. 3 (ed. O. Waldhauer). Berlin: W. de Gruyter, 1936.
BABesch = *Bulletin van de Vereeniging tot Bevordering der Kennis van de Antike Beschaving.*
Bard. = Bardesan. *The Book of the Laws of Countries*, in *Spicilegium Syriacum* (ed. and tr. W. Cureton). London: Rivingtons, 1855, 1–34.
BASP = *Bulletin of the American Society of Papyrologists.*
BCH = *Bulletin de Correspondance Hellénique.*
BdI = *Bullettino del Istituto di Corrispondenza Archeologica.*
BGU = *Agyptische Urkunden aus den Königlichen [Staatlichen] Museen zu Berlin, Griechische Urkunden*, vol. 1 (nos 1–361), 1895; vol. 2 (nos 362–696), 1898; vol. 9 (nos 1891–1900), 1937; vol. 11:1 (nos 2012–131), 1966.
BLund = *Bulletin de la Société Royale des Lettres de Lund.*
BMCG = *Catalogue of the Engraved Gems and Cameos Greek, Etruscan and Roman in the British Museum* (ed. H.B. Walters). London: B.M. Publications, 1926.
BMCGC = *Catalogue of the Greek Coins in the British Museum*, vols 1–29 (many eds). London: B.M. Publications, 1873–1927.
BMCGRL = *Catalogue of the Greek and Roman Lamps in the British*

		Museum (ed. H.B. Walters). London: B.M. Publications, 1914.
BMCL	=	*A Catalogue of the Lamps in the British Museum 2: Roman Lamps made in Italy* (ed. D.M. Bailey). London: B.M. Publications, 1980.
BMCPCG	=	*Catalogue of the Engraved Gems of the Post-Classical Periods in the Department of British and Mediaeval Antiquities and Ethnography in the British Museum* (ed. O.M. Dalton). London: B.M. Publications, 1915.
BMCRE	=	*Coins of the Roman Empire in the British Museum*, vols 1–6 (ed. H. Mattingly and R.A.G. Carson). London: B.M. Publications, 1923–62.
BMCRR	=	*Coins of the Roman Republic in the British Museum*, vols 1–3 (ed. H.A. Grueber). London: B.M. Publications, 1970.
BMCS	=	*A Catalogue of Sculpture in the Department of Greek and Roman Antiquities, British Museum*, vol. 3 (ed. A.H. Smith). London: B.M. Publications, 1904.
BMCSP	=	*Catalogue of the Silver Plate Greek, Etruscan and Roman in the British Museum* (ed. H.B. Walters). London: B.M. Publications, 1921.
BMQ	=	*British Museum Quarterly.*
BR	=	*Bible Review.*
BullComm	=	*Bullettino della Commissione Archeologica Comunale di Roma.*
C & M	=	*Classica et Mediaevalia.*
CACFC	=	*Catalogue of the Antiquities (Greek, Etruscan and Roman) in the Collection of the Late Wyndham Francis Cook, Esqre*, vol. 2 (ed. C.H. Smith and C.A. Hutton). London: Metchim and Son, 1908 (for private circulation).
CAH	=	*Cambridge Ancient History.*
CCPG	=	*De Clercq Collection 7.2: Les Pierres Gravées* (ed. A. de Ridder). Paris: E. Leroux, 1911.
CCPGBI	=	*Catalogue général et raisonné des camées et pierres gravées de la Bibliothèque Impériale* (ed. M. Chabouillet). Paris: J. Claye, 1858.
CEGMM	=	*Catalogue of Engraved Gems: Greek, Etruscan and Roman* (Metropolitan Museum of Art, New York – ed. G.M.A. Richter). Rome: 'L'Erma' di Bretschneider, 1956.
Censor.	=	Censorinus. *De Die Natali Liber* (ed. F. Hultsch). Leipzig: B.G. Teubner, 1867 (French tr. G. Rocca-Serra. Paris: Librairie Philosophique J. Vrin, 1980).
CGJM	=	*Catalogue of Engraved Gems and Rings in the Collection of Joseph Mayer, F.S.A.* (ed. C.T. Gatty). London: Bradbury, Agnew, 1879.
ChLA	=	*Chartae Latinae Antiquiores*, vols 1–25 (ed. A. Bruckner and R. Marichal). Olten and Lausanne: Urs Graf, 1954– .

Cic.	=	Cicero. *Opera*, vols 1–28. in *LCL* (Eng. tr. H. Rackham *et al.*), 1913–77; *Acad.* = *Academica*, *Div.* = *De Divinatione*, *Leg.* = *De Legibus*, *Phil.* = *Philippicae*, *Verr.* = *In Verrem*.
CIJ	=	*Corpus Inscriptionum Judaicarum*, vol. 1 (ed. J.-B. Frey). Rome: Pontificio Istituto di Archeologia Cristiana, 1936.
CIL	=	*Corpus Inscriptionum Latinarum*.
CJ	=	*Classical Journal*.
CMT	=	*Catalogo del Museo Torlonia di Sculture Antiche* (ed. P.E. Visconti). Rome: Tipografia Tiberina, 1880 (Plates vol. 3. Rome: Stabilimento Fotografico Danesi, 1884).
Corin.	=	*Corinth: Latin Inscriptions 1896–1926*, vol. 8:2 (ed. A.B. West). Cambridge, Mass.: Harvard University Press, 1931.
CP	=	*Classical Philology*.
CPABN	=	*Catalogue des plombs de l'antiquité, du moyen age et des temps modernes conservés au Département des Médailles et Antiques à la Bibliothèque Nationale* (ed. M. Rostovtsew and M. Prou). Paris: C. Rollin and Feuardent, 1900.
CPJ	=	*Corpus Papyrorum Judaicarum*, vol. 2 (ed. V.A. Tcherikover and A. Fuks). Cambridge, Mass.: Harvard University Press, 1960.
CQ	=	*Classical Quarterly*.
CR	=	*Classical Review*.
CRAI	=	*Comptes Rendus, Académie des Inscriptions & Belles-Lettres*.
Crin.	=	Crinagoras. *Epigrams*, in *Greek Anthology*, vols 1–5, in *LCL* (Eng. tr. W.R. Paton), 1916–18.
CSIR	=	*Corpus Signorum Imperii Romani*.
CSIRPol	–	*CSIR, Pologne 1: les portraits romains dans les collections polonaises* (ed. A. Sadurska). Warsaw: PWN – Editions Scientifiques de Pologne, 1972.
CV	=	*Classical Views* (= *Echos du Monde Classique*).
CW	=	*Classical Weekly*.
DAT	=	*Documents Illustrating the Reigns of Augustus and Tiberius* (2nd edn, V. Ehrenberg and A.H.M. Jones; repr. with addenda by D.L. Stockton). Oxford: Clarendon Press, 1976.
DCAMG	=	*A Descriptive Catalogue of a General Collection of Ancient and Modern Engraved Gems, Cameos as well as Intaglios* (ed. R.E. Raspe), London, 1791.
DGCN	=	*Documents Illustrating the Principates of Gaius, Claudius and Nero* (ed. E.M. Smallwood). Cambridge: Cambridge University Press, 1967.
DGRBM	=	*A Dictionary of Greek and Roman Biography and Mythology*, vol. 1 (ed. W. Smith). London: J. Murray, 1876.
Dig.	=	*Corpus Iuris Civilis 1: Digesta recognovit Th. Mommsen*

		(ed. P. Krueger). Berlin: Weidmann, 1922.
Dio	=	Dio Cassius. *Roman History*, vols 1–9, in *LCL* (Eng. tr. E. Cary), 1914–27.
Diod.	=	Diodorus Siculus. *Library of History*, vols 1–12, in *LCL* (Eng. tr. C.H. Oldfather *et al.*), 1933–67.
DRC	=	*A Dictionary of Roman Coins, Republican and Imperial* (ed. S.N. Stevenson *et al.*). London: G. Bell and Sons, 1889 (repr. B.A. Seaby, 1964).
EA	=	*Photographische Einzelaufnahmen Antiker Sculpturen*, vols 4–5 (ed. P. Arndt and W. Amelung). Munich: Bruckmann, 1899–1902.
EAA	=	*Enciclopedia dell'Arte Antica, Classica e Orientale* (ed. R. Bianchi-Bandinelli). Rome: Fondata da G. Treccani, 1958.
EC	=	*Les Etudes Classiques*.
EDRL	=	*Encyclopedic Dictionary of Roman Law* (trans. of the Amer. Philos. Soc., n.s., vol. 43:2 -- ed. A. Berger). Philadelphia, Pa: The American Philosophical Society, 1953.
Eph.Epigr.	=	*Ephemeris Epigraphica: Corporis Inscriptionum Latinarum Supplementum Edita Iussu Instituti Archaeologici Romani*, vols 1–9. Berlin: G. Reimer.
Eur.	=	Euripides. *Children of Hercules*, vol. 3, in *LCL* (Eng. tr. A.S. Way), 1912.
Flor.	=	Florus. *Epitome*, in *LCL* (Eng. tr. E.S. Forster), 1929.
Front.	=	Frontinus. *De Aquis*, in *LCL* (Engl. tr. M.B. McElwain), 1925.
G & R	=	*Greece and Rome*.
Gai	=	Gaius. *Institutes* (tr. W.M. Gordon and O.F. Robinson). Ithaca, NY: Cornell University Press, 1988.
Gal.	=	*The Epistle to the Galatians*, in *Novum Testamentum Graece* (26th edn, Nestle-Aland). Stuttgart: Deutsche Bibelstiftung, 1981, 493–503.
Galen	=	Galen. *De Compositione Medicamentorum Secundum Locos*, in *Opera Omnia*, vol. 12, 378–1007 (ed. C.G. Kühn). Hildesheim: G. Olms, 1965.
GBR	=	*La Galleria Borghese a Roma* (ed. P. della Pergola). Rome: Garzanti, 1966.
Gel.	=	Aulus Gellius. *Noctes Atticae*, vols 1–3, in *LCL* (Eng. tr. J.C. Rolfe), 1927.
GUS	=	*Galleria degli Uffizi: le sculture*, vol. 2 (ed. G.A. Mansuelli). Rome: Istituto Poligrafico dello Stato, 1961.
Herod.	=	Herodotus. *History*, vols 1–4, in *LCL* (Eng. tr. A.D. Godley), 1920–4.
Hes.	=	Hesiod. *Opera*, in *LCL* (Eng. tr. H.G. Evelyn-White), 1936; *Op. et Dies = Opera et Dies*, *Theog. = Theogony*.
Hon.	=	Honestus. *Epigrams* in Gow and Page 1968, 269–79.

HSRC	=	*Histoire Sociale. Revue Canadienne.*
HTR	=	*Harvard Theological Review.*

HunterColl. = *Catalogue of Greek Coins in the Hunterian Collection, University of Glasgow*, vol. 2 (ed. G. MacDonald). Glasgow: J. Maclehose and Son, 1901.

IG = *Inscriptiones Graecae.*

IGRR = *Inscriptiones Graecae ad res Romanas Pertinentes.*

IJNA = *International Journal of Nautical Archaeology.*

IK = *Inschriften Griechischer Städte aus Kleinasien 3: Die Inschriften von Ilion* (ed. P. Frisch). Bonn: R. Habelt, 1975.

ILAlg. = *Inscriptions Latines de L'Algérie*, vol. 2 (ed. St Gsell). Paris: E. Champion, 1958.

ILS = *Inscriptiones Latinae Selectae.*

Inscr.It. = *Inscriptiones Italiae*, vols 13:1 and 2 (ed. A. Degrassi). Rome: Libreria dello Stato, 1947–63.

JARCE = *Journal of the American Research Center in Egypt.*

JdI = *Jahrbuch des Deutschen Archäologischen Instituts.*

JEA = *Journal of Egyptian Archaeology.*

Jer. = Jerome. *Sancti Hieronymi Epistulae*, vols 1–8 (ed. J. Labourt). Paris: Budé, 1949–63.

JHS = *Journal of Hellenic Studies.*

Jn. = *The Gospel According to John*, in *Novum Testamentum Graece* (26th edn, Nestle-Aland). Stuttgart: Deutsche Bibelstiftung, 1981, 247–319.

Jos. = Josephus. *Opera*, vols 1–10, in *LCL* (Eng. tr. H. St. J. Thackeray *et al.*), 1926–65; *Apion* = *Against Apion*, *Ant.* = *Jewish Antiquities*, *Vita* = *The Life*, *War* = *The Jewish War.*

JRS = *Journal of Roman Studies.*

Juv. = Juvenal. *The Sixteen Satires* (Penguin Classics – Eng. tr. P. Green). Harmondsworth: Penguin Books, 1974.

JWCI = *Journal of Warburg and Courtauld Institutes.*

KASSE = *Katalog der Antiken Skulpturen in Schloss Erbach* (Archäol. Forschun., no. 3 – ed. K. Fittschen). Berlin: G. Mann, 1977.

KKHM = *Die Kammen im Kunsthistorischen Museum* (ed. F. Eichler and E. Kris). Vienna: Von Anton Schroll, 1927.

KRPCM = *Katalog der Römischen Porträts in den Capitolinischen Museen und den Anderen Kommunalen Sammlungen der Stadt Rom: Kaiserinnen und Prinzessinnenbildnisse Frauenporträts*, vol. 3 (ed. K. Fittschen and P. Zanker). Mainz-on-Rhine: Philipp von Zabern, 1983.

KSAS = *Katalog der Sammlung Antiker Skulpturen: Römische Bildnisse* (ed. C. Blümel). Berlin: Verlag für Kunstwissenschaft, 1933.

LA = *Liber Annuus* (Jerusalem).

LCL = *Loeb Classical Library.* London: W. Heinemann, 1912–

LCM = *Liverpool Classical Monthly.*

LEX = *Ausführliches Lexicon der griechischen und römischen Mythologie*, vol. 1 (ed. W.H. Roscher). Leipzig: Druck und Verlag von B.G. Teubner, 1897.

LipSVM = *Die Skulpturen des Vaticanischen Museums*, vol. 3:2 (ed. G. Lippold). Berlin: W. de Gruyter, 1956.

Livy = Livy. *Epitome*, vols 1–14, in *LCL* (Eng. tr. B.O. Foster *et al.*), 1919–59.

Lk. = *The Gospel According to Luke*, in *Novum Testamentum Graece* (26th edn, Nestle-Aland). Stuttgart: Deutsche Bibelstiftung, 1981, 150–246.

MAAR = *Memoirs of the American Academy in Rome.*

MarGems = *The Marlborough Gems* (ed. M.H. Nevil Story-Maskelyne). London: Bradbury, Evans, 1870 (for private distribution).

MAVR = *Museo Archeologico di Venezia: i ritratti* (ed. G. Traversari). Rome: La Libreria dello Stato.

McCleanColl = *Catalogue of the McClean Collection of Greek Coins, Fitzwilliam Museum*, vols 2–3 (ed. S.W. Grose). Cambridge: Cambridge University Press, 1926–9.

MdI = *Mitteilungen des Deutschen Archäologischen Instituts (Römische Abteilung).*

MEFRA = *Mélanges de l'École Française de Rome.*

MEPR = *Musée de l'Ermitage, le portrait romain: album et catalogue illustré de toute la collection* (ed. A. Votschinina). Leningrad: Éditions d'Art Aurore, 1974 (Russian and French).

Mk. = *The Gospel According to Mark*, in *Novum Testamentum Graece* (26th edn, Nestle-Aland). Stuttgart: Deutsche Bibelstiftung, 1981, 88–149.

MNRR = *Museo Nazionale Romano: i ritrati* (ed. B. M. Felletti-Maj). Rome: Libreria dello Stato, 1953.

MNRS = *Museo Nazionale Romano: le sculture*, vols 1:1, 1:5 (ed. A. Giuliano). Rome: De Luca Editore, 1979, 1983.

MonAL = *Monumenti Antichi pubblicati dall'Accademia dei Lincei.*

MonPiot = *Fondation Eugène Piot. Monuments et Mémoires.*

Mt. = *The Gospel According to Matthew*, in *Novum Testamentum Graece* (26th edn, Nestle-Aland). Stuttgart: Deutsche Bibelstiftung, 1981, 1–87.

NC = *Numismatic Chronicle.*

NomChr. = *Nomismatika Chronika* (Greek).

NT = *Novum Testamentum.*

NZ = *Numismatische Zeitschrift.*

OGIS = *Orientis Graeci Inscriptiones Selectae.*

Ovid = Ovid. *Opera*, vols 1–6, in *LCL* (Eng. tr. J.H. Mozley *et al.*), 1914–31; *Ars Amat.* = *Ars Amatoria*, *Cons. ad Liv.* = *Consolatio ad Liviam*, *Fast.* = *Fasti*, *Met.* = *Metamorphoses*, *Pont.* = *Ex Ponto*, *Trist.* = *Tristia.*

P.Aberd. = *Catalogue of Greek and Latin Papyri and Ostraca in the*

Possession of the University of Aberdeen (ed. E.G. Turner). Aberdeen: Aberdeen University Press, 1939.

P.Berl.Leihg. = *Berlin Leihgabe Griechischer Papyri.* Vol. 1 (ed. T. Kalén). Uppsala: A.-B. Lundequistska Bokhandeln, 1932. Vol. 2 (ed. A. Tomsin). Uppsala: Almqvist and Wiksell, 1977.

P.Bour. = *Les Papyrus bouriant* (ed. P. Collart). Paris: E. Champion, 1926.

P.Chic. = *Chicago Literary Papyri* (ed. E.J. Goodspeed). Chicago, Ill.: Chicago University Press, 1908.

P.Col. = *Columbia Papyri V: Tax Documents from Theadelphia* (no. 1 verso – ed. J. Day and C.W. Keyes). New York: W. H. Allen, 1956.

P.Fay. = *Fayûm Towns and their Papyri* (Graeco-Roman Mem., no. 3 – ed. B.P. Grenfell *et al.*). London: Egypt Exploration Society, 1900.

P.Giss.Univ. = *Mitteilungen aus der Papyrussammlung der Giessener Universitätsbibliothek 6: Griechische Verwaltungsurkunden von Tebtynis aus dem Anfang des Dritten Jahrhunderts n. Chr.* (nos 47–53 – ed. G. Rosenberger). Giessen: A. Töpelmann, 1939.

P.Hamb. = *Griechische Papyrusurkunden der Hamburger Staats- und Universitätsbibliothek 1* (ed. P.M. Meyer). Leipzig and Berlin (repr. Milan: Cisalpino – La Goliardica), 1911.

P.Köln = *Kölner Papyri* (Pap. Colon., no. 7), vol. 6 (ed. M. Gronewald *et al.*). Opladen: Westdeutscher Verlag, 1986.

P.Lond. = *Greek Papyri in the British Museum.* Vol. 2 (nos 139–484 – ed. F.G. Kenyon). London: B.M. Publications, 1898. Vol. 3 (nos 485–1331 – ed. F.G. Kenyon and H.I. Bell). London: B.M. Publications, 1907.

P.Mich. = *Michigan Papyri 4:1, Tax Rolls from Karanis* (nos 223–5 – ed. H.C. Youtie). Ann Arbor, Mich.: University of Michigan Press, 1936.

P.Mil.Vogl. = *Papiri della Università degli Studi di Milano*, vol. 2 (nos 29–110 – ed. A. Vogliano *et al.*). Milan: Cisalpino – La Goliardica, 1961.

P.Oslo = *Papyri Osloenses*, vol. 3 (nos 65–200 – ed. S. Eitrem and L. Amundsen). Oslo: J. Dybwad, 1936.

P.Oxy. = *The Oxyrhynchus Papyri.* Vol. 2 (nos 208–400 – ed. B.P. Grenfell and A.S. Hunt). London: Egypt Exploration Society, 1899. Vol. 17 (nos 2065–156 – ed. A.S. Hunt). London: Egypt Exploration Society, 1927. Vol. 25 (nos 2426–37 – ed. E. Lobel and E.G. Turner). London: Egypt Exploration Society, 1959.

P.Phil. = *Papyrus de Philadelphie* (Publ. Soc. Fouad, no. 7 – ed. J. Scherer). Cairo: Imprimerie de l'Institut Français d'Archéologie Orientale.

P.Princ. = *Papyri in the Princeton University Collections*, vol. 1 (nos 1–14 – ed. A.C. Johnson and H.B. van Hoesen). Baltimore, Md: Johns Hopkins University Press, 1931.

P.Rainer = *Mitteilungen aus der Sammlung der Papyrus Erzherzog Rainer*, vol. 4 (ed. J. Karabacek). Vienna: A. Hölder, 1888.

P.Ros.Georg. = *Papyri Russischer und Georgischer Sammlungen: Ptolemäische und Frührömische Texte*, vol. 2 (nos 1–43 – ed. O. Krüger). Tiflis: Universitätslithographie, 1929.

P.Ryl. = *Catalogue of the Greek Papyri in the John Rylands Library, Manchester: Documents of the Ptolemaic and Roman Periods*, vol. 2 (nos 62–456 – ed. J. de M. Johnson et al.). Manchester: Manchester University Press, 1915.

P.Stras. = *Papyrus Grecs de la Bibliothèque Nationale et Universitaire de Strasbourg*. Vol. 4 (nos 169–300 – ed. J. Schwartz). Strasbourg: Bibliothèque Nationale, 1963. Vol. 6 (nos 501–600 – ed. J. Schwartz). Strasbourg: Bibliothèque Nationale, 1971–5.

P.Tebt. = *The Tebtunis Papyri*, vol. 2 (nos 265–689 – ed. B.P. Grenfell et al.). London: H. Frowde, 1907.

P.Vindob. = *Fünfunddreissig Wiener Papyri* (Stud. Amst., no. 6 – ed.
Tandem   P.J. Sijpesteijn and K.A. Worp). Zutphen: Terra, 1976.

Paus. = Pausanias. *Description of Greece*, vols 1–5, in *LCL* (Eng. tr. W.H.S. Jones et al.), 1918–35.

PBA = *Proceedings of the British Academy*.

PBSR = *Papers of the British School at Rome*.

PCPhilS = *Proceedings of the Cambridge Philological Society*.

PDAR = *Pictorial Dictionary of Ancient Rome*, vols 1–2 (ed. E. Nash). London: A. Zwemmer, 1961–2.

PECS = *The Princeton Encyclopedia of Classical Sites* (ed. R. Stillwell). Princeton, NJ: Princeton University Press, 1976.

PEQ = *Palestine Exploration Quarterly*.

PFOS = *Prosopographie des femmes de l'ordre Sénatorial (Ier–IIe siècles)* (ed. M.-Th. Raepsaet-Charlier). Louvain: Peeters, 1987.

Philo = Philo. *Opera*, vols 1–10 (plus two suppl.), in *LCL* (Engl. tr. F.H. Colson et al.), 1929–62; *Flac.* = *Against Flaccus* or *In Flaccum*, *Leg.* = *On the Embassy to Gaius* or *Legatio*.

PIR[2] = *Prosopographia Imperii Romani: Saec. I, II, III* (2nd edn, ed. E. Groag et al.). Berlin: W. de Gruyter, 1933– .

Pliny = The Elder Pliny. *Naturalis Historiae*, vols 1–11, in *LCL* (Eng. tr. H. Rackham et al.), 1938–63.

Pliny = The Younger Pliny. *Ep.* = *Epistulae. The Letters* (Penguin Classics – Eng. tr. B. Radice). Harmondsworth: Penguin Books, 1969.

215

BIBLIOGRAPHY

Plut.   = Plutarch. *Opera*, vols 1–28, in *LCL* (Eng. tr. B. Perrin
                et al.), 1914–69; *Anton.* = *Demetrius and Antony, Fab.
                Max.* = *Pericles and Fabius Maximus, Marc.* = *Pelopidas
                and Marcellus, Mor.* = *Moralia, Num.* = *Lycurgus and
                Numa, Pomp.* = *Agesilaus and Pompey.*
PopSt   = *Population Studies.*
PP   = *La Parola del Passato.*
PRCarl.   = *Les Portraits romains 1: république et dynastie Julienne*
                (ed. V.H. Poulsen). Copenhagen: Ny Carlsberg
                Glyptothèque, 1962.
QUCC   = *Quaderni Urbinati di Cultura Classica.*
RBN   = *Revue Belge de Numismatique et de Sigillographie.*
RE   = *Real-Encyclopädie der Classischen Altertumswissenschaft*
                (ed. A. Pauly *et al.*). Stuttgart: J. B. Metzler, 1893– .
REL   = *Revue des Etudes Latines.*
RendAccIt   = *Atti della Reale Accademia d'Italia Rendiconti della Classe
                di Scienze Morali e Storiche.*
RendPondAcc= *Rendiconti della Pontificia Accademia di Archeologia.*
Res Gest.   = *Res Gestae Divi Augusti*, in *LCL* (Eng. tr. F.W. Shipley),
                1924.
RFIC   = *Rivista di Filologia e di Istruzione Classica.*
RGE   = *Rome and the Greek East to the Death of Augustus* (trans.
                Doc. of Gr. and Rom., no. 4 – ed. R.K. Sherk).
                Cambridge: Cambridge University Press, 1984.
RGRS   = *Ritratti Greci e Romani della Sicilia: catalogo* (ed.
                N. Bonacasa). Palermo: Fondazione I. Mormino del
                Banco di Sicilia, 1964.
RHD   = *Revue Historique de Droit Français et Etranger.*
RivIt   = *Rivista d'Italia.*
RP   = *La Revue de Paris.*
RSA   = *Rivista Storica dell'Antichità.*
SAMSG   = *La Sculpture Antique du Musée Stéphane Gsell* (Les Conf.,
                Visites du Musée St Gsell 1956–7 – ed. M. Leglay).
                Algiers: Gouvernement Général de l'Algérie, 1957.
Sard.   = *Sardis: Greek and Latin Inscriptions*, vol. 8:1 (ed. W.H.
                Buckler and D.M. Robinson). Leiden: E.J. Brill, 1932.
SB   = *Sammelbuch Griechischer Urkunden aus Aegypten.* Vol. 1
                (nos 1–6000 – ed. F. Preisigke). Strasbourg and
                Berlin: O. Harrassowitz, 1913–15. Vol. 10 (nos
                10209–10763 – ed. H.-A. Rupprecht). Weisbaden:
                O. Harrassowitz, 1971. Vol. 12 (nos 10764–11263 –
                ed. H.-A. Rupprecht). Wiesbaden: O. Harrassowitz,
                1976–7.
SchMünz   = *Schweizer Münzblätter.*
Scrib. Largus = Scribonius Largus. *Compositiones* (ed. G. Helmreich).
                Leipzig: B.G. Teubner, 1887.
SEG   = *Supplementum Epigraphicum Graecum.*
Sel. Pap.   = *Select Papyri*, vols 1–3, in *LCL* (Eng. tr. A.S. Hunt *et
                al.*), 1932–42.

BIBLIOGRAPHY

BIBLIOGRAPHY

Sen. = Seneca. *Opera*, vols 1–10, in *LCL* (Eng. tr. J.W. Basore *et al.*), 1917–72; *Apocol.* = *Apocolocyntosis, Cons. ad Marc.* = *De Consolatione ad Marciam, De Brev. Vitae* = *De Brevitate Vitae, De Ira* = *De Ira, De Tranq.* = *De Tranquillitate, Epist. mor.* = *Epistulae morales.*

SGRMCV = *Sculture Grece e Romane del Museo Civico di Vicenza* (ed. V. Galliazzo). Treviso: Marton, 1976.

SGRML = *La Sculpture grecque et romaine au Musée du Louvre* (ed. J. Charbonneaux). Paris: Editions des Musées Nationaux, 1963.

S.H.A. = *Scriptores Historiae Augustae*, vols 1–3, in *LCL* (Eng. tr. D. Magie), 1922–32.

SMMV = *Sculture del magazzino del Museo Vaticano* (Monum. Vat. di Archeol. e d'Arte, no. 4 – ed. G. Kaschnitz-Weinberg). Vatican: Pontificia Accademia Romana di Archeologia, 1937.

SNG = *Sylloge Nummorum Graecorum.*

SNGD = *SNG Deutschland: Sammlung von Aulock.* Berlin: G. Mann, 1957– .

SNGDen = *SNG Denmark: The Royal Collection of Coins and Medals of the Danish National Museum.* Copenhagen: Munksgaard, 1943– .

Sol. = Solinus. *Collectanea Rerum Memorabilium* (ed. T. Mommsen). Berlin: Weidmann, 1895.

Stat. = Statius. *Opera*, vols 1–2, in *LCL* (Eng. tr. J. H. Mozley), 1928; *Silv.* = *Silvae, Theb.* = *Thebais.*

STh = *Studia Theologica cura ordinum Theologorum Scandinavicorum Edita.*

Strabo = Strabo. *Geography*, vols 1–8, in *LCL* (Eng. tr. H.L. Jones), 1917–32.

Suet. = Suetonius. *De Vita Caesarum*, vols 1–2, in *LCL* (Eng. tr. J.C. Rolfe), 1914; *Aug.* = *Augustus, Cal.* = *C. Caligula, Cl.* = *Claudius, Dom.* = *Domitianus, De Gram.* = *De Grammaticis, Nero* = *Nero, Tib.* = *Tiberius, Vesp.* = *Vespasianus, Vit.* = *Vitellius.*

Sylloge = *Tesserarum Urbis Romae et Suburbi Plumbearum Sylloge* (ed. M. Rostowzew). St Petersburg: Académie Impériale des Sciences, 1903.

Tac. = Tacitus. *Opera*, vols 1–5, in *LCL* (Eng. tr. M. Hutton *et al.*), 1914–37; *Ann.* = *Annales, Germ.* = *Germania, Hist.* = *Historiae.*

TAPA = *Transactions and Proceedings of the American Philological Association.*

TCWA = *Transactions of the Cumberland and Westmorland Antiquarian and Archaeological Society.*

TDAR = *A Topographical Dictionary of Ancient Rome* (ed. S.B. Platner and T. Ashby). London: H. Milford, 1929.

TEAS = *Transactions of the Essex Archaeological Society.*

Tripol. = 'Due Iscrizioni Imperiali Neopuniche di Leptis

Magna' (ed. G.L. della Vida), *AfrIt* 6 (1935), 15–27. (See now *Iscrizioni Puniche della Tripolitania (1927–1967)* (ed. G.L. della Vida and M.G.A. Guzzo), 1987, 53–7, no. 22, pls 10–14).

TRSE	= *Transactions of the Royal Society of Edinburgh.*
TrZ	= *Trierer Zeitschrift.*
TS	= *Tabula Siarensis.*
UBHJ	= *University of Birmingham Historical Journal.*
V. Max.	= Valerius Maximus. *Factorum et Dictorum Memorabilium* (ed. C. Kempf). Leipzig: B.G. Teubner, 1888.
Varro	= Varro. *Rerum Rusticarum*, in *LCL* (Eng. tr. H.B. Ash), 1934.
Veget.	= Vegetius Renatus. *Epitoma Rei Militaris* (2nd edn, C. Lang). Leipzig: B.G. Teubner, 1885.
Vell.	= Velleius Paterculus. *Historiae Romanae*, in *LCL* (ed. F.W. Shipley), 1924.
Virg.	= Virgil. *Aeneid*, vols 1–2, in *LCL* (Eng. tr. H.R. Fairclough), 1916–18.
W.Chr.	= *Grundzüge und Chrestomathie der Papyruskunde*, vols 1–2 (ed. L. Mitteis and U. Wilcken). Leipzig and Berlin (repr. Hildesheim: G. Olms), 1912.
YCS	= *Yale Classical Studies.*
ZFN	= *Zeitschrift für Numismatik.*
ZPE	= *Zeitschrift für Papyrologie und Epigraphik.*

(B) SECONDARY SOURCES

Akveld, W.F., 1961. *Germanicus*. Groningen: J.B. Wolters.

Aland, K. and Aland, B., 1987. *The Text of the New Testament* (Eng. tr. E. F. Rhodes). Leiden: E.J. Brill.

Andreae, B., 1983. 'Le Sculture', in *Baia: Il Ninfeo Imperiale Sommerso di Punta Epitaffio* (ed. G. Tocco-Sciarelli). Naples: Banca Sannitica, 46–66.

Angeli-Bertinelli, M.G., 1987. 'Germanico nella documentazione epigrafica', in *Germanico: la persona, la personalità, il personaggio* (ed. G.Bonamente and M.P. Segoloni). Rome: G. Bretschneider, 25–51.

Anti, C., 1928. 'Un nuovo ritratto di Agrippina Maggiore', *AfrIt* 2, 3–16.

Arnaud-Lindet, M.-P., 1980. 'Crimen Seiani. Sur quelques vers de Juvénal', *RHD* 58, 411–22.

Ashby, T., 1910. 'The Classical Topography of the Roman Campagna', *PBSR* 5, 213–425.

——, 1915. 'Roman Malta', *JRS* 5, 23–79.

——, 1935. *The Aqueducts of Ancient Rome*. Oxford: Clarendon Press.

Aune, D.E., 1980. 'Magic in Early Christianity', in *ANRW* 2.23:2, 1507–57.

Aurigemma, S., 1940. 'Sculture del Foro Vecchio di Leptis Magna raffiguranti la Dea Roma e Principi della Casa dei Giulio-Claudi', *AfrIt* 8, 1–94.

Avigad, N., 1983. *Discovering Jerusalem*. Nashville, Tenn.: T. Nelson.

Babcock, C.L., 1965. 'The Early Career of Fulvia', *AJP* 86, 1–32.

Badian, E., 1980/1. 'Notes on the "Laudatio" of Agrippa', *CJ* 76, 97–109.

Bailie, J.K., 1846. *Fasciculus Inscriptionum, Graecarum Potissimum*, vol. 2. Dublin: Hodges and Smith.

Baldwin, B., 1981. 'The Authorship of the (Aratus) Ascribed to Germanicus', *QUCC* (n.s.) 7, 163–72.

Balsdon, J.P.V.D., 1934. *The Emperor Gaius*. Oxford: Oxford University Press.

——, 1936. 'Gaius and the Grand Cameo of Paris', *JRS* 26, 152–60.

——, 1962. *Roman Women their History and Habits*. London: The Bodley Head.

——, 1969. *Life and Leisure in Ancient Rome*. London: The Bodley Head.

Beard, M., 1980. 'The Sexual Status of Vestal Virgins', *JRS* 70, 12–27.

Belfort, A. de, 1889. 'Essai de classification des tessères romaines en bronze', *AnnNum* 13, 69–92.

Bellinger, A.R., 1961. *Troy: The Coins* (Suppl. Monogr., no. 2). Princeton, NJ: Princeton University Press.

Bengtson, H., 1977. *Marcus Antonius: Triumvir und Herrscher des Orients*. Munich: C. H. Beck'sche.

Benoit, M.F., 1962a. 'Les fouilles de Cimiez', *CRAI*, 207–19.

——, 1962b. 'Circonscription d'Aix-en-Provence (Région Sud)', *Gallia* 20, 687–716.

——, 1966. 'La Statue d'Antonia nièce d'Auguste et le culte de la "domus divina" au IIIe siècle à Cimiez', in *Mélanges André Piganiol*, vol. 1 (ed. R. Chevallier). Paris: SEVPEN, 369–81.

——, 1977. *Fouilles de Cemenelum I: Cimiez la ville antique (monuments, histoire)*. Paris: Editions E. de Boccard.

Bernoulli, J.J., 1886. *Römische Ikonographie*, vol. 2:1. Berlin and Stuttgart: W. Spemann.

Bianchi-Bandinelli, R., Vergana-Caffarelli, E. and Caputo, G., 1966. *The Buried City: Excavations at Leptis Magna* (Eng. tr. D. Ridgway). London: Weidenfeld and Nicolson.

Bicknell, P.J., 1963. 'Agrippina's Villa at Bauli', *CR* 13: 261–2. (See also *CR* 14 (1964), 360.)

Bilde, P., 1978. 'The Roman Emperor Gaius's Attempt to Erect his Statue in the Temple of Jerusalem', *STh* 32, 67–93.

Bird, H.W., 1969. 'L. Aelius Seianus and his Political Significance', *Latomus* 28, 61–98.

Boak, A.E.R., 1935. *Soknopaiou Nesos: The University of Michigan Excavations at Dimê in 1931–32*. Ann Arbor, Mich.: University of Michigan Press.

Bodnar, E.W., 1960. *Cyriacus of Ancona and Athens* (Latomus no. 43). Brussels: Berchem.

Bonanno, A., 1976. *Portraits and Other Heads on Roman Historical Relief up to the Age of Septimius Severus* (B.A.R., suppl. no. 6). Oxford: British Archaeological Reports.

Bonniec, H. Le, 1958. *La Culte de Cérès à Rome: des origines à la fin de la République*. Paris: Librairie C. Klincksieck.

Bowman, A.K., 1976. 'Papyri and Roman Imperial History, 1960–1975', *JRS* 66, 153–73.

Braun, E., 1839. '(b.) Adriano ed Antonino Pio sopra tensa trionfale', *AdI*, 11, 238–51.

——, 1852. 'I. Scavi: b. Colombario di Vigna Codini', *BdI*, 81–3.

Braund, D.C., 1984. *Rome and the Friendly King: The Character of the Client Kingship*. London and Canberra: Croom Helm.

——, 1985. *Augustus to Nero: A Sourcebook on Roman History 31 BC–AD 68*. London and Sydney: Croom Helm.

Bremen, R. van, 1983. 'Women and Wealth', in *Images of Women in Antiquity* (ed. A. Cameron and A. Kuhrt). London and Canberra: Croom Helm, 223–42.

Broughton, T.R.S., 1934. 'Roman Landholding in Asia Minor', *TAPA* 65, 207–39.

Bruce, F.F., 1988. 'The Enigma of Paul: Why Did the Early Church's Great Liberator Get a Reputation as an Authoritarian?', *BR* 4:4, 32–3.

Bruns, G., 1946. *Antike Terrakotten*. Berlin: G. Mann.

Burn, R., 1871. *Rome and the Campagna: An Historical and Topographical Description of the Site, Buildings, and Neighbourhood of Ancient Rome*. Cambridge: Deighton, Bell.

Burnett, A., 1987. 'The Coinage of Agrippa I of Judaea and a New Coin of Herod of Chalcis', in *Mélanges Pierre Bastien* (ed. H. Huvelin, M. Christol and G. Gautier). Wetteren, Belgium: NR, 25–38.

Cantineau, J., 1931. 'Textes Palmyréniens provenant de la fouille du temple de Bèl', *Syria* 12, 116–41.

Carettoni, G., 1983a. 'La decorazione pittorica della casa di Augusto sul Palatino', *MdI* 90, 373–419.

——, 1983b. *Das Haus des Augustus auf dem Palatin*. Mainz-on-Rhine: Philipp von Zabern.

Carettoni, G., Colini, A.M., Cozza, L. and Gatti, G., 1960. *La pianta marmorea di Roma antica, forma urbis Romae*.Rome: SPQR.

Caro, S. de and Greco, A., 1981. *Campania* (Guide Archeol. Laterza, no. 10). Bari: G. Laterza.

Cartledge, P., 1981. 'Spartan Wives: Liberation or Licence?', *CQ* 31, 84–105.

Casson, L., 1951. 'Speed Under Sail of Ancient Ships', *TAPA* 82, 136–48.

——, 1971. *Ships and Seamanship in the Ancient World*. Princeton, NJ: Princeton University Press.

Castagnoli, F., 1942. 'Due Archi Trionfali della Via Flaminia presso Piazza Sciarra', *BullComm* 70, 57–82.

——, 1968. *Topografia e urbanistica di Roma antica*. Bologna: Istituto di Studi Romani.

——, 1984. 'L'Arco di Germanico in "Circo Flaminio" ', *ArchClass* 36, 329–32.

Chaisemartin, N. de, 1987. 'Recherches sur la frise de l'Agora de Tibère', in *Aphrodisias de Carie* (ed. J. de la Genière and K. Erim). Paris: Editions Recherche sur les Civilisations, 135–54.

Charlesworth, M.P., 1934. 'Germanicus and Drusus', *CAH* 10, 618–26.

Cichorius, C., 1922. *Römische Studien*. Leipzig and Berlin: B.G. Teubner.

Clark, G., 1981. 'Roman Women', *G & R* 28, 193–212.

Clavel, M., 1970. *Béziers et son territoire dans l'antiquité*. Paris: Société d'Edition Les Belles Lettres.

Clayton, P.A., 1988. 'The Pharos at Alexandria', in *The Seven Wonders of the Ancient World* (ed. P.A. Clayton and M.J. Price). London and New York: Routledge, 138–57.

Coarelli, F., 1988. *Il Foro Boario*. Rome: Edizioni Quasar.

Cohen, H., 1930. *Description historique des monnaies frappées sous l'Empire romain communement appelées médailles impériales*, vols 1–8. Leipzig: G. Fock.

Connolly, P., 1975. *The Roman Army*. London: Macdonald.

Conzalez, J., 1984. 'Tabula Siarensis, Fortunales et Municipia Civium Romanorum', *ZPE* 55, 55–100.

Conzalez, J. and Fernandez, F., 1981. 'Tabula Siarensis', *Iura* 32 [1985], 1–36.

Cook, B.F., 1976. *Greek and Roman Art in the British Museum*. London: B.M. Publications.

Corbett, P.E. and Strong, D.E., 1961. 'Three Roman Silver Cups', *BMQ* 23, 68–86.

Coventry, A., 1853. 'Notice of an Antique Marble Bust', *TRSE* 20:3, 417–23 (read on 16 February 1852).

Cramer, F.H., 1951. 'Expulsion of Astrologers from Ancient Rome', *C & M* 12, 9–50.

——, 1954. *Astrology in Roman Law and Politics*. Philadelphia, Pa: The American Philosophical Society.

Crawford, D.J., 1976. 'Imperial Estates', in *Studies in Roman Property* (ed. M.I. Finley). Cambridge: Cambridge University Press, 35–70.

Crawford, M., 1975. *Roman Republican Coinage*, vols 1–2. Cambridge: Cambridge University Press.

——, 1983. 'Numismatics', in *Sources for Ancient History* (ed. M. Crawford). Cambridge: Cambridge University Press, 185–233.

Crook, J.A., 1986. 'Women in Roman Succession', in *The Family in Ancient Rome: New Perspectives* (ed. B. Rawson). London and Sydney: Croom Helm, 58–82.

Curtius, L., 1948. 'Ikonographische Beiträge zum Porträt der Römischen Republik und der Julisch-Claudischen Familie: XIV. Germanicus', *MdI* 1, 69–94.

D'Arms, J.H., 1970. *Romans on the Bay of Naples: A Social and Cultural Study of the Villas and their Owners from 150 BC to AD 400*. Cambridge, Mass.: Harvard University Press.

Dixon, S., 1983. 'A Family Business: Women's Role in Patronage and Politics at Rome, 80–44 BC', *C & M* 34, 91–112.

——, 1985. 'Polybius on Roman Women and Property', *AJP* 106, 145–70.

——, 1988. *The Roman Mother*. London and Sydney: Croom Helm.

Donaldson, T.L., 1859. *Architectura Numismatica* (reprint edn 1965).

Chicago, Ill.: Argonaut Inc.

Duff, A.M., 1928. *Freedmen in the Early Roman Empire*. Oxford: Oxford University Press.

Eitrem, S. and Holst, H., 1928. 'Three Greek Papyri in Oslo', *Klio* 22, 222–8.

Eliot, C.W.J., 1955. 'New Evidence for the Speed of the Roman Imperial Post', *Phoenix* 9, 76–80.

Erhart, K.P., 1978. 'A Portrait of Antonia Minor in the Fogg Art Museum and its Iconographic Tradition', *AJA* 82, 192–212.

Erim, K.T., 1986. *Aphrodisias: City of Venus Aphrodite*. London: Muller, Blond and White.

Espérandieu, E., 1910. *Recueil général des bas-reliefs, statues et bustes de la Gaule romaine*, vol. 3. Paris: Imprimerie Nationale.

Esser, A., 1958. *Cäsar und die Julisch-Claudischen Kaiser im biologisch-ärtzlichen Blickfeld*. Leiden: E. J. Brill.

Farnell, L.R., 1896. *The Cults of the Greek States*, vol. 1. Oxford: Clarendon Press.

——, 1909. *The Cults of the Greek States*, vol. 5. Oxford: Clarendon Press.

Feldman, L.H., 1962. 'The Sources of Josephus' "Antiquities" ', *Latomus* 21, 320–33.

Felletti-Maj, B.M., 1958. 'Antonia Minore (Antonia Augusta)', in *EAA* 1, 441.

Ferguson, J., 1970. *The Religions of the Roman Empire*. London: Thames and Hudson.

Ferrero, G., 1925. *The Women of the Caesars* (Eng. tr. C. Gauss). New York: Putnam's Sons.

Finegan, J., 1975. *Encountering New Testament Manuscripts*. London: SPCK.

Finley, M.I., 1968. 'The Silent Women of Rome', in *Aspects of Antiquity: Discoveries and Controversies* (ed. M.I. Finley). London: Chatto and Windus, 129–42.

Fishwick, D., 1987. *The Imperial Cult in the Latin West*, vol. 1:1 (Etud. prélim. aux relig. orient. dans l'Empire Rom.). Leiden: E.J. Brill.

Fittschen, K., 1975. 'Zur Panzerstatue in Cherchel', *JdI* 90,175–210.

——, 1987. 'I ritratti di Germanico', in *Germanico: la persona, la personalità, il personaggio* (ed. G. Bonamente and M.P. Segoloni). Rome: G. Bretschneider, 205–18.

Forrer, L., 1969. *Portraits of Royal Ladies on Greek Coins*. Chicago, Ill.: Argonaut Inc. (first published in *NC* 1938).

Fowler, W.W., 1920. *Roman Essays and Interpretations*. Oxford: Oxford University Press.

Fraccaro, P., 1940. 'C. Herennius Capito di Teate Procurator di Livia, di Tiberio e di Gaio', *Athenaeum* 18, 136–44.

Franke, P.R., Leschhorn, W. and Stylow, A.U., 1981. *SNGD Sammlung v. Aulock: Index*. Berlin: G. Mann.

Frederiksen, M., 1984. *Campania*. Rome: The British School.

Friedländer, L., 1968. *Roman Life and Manners under the Early Empire*, vols 1–4 (7th edn, Eng. tr. L. A. Magnus). London: Routledge and Kegan Paul.

Friggeri, R., 1977/8. 'La Domus di Antonia Caenis e il Balineum Caenidianum', *RendPontAcc* 50, 145–54.

Frost, H., 1983. 'The Nymphaeum at Baia', *IJNA* 12, 81–3.

Furnee-van Zwet, L., 1956. 'Fashions in Women's Hair-Dress in the First Century of the Roman Empire', *BABesch* 31, 1–19.

Furtwängler, A., 1895. *Masterpieces of Greek Sculpture* (ed. E. Sellers). London: W. Heinemann.

——, 1900. *Die antiken Gemmen Geschichte der Steinschneidekunst im klassischen Altertum*, vols 1–2. Leipzig and Berlin: Giesecke and Devrient.

Gaebler, H., 1935. *Die Antiken Münzen von Makedonia und Paionia* (Die Antiken Münzen Nord-Griechenlands, vol. 3:2). Berlin: W. de Gruyter.

Gagé, J., 1968. *'Basiléia' : les Césars, les rois d'Orient et les 'mages'*. Paris: Société d'Edition Les Belles Lettres.

Gaggero, R., 1927. 'La madre di Germanico', *RivIt* 2, 145–68.

Gain, D.B., 1976. *The Aratus Ascribed to Germanicus Caesar*. London: The Athlone Press.

Galli, E. 1919. *Fiesole: Gli Scavi il Museo Civico*. Milan: Alfieri and Lacroix.

Gallotta, B., 1987. *Germanico*. Rome: 'L'Erma' di Bretschneider.

Garcia y Bellido, A., 1966. 'Los Retratos de Livia, Drusus Minor y Germanicus de Medina Sidonia', in *Mélanges André Piganiol*, vol. 1 (ed. R. Chevallier). Paris: SEVPEN, 481–94.

Gardner, J.F., 1986. *Women in Roman Law and Society*. London and Sydney: Croom Helm.

Gazda, E.K. (ed.), 1983. *Karanis an Egyptian Town in Roman Times: Discoveries of the University of Michigan Expedition to Egypt 1924–1935*. Ann Arbor, Mich.: Kelsey Museum.

Gerkan, A. von, 1941. 'Die Neronische Scaenae Frons des Dionysostheaters in Athen', *JdI* 56, 163–77.

Gigante, M., 1984. 'Thanatos non Eros a Baiae?', *PP* 39, 230–40.

Gow, A.S.F. and Page, D.L., 1968. *The Greek Anthology: The Garland of Philip and some Contemporary Epigrams*, vol. 1. Cambridge: Cambridge University Press.

Graillot, H., 1912. *Le Culte de Cybèle*. Paris: Fontemoing.

Graindor, P., 1927. *Athènes sous Auguste*. Cairo: Imprimerie Misr.

Grant, M., 1950a. *Aspects of the Principate of Tiberius: Historical Comments on the Colonial Coinage issued outside Spain* (Num. Notes and Monogr., no. 116). New York: The American Numismatic Society.

——, 1950b. *Roman Anniversary Issues: An Exploratory Study of the Numismatic and Medallic Commemoration of Anniversary Years 49 BC–AD 375*. Cambridge: Cambridge University Press.

——, 1956. 'The Pattern of Official Coinage in the Early Principate', in *Essays in Roman Coinage Presented to Harold Mattingly* (ed. R.A.G. Carson and C.H.V. Sutherland). Oxford: Oxford University Press, 96–112.

——, 1968. *Roman History from Coins*. Cambridge: Cambridge University Press.

——, 1972. *Cleopatra*. London: Weidenfeld and Nicolson.

Graves, R., 1955. *The Greek Myths*, vol. 2. Harmondsworth: Penguin.

Grether, G., 1946. 'Livia and the Roman Imperial Cult', *AJP* 67, 222–52.

Griffin, M.T., 1982. 'The Lyons Tablet and Tacitean Hindsight', *CQ* 32, 404–18.

Gross, W.H., 1962. *Iulia Augusta: Untersuchungen zur Grundlegung einer Livia-Ikonographie* (Abh. Göttingen Akad., Phil.-Hist. Klasse, vol. 3:52). Göttingen: Vandenhoeck and Ruprecht.

Günther, R.T., 1913. *Pausilypon, the Imperial Villa near Naples*. Oxford: Oxford University Press (by Horace Hart).

Hafner, G., 1955. 'Zum Augustus Relief in Ravenna', *MdI* 62, 160–73

Hamburger, A., 1986. 'Surface-Finds from Caesarea Maritima – Tesserae', in *Excavations at Caesarea Maritima 1975, 1976, 1979 – Final Report* (Qedem, no. 21 – ed. L.I. Levine and E. Netzer). Jerusalem: The Hebrew University, 187–204.

Hanell, K., 1935/6. 'Zur Diskussion über die Ara Pacis', *BLund* 5, 9–22.

Hanfmann, G.M.A., 1983. *Sardis from Prehistoric to Roman Times: Results of the Archaeological Exploration of Sardis 1958–1975*. Cambridge, Mass.: Harvard University Press.

Hanson, C. and Johnson, F.P., 1946. 'On Certain Portrait Inscriptions', *AJA* 50, 389–400.

Haslam, M.W., 1979/80. 'Augustus' Funeral Oration for Agrippa', *CJ* 75, 193–9.

Hauben, H., 1979. 'A Jewish Shipowner in the Third-Century Ptolemaic Egypt', *AncSoc* 10, 167–70.

Haynes, D.E.L., 1959. *The Antiquities of Tripolitania*. London: The Trinity Press.

Heintze, H. von, 1964. 'Review of Gross' Iulia Augusta', *AJA* 68, 318–20.

Henig, M., 1974. *A Corpus of Roman Engraved Gemstones from the British Sites* (B.A.R., Suppl. 8i and 8ii). Oxford: British Archaeological Reports.

——, 1983. 'The Luxury Arts: Decorative Metalwork, Engraved Gems and Jewellery', in *A Handbook of Roman Art: A Survey of the Visual Arts of the Roman World* (ed. M. Henig). Oxford: Phaidon, 139–65.

——, 1988. 'Ancient Engraved Gems', in *Joseph Mayer of Liverpool, 1803–1886* (ed. M. Gibson and S.M. Wright). London: Society of Antiquaries, 94–105.

Hennig, D., 1972. 'Zur Ägyptenreise des Germanicus', *Chiron* 2, 349–65.

——, 1975. *L. Aelius Seianus: Untersuchungen zur Regierung des Tiberius* (Vestigia, no. 21). Munich: C.H. Beck'sche.

Henzen, G., 1847. 'I. Scavi e Viaggi: a. Scavi di Roma', *BdI*, 49–51.

——, 1868. *Scavi nel Bosco Sacro dei Fratelli Arvali*. Rome: Tipografia Tiberina.

——, 1874. *Acta Fratrum Arvalium Quae Supersunt*. Berlin: G. Reimer.

Hill, G.F., 1909. *Historical Roman Coins: from the Earliest Times to the Reign of Augustus*. London: Constable.

Hinks, R.P., 1976. *Greek and Roman Portrait Sculpture*. London: B.M.

Publications.

Hirschfeld, O., 1902. 'Der Grundbesitz der römischen Kaiser in den ersten drei Jahrhunderten', *Klio* 2, 45–72; 284–315.

Hobson, D., 1983. 'Women as Property Owners in Roman Egypt', *TAPA* 113, 311–21.

Hoffman-Lewis, M.W., 1955. *The Official Priests of Rome under the Julio-Claudians*. Rome: The American Academy in Rome.

Holloway, R.R., 1984. 'Who's Who on the Ara Pacis?', in *Alessandria e il mondo Ellenistico-Romano: studi in onore di Achille Adriani*, vol. 3 (Stud. e Mat., Univ. Palermo, no. 6). Rome: 'L'Erma' di Bretschneider, 625–8.

Hopkins, K., 1964/5. 'The Age of Roman Girls at Marriage', *PopSt* 18, 309–27.

——, 1966. 'On the Probable Age Structure of the Roman Population', *PopSt* 20, 245–64.

——, 1983. *Death and Renewal* (Sociol. Stud. in Rom. Hist., vol. 2). Cambridge: Cambridge University Press.

Humphrey, J.H., 1979. 'The Three Daughters of Agrippina Maior', *AJAH* 4, 125–43.

——, 1986. *Roman Circuses*. London: B.T. Batsford.

Husselman, E.M., 1979. *Karanis: Topography and Architecture* (Kelsey Museum of Archaeol., Stud. no. 5). Ann Arbor, Mich.: University of Michigan Press.

Huzar, E.G., 1986. *Mark Antony: A Biography*. London and Sydney: Croom Helm.

Ian, L., 1970. *C. Plini Secundi Naturalis Historiae Libri XXXVII: Indices* (repr. edn C. Mayhoff). Stuttgart: B.G. Teubner.

Ingholt, H., 1963. 'A Colossal Head from Memphis, Severan or Augustan?', *JARCE* 2, 125–45.

Ingholt, H., Seyrig, H. and Starcky, J., 1955. *Recueil des tessères de Palmyre*. Paris: Institut Français d'Archéologie de Beyrouth.

Jacopi, G., 1939. 'Gli scavi della missione archeologica italiana ad Afrodisiade nel 1937', *MonAL* 38, cols 73–232.

James, P.J., Thorpe, I.J., Kokkinos, N. and Frankish, J.A., 1987. *Bronze to Iron Age Chronology in the Old World: Time for a Reassessment?* (Stud. in Anc. Chronol., vol. 1). London: Institute of Archaeology.

James, P.J., Thorpe, I.J., Kokkinos, N., Morkot, R. and Frankish J., 1991. *Centuries of Darkness: A Challenge to the Conventional Chronology of Old World Archaeology*. London: Jonathan Cape.

Jamot, P., 1902. 'Fouilles de Thespies: le monument des muses dans le bois de l'Helicon et le poète Honestus', *BCH* 26, 127–60.

Javier-Lomas, F., 1978. 'Tabula Hebana', *Habis* 9, 323–54.

Jex-Blake, E. and Sellers, E., 1896. *The Elder Pliny's Chapters on the History of Art*. London: Macmillan.

Jones, A.H.M., 1971. *The Cities of the Eastern Roman Provinces* (2nd edn). Oxford: Oxford University Press.

Jones, B.W. and Milns, R.D., 1984. *The Use of Documentary Evidence in the Study of Roman Imperial History*. Sydney: Sydney University Press.

Jucker, H., 1961. *Das Bildnis im Blätterkelch* (Bibl. Helv. Rom., no. 3).

Lausanne and Freiburg: Urs Graf.

——, 1976. 'Der Grosse Pariser Kameo: Eine Huldigung an Agrippina, Claudius und Nero', *JdI* 91, 211–50.

Katzoff, R., 1973. 'Where was Agrippina Murdered?', *Historia* 22, 72–8.

King, C.W., 1872. *Antique Gems and Rings*, vol. 1. London: Bell and Daldy.

——, 1873. *Early Christian Numismatics and Other Antiquarian Tracts*. London: Bell and Daldy.

Kiss, Z., 1975. *L'Ikonographie des princes Julio-Claudiens au temps d'Auguste et de Tibère* (Travaux du Centre d'Archéol. Médit. de l'Acad. Polon. des Sciences, vol. 17). Warsaw: PWN – Editions Scientifiques de Pologne.

Kleiner, D.E.E., 1978. 'The Great Friezes of the Ara Pacis Augustae: Greek Sources, Roman Derivatives, and Augustan Social Policy', *MEFRA* 90, 753–85.

Kleiner, D.E.E. and Kleiner, F.S., 1974. 'Review of Polaschek's "Studien zur Ikonographie der Antonia Minor" and "Porträttypen einer Claudischen Kaiserin" ', *AJA* 78, 443–4.

Koenen, L., 1970. 'Die "Laudatio Funebris" des Augustus für Agrippa auf einem neun Papyrus', *ZPE* 5, 217–83.

Kokkinos, N., 1977/8. 'Jesus in History', *Ainigmata* 21.58–60, 64; 22.61–2; 24.57–62; 28.50–3; 32. 55–8, 64; 33.48–9, 63; 37.58–61 (in Greek).

——, 1978a. 'The Inauthenticity of the Essene Epistle sent from Jerusalem to Alexandria', *Ainigmata* 38/39.19–21, 26 (in Greek).

——, 1978b. 'The Dead Sea Scrolls Recently', *Ainigmata* 40.17–33 (in Greek).

——, 1980. *The Enigma of Jesus the Galilean*. Athens: Chrysê Tomê (in Greek).

——, 1981, 'The Inauthenticity of the Shroud', *Ainigmata* 70.32–7 (in Greek).

——, 1981/2. 'The Nag Hammadi Codices and the Gnostic Secret', *Ainigmata* 71.40–4; 72/73.46–50; 74/76.85–9 (in Greek).

——, 1983. 'Crucifixion in AD 36: The Keystone for Dating the Birth of Jesus' (paper read at the Nativity Conf., Mississippi State University) – published in *Chronos, Kairos, Christos: Nativity and Chronological Studies Presented to Jack Finegan* (ed. J. Vardaman and E.M. Yamauchi). Winona Lake: Eisenbrauns, 1989, 133–63.

——, 1985. 'A Coin of Herod the Great Commemorating the City of Sebaste', *LA* 35, 303–6.

——, 1986a. 'A Retouched New Date on a Coin of Valerius Gratus', *LA* 36, 241–6.

——, 1986b. 'Which Salome Did Aristobulus Marry?', *PEQ* 118, 33–50.

——, 1987. 'Re-assembling the Inscription of Glaphyra from Athens', *ZPE* 68, 288–90.

——, 1990. 'A Fresh Look at the "Gentilicium" of Felix Procurator of Judaea', *Latomus* 49, 126–41.

——, forthcoming 1. 'The Herods in Greece'.

226

——, forthcoming 2. 'The Herodian Dynasty: Origins, Role in Society and Eclipse'. D.Phil. thesis, Oxford University.

——, forthcoming 3. 'Annius Rufus, Valerius Gratus and the Herodian Kore in a Neglected Inscription from Sebaste?'.

——, forthcoming 4. 'The Daughter of Claudius Lysias (who Arrested Paul in Jerusalem) in a Neglected Greek Text?'.

Köstermann, E., 1958. 'Die Mission des Germanicus in Orient', *Historia* 7, 331–75.

Koumanoudes, S.A., 1885. 'Inscriptions from the Excavations of the Athenian Agora', *ArchEph*, 204–19 (in Greek).

Kraeling, C.H., 1962. *Ptolemais: City of the Libyan Pentapolis*. Chicago, Ill.: Chicago University Press.

Kubitschek, W., 1921. 'Neue Münzen', *NZ* 14, 151–2.

Lachenal, L. de, 1983. 'Juno Ludovisi: Testa di Antonia Minor? (inv. no. 8631)', in *MNRS* 1:5, 133–7.

Laguerre, C.-G., 1975. *Les Inscriptions antiques de Nice-Cimiez (Cemenelum, Ager Cemenelensis)*. Paris: Editions E. de Boccard.

Lanciani, R., 1888. *Ancient Rome in the Light of Recent Discoveries*. London: Macmillan.

——, 1897. *The Ruins and Excavations of Ancient Rome: A Companion Book for Students and Travelers*. Boston and New York: Houghton and Mifflin.

Lebek, W.D., 1986. 'Schwierige Stellen der Tabula Siarensis', *ZPE* 66, 31–48.

——, 1987. 'Die drei Ehrenbögen für Germanicus: Tab. Siar. frg.I 9–34; *CIL* VI 31199a 2–17', *ZPE* 67, 129–48.

Lefkowitz, M.R., 1983. 'Influential Women', in *Images of Women in Antiquity* (ed. A. Cameron and A. Kuhrt). London and Canberra: Croom Helm, 49–64.

Letta, C. and d'Amato, S., 1975. *Epigrafia della Regione dei Marsi*. Milan: Cisalpino-Goliardica.

Levick, B., 1966. 'Drusus Caesar and the Adoptions of AD 4', *Latomus* 25, 227–44.

——, 1976. *Tiberius the Politician*. London: Thames and Hudson.

Lewis, N., 1974. 'Notationes Legentis', *BASP* 11, 44–59 (for Livia see n. 6, 52–4).

——, 1983. *Life in Egypt under Roman Rule*. Oxford: Clarendon Press.

Lewis, N. and Reinhold, M., 1955. *Roman Civilization Sourcebook II: The Empire*. New York: Columbia University Press.

Lindsay, J., 1963. *Daily Life in Roman Egypt*. London: F. Muller.

——, 1971. *Cleopatra*. London: Constable.

Lugli, G., 1970. *Itinerario di Roma Antica*. Milan: Periodici Scientifici.

MacKendrick, P., 1980. *The North African Stones Speak*. London: Croom Helm.

MacLennan, H., 1935. *Oxyrhynchus: An Economic and Social Study*. Princeton, NJ: Princeton University Press.

MacMullen, R., 1976. 'Two Notes on Imperial Properties', *Athenaeum* 54, 19–36.

Macurdy, G.H., 1932. *Hellenistic Queens: A Study of Woman-Power in*

Macedonia, Seleucid Syria, and Ptolemaic Egypt. Baltimore, Md and London: Johns Hopkins University Press and H. Milford.

Magie, D., 1950. *Roman Rule in Asia Minor to the End of the Third Century after Christ*, vols. 1–2. Princeton, NJ: Princeton University Press.

Maiuri, A., 1934. *I Campi Flegréi* (Itin. dei Musei e Monum. d'Italia, no. 32 – 4th edn 1963). Rome: La Libreria dello Stato.

——, 1941. 'Note di topografia campana: I. Bauli', *RendAccIt* (7th ser.) 2, 249–60.

Mann, E.M., 1926. 'Some Private Houses in Ancient Rome', *CW* 19.16: 127–32.

Marsh, F.B., 1931. *The Reign of Tiberius*. London: H. Milford.

Marwood, M., 1988. *The Roman Cult of Salus*. Oxford: B.A.R.(Inter. ser. 465).

Matthews, J.F., 1984. 'The Tax of Palmyra: Evidence for Economic History in a City of the Roman East', *JRS* 74, 157–80.

Mattingly, H., 1928. *Roman Coins: From the Earliest Times to the Fall of the Western Empire* (2nd edn 1960). London: Eyre Methuen.

Maxfield, V.A., 1981. *The Military Decorations of the Roman Army*. London: B.T. Batsford.

Mazar, B, 1971. *The Excavations in the Old City of Jerusalem near the Temple Mount* (Second Preliminary Report, 1969–70 Seasons). Jerusalem: The Israel Exploration Society.

McClees, H., 1920. *A Study of Women in Attic Inscriptions*. New York: Metropolitan Museum.

McDermott, M., 1948. 'C.I.L., IX, 3660–3663', in *Mélanges de philologie, de littérature et d'histoire anciennes offerts à J. Marouzeau*. Paris: Les Belles Lettres, 421–6.

Meise, E., 1969. *Untersuchungen zur Geschichte der Julisch-Claudischen Dynastie*. Munich: C. H. Beck'sche.

Meshorer, Y., 1982. *Ancient Jewish Coinage 2: Herod the Great through Bar Cochba*. New York: Amphora Books.

——, 1985. *City-Coins of Eretz-Israel and the Decapolis in the Roman Period*. Jerusalem: The Israel Museum.

Metzger, B.M., 1968. *The Text of the New Testament: Its Transmission, Corruption, and Restoration* (2nd edn). Oxford: Clarendon Press.

Michaelis, A., 1882. *Ancient Marbles in Great Britain*. Cambridge: Cambridge University Press.

Middleton, J.H., 1892. *The Remains of Ancient Rome*, vol. 1. London and Edinburgh: Adam and Charles Black.

Millar, F., 1977. *The Emperor in the Roman World (31 BC–AD 337)*. London: Duckworth.

——, 1983. 'Epigraphy', in *Sources for Ancient History* (ed. M. Crawford). Cambridge: Cambridge University Press, 80–136.

——, 1988. 'Imperial Ideology in the Tabula Siarensis', in *Estudios Sobre la Tabula Siarensis* (ed. J. Gonzàlez and J. Arce). Madrid: CSIC, 11–19.

Milne, J.G., 1916. 'Greek and Roman Tourists in Egypt', *JEA* 3, 76–80.

Mionnet, T.E., 1808. *Description de médailles antiques grecques et romaines*,

vol. 3. Paris: De l'Imprimerie de Testu, Imprimeur de sa Majesté.
——, 1822. *Description de médailles antiques grecques et romaines*, vol. 1. Paris: M.P. Guyot.

Mitchiner, M., 1984. 'Rome: Imperial Portrait Tesserae from the City of Rome and Imperial Tax Tokens from the Province of Egypt', *NC* 144, 95–114.

Moehring, H.R., 1959. 'The Persecution of the Jews and the Adherents of the Isis Cult at Rome AD 19', *NT* 3, 293–304.

Momigliano, A., 1934. *Claudius the Emperor and his Achievement*. Oxford: Oxford University Press.

Mommsen, T., 1878. 'Die Familie des Germanicus', *Hermes* 13, 245–65.

Moretti, L., 1980. 'Epigraphica', *RFIC* 108, 442–54.

Moscovich, M.J., 1983. 'Hostage Princes and Roman Imperialism in the Second Century BC', *CV* 27, 297–309.

Mullens, H.G., 1942. 'The Women of the Caesars', *G & R* 2, 59–67.

Murray, W.M. and Petsas, P.M., 1988. 'The Spoils of Actium', *Archaeology* 41, 28–35.

Nicols, J., 1975. 'Antonia and Sejanus', *Historia* 24, 48–58.

Nony, D., 1986. *Caligula*. Paris: Fayard.

Olinder, B., 1974. *Porticus Octavia in Circo Flaminio. Topographical Studies in the Campus Region of Rome* (Acta Inst. Rom. Regni Suec., no. 11). Stockholm: P. Åström.

Oliver, J.H., 1971. 'On the Edict of Germanicus declining Divine Acclamations', *RSA* 1, 229–30.

Oost, S.I., 1958. 'The Career of M. Antonius Pallas', *AJP* 79, 113–39.

Orelli, G.C., 1856. *Inscriptionum Latinarum Selectarum amplissima collectio*, vol. 3. Zurich: Typis Orellii, Fuesslini et Sociorum.

Pala, C., 1976. *Nomentum* (Forma Italiae, Regio I, vol. 12). Rome: De Luca Editore.

Pani, M., 1987. 'La missione di Germanico in Oriente: politica estera e politica interna' in *Germanico: la persona, la personalità, il personaggio* (ed. G. Bonamente and M.P. Segoloni). Rome: G. Bretschneider, 1–23.

Paraskevaides, P.S., 1978. *Roman Lesbos*. Athens: privately printed (in Greek).

Parassoglou, G.M., 1978. *Imperial Estates in Egypt* (Amer. Stud. in Papyr., no. 18). Amsterdam: A.M. Hakkert.

Parke, H.W., 1985. *The Oracles of Apollo in Asia Minor*. London, Sydney and Dover: Croom Helm.

Parker, E.R., 1946. 'Education of Heirs in Julio-Claudian Family', *AJP* 67, 29–50.

Pellegrini, G., 1865. *Edificio dei Fratelli Arvali*. Rome: Tipografia Tiberiana.

Pembroke, S., 1967. 'Women in Charge: The Function of Alternatives in Early Greek Tradition and the Ancient Idea of Matriarchy', *JWCI* 30, 1–35.

Perowne, S., 1974. *The Caesar's Wives: Above Suspicion?* London: Hodder and Stoughton.

Petrie, F., Gardiner, A., Petrie, H. and Murray, M.A., 1925. *Tombs of the Courtiers and Oxyrhynkhos* (B.S.A.E., no. 37). London: The British School of Archaeology in Egypt.

Picciotti-Giornetti, V., 1979. 'Busto di Giovane Donna: Antonia Minore? (Sala della Farnesina, inv. no. 620)', in *MNRS* 1:1, 338–40.

Pick, B. and Regling, K., 1910. *Die antiken Münzen von Dacien und Moesien* (*Die antiken Münzen Nord-Griechenlands*, vol. 1.2:1). Berlin: G. Reimer.

Polaschek, K., 1973. *Studien zur Ikonographie der Antonia Minor* (Stud. Archaeol., no. 15). Rome: 'L'Erma' di Bretschneider.

Pollard, J., 1977. *Birds in Greek Life and Myth*. London: Thames and Hudson.

Pomeroy, S.B., 1975. *Goddesses, Whores, Wives and Slaves: Women in Classical Antiquity*. New York: Schocken.

——, 1981. 'Women in Roman Egypt: A Preliminary Study Based on Papyri', in *Reflections of Women in Antiquity* (ed. H.P. Foley). New York, London and Paris: Gordon and Breach Science Publishers, 303–22.

Potter, D.S., 1987. 'The "Tabula Siarensis", Tiberius, the Senate, and the Eastern Boundary of the Roman Empire', *ZPE* 69, 269–76.

Pottier, E. and Hauvette-Besnault, A., 1880. 'Inscriptions de Lesbos', *BCH* 4, 417–48.

Poulsen, F., 1928. *Porträtstudien in Norditalienischen Provinzmuseen*. Copenhagen: A.F. Host.

Poulsen, V.H., 1946. 'Studies in Julio-Claudian Iconography', *ActaA* 17, 1–48.

——, 1960. *Claudische Prinzen: Studien zur Ikonographie des Ersten Römischen Kaiserhauses*. Baden-Baden: B. Grimm.

Price, S.R.F., 1984a. 'Gods and Emperors: The Greek Language of the Roman Imperial Cult', *JHS* 104, 79–95.

——, 1984b. *Rituals and Power: The Roman Imperial Cult in Asia Minor*. Cambridge: Cambridge University Press.

Purcell, N., 1986. 'Livia and the Womanhood of Rome', *PCPhilS* 212, 78–105.

Raditsa, L.F., 1980. 'Augustus' Legislation Concerning Marriage, Procreation, Love Affairs and Adultery', in *ANRW* 2.13, 278–339.

Raepsaet-Charlier, M.-T., 1982. 'Epouses et familles de magistrats dans les provinces romaines aux deux premiers siècles de l'Empire', *Historia* 31, 56–69.

Ramsay, A.M., 1925. 'The Speed of the Roman Imperial Post', *JRS* 15, 60–74.

Rapke, T.T., 1982. 'Tiberius, Piso, and Germanicus', *AClass* 25, 61–9.

Rathbone, D.W., 1986. 'The Dates of the Recognition in Egypt of the Emperors from Caracala to Diocletianus', *ZPE* 62, 101–31.

Raubitschek, A.E., 1946. 'Octavia's Deification at Athens', *TAPA* 77, 146–50.

Redfield, J., 1977/8. 'The Women of Sparta', *CJ* 73, 146–61.

Reinach, S., 1922. *Répertoire de peintures grecques et romaines*. Paris: E. Leroux.

Reinhold, M., 1972. 'Marcus Agrippa's Son-in-Law P. Quinctilius Varus', *CP* 67, 119–21.

Reynolds, J.M., 1980. 'The Origins and Beginnings of the Imperial Cult at Aphrodisias', *PCPhilS* 206, 70–84.

——, 1981. 'New Evidence for the Imperial Cult in Julio-Claudian Aphrodisias', *ZPE* 43, 317–27.

Reynolds, J.M., Beard, M. and Roueché, C., 1986. 'Roman Inscriptions 1981–5', *JRS* 76, 124–46.

Reynolds, J.M. and Ward-Perkins, J.B. (eds), 1959. *The Inscriptions of Roman Tripolitania*. Rome: The British School at Rome.

Riad, H., 1980. *Guide aux Monuments Alexandrins*. Alexandria: The Archaeological Museum.

Richmond, O.L., 1914. 'The Augustan Palatium', *JRS* 4, 193–226.

Richter, G.M.A., 1971. *Engraved Gems of the Romans*. London: Phaidon.

Rodriguez-Almeida, F., 1981. *Forma Urbis Marmorea: Aggiornamento Generale 1980*. Rome: Edizioni Quasar.

Rogers, R.S., 1931. 'The Date of the Banishment of the Astrologers', *CP* 26, 203–4.

——, 1932. 'Fulvia Paulina C. Sentii Saturnini', *AJP* 53, 252–6.

——, 1945/6. 'Tiberius' Travels, AD 26–37', *CW* 39, 42–4.

——, 1947. 'The Roman Emperors as Heirs and Legatees', *TAPA* 78, 140–58.

Rösch, G. 1978. *ΟΝΟΜΑ ΒΑΣΙΛΕΙΑΣ*: Studien zum Offiziellen Gebrauch der Kaisertitel in spätantiker und frühbyzantinischer Zeit. Vienna: Österreichischen Akademie der Wissenschaften.

Rostovtzeff, M. (also Rostowzew, as well as Rostovtsew under *CPABN*), 1922. *A Large Estate in Egypt in the Third Century BC, A Study in Economic History* (Stud. in Soc. Sciences and Hist., no. 6). Madison, Wis.: University of Wisconsin Press.

——, 1957. *The Social and Economic History of the Roman Empire* (2nd edn, rev. P.M. Fraser). Oxford: Oxford University Press.

Rostowzew, M., 1905. *Römische Bleitesserae* (Klio: Beiträge 3). Leipzig: Klio.

——, 1910. *Studien zur Geschichte des römischen Kolonates* (Archiv für Papyr. und Verwandte Gebiere, no. 1). Leipzig and Berlin: B.G. Teubner.

Rumpf, A, 1941. *Antonia Augusta* (Abh. der Preuss. Akad. der Wissen., Phil.-Hist. Klasse, no. 5). Berlin: W. de Gruyter.

Ryberg, I.S., 1955. *Rites of the State Religion in Roman Art* (*MAAR*, no. 22). Rome: The American Academy in Rome.

Sallet, A. von, 1879. 'Kopf der Antonia auf Münzen des jüngeren Drusus', *ZfN* 6, 60–3.

Scheid, J., 1975. 'Scribonia Caesaris et les Julio-Claudiens: problèmes de vocabulaire de parenté', *MEFRA* 87, 349–75.

Schilling, R., 1954. *La Religion romaine de Vénus: depuis les origines jusqu'au temps d'Auguste*. Paris: E. de Boccard.

Schliemann, H., 1884. *Troja: Results of 1882* (reprint edn 1976). New York: Arno Press.

Scramuzza, V.M., 1940. *The Emperor Claudius*. Cambridge, Mass.:

Harvard University Press.

Seager, R., 1972. *Tiberius*. London: Eyre Methuen.

Sensi, L., 1980/1. 'Ornatus e status sociale delle donne Romane', *AFLPer* 18, 55–90.

——, 1984/5. 'I ritratti Romani di Spoleto', *AFLPer* 22, 229–76.

——, 1987. 'Il ritratto di Germanico da Mentana: alcune considerazioni', in *Germanico: la persona, la personalità, il personaggio* (ed. G. Bonamente and M.P. Segoloni). Rome: G. Bretschneider, 219–27.

Shaw, B.D., 1987. 'The Age of Roman Girls at Marriage: Some Reconsiderations', *JRS* 77, 30–46.

Sherk, R.K., 1988. *The Roman Empire: Augustus to Hadrian*. Cambridge: Cambridge University Press.

Shipley, F.W., 1931. 'Chronology of the Building Operations in Rome from the Death of Caesar to the Death of Augustus', *MAAR* 9, 7–60.

Sidari, D., 1979/80. 'La missione di Germanico in Oriente nel racconto di Tacito', *AIV* 138, 599–628.

Simon, E., 1982a. 'Augustus und Antonia Minor in Kurashiki/Japan', *AA*, 332–43.

——, 1982b. *The Kurashiki Ninagawa Museum: Greek, Etruscan, and Roman Antiquities*. Mainz-on-Rhine: Philipp von Zabern.

Singer, M.W., 1948. 'The Problems of Octavia Minor and Octavia Maior', *TAPA* 79, 268–74.

Smallwood, E.M., 1956. 'Some Notes on the Jews under Tiberius', *Latomus* 15, 314–29.

——, 1957. 'The Chronology of Gaius' Attempt to Desecrate the Temple', *Latomus* 16, 3–17.

——, 1976. *The Jews Under Roman Rule: From Pompey to Diocletian*. Leiden: E.J. Brill.

Smith, R.R.R., 1987. 'The Imperial Reliefs from the Sebasteion at Aphrodisias', *JRS* 77, 88–138.

Snyder, W.F., 1940. 'Public Anniversaries in the Roman Empire: The Epigraphical Evidence for their Observance during the First Three Centuries', *YCS* 7, 223–317.

Sperber, D., 1986. *Nautica Talmudica*. Ramat-Gan: Bar-Ilan University.

Strong, A., 1907. *Roman Sculpture from Augustus to Constantine*. London: Duckworth.

Strong, D., 1976. *Roman Art* (The Pelican History of Art). Harmondsworth: Penguin Books.

Stuart, M., 1939. 'How Were Imperial Portraits Distributed?', *AJA* 43, 601–17.

Sullivan, R.D., 1980. 'Dynasts in Pontus', *ANRW* 2.7:2, 913–30.

Sumner, G.V., 1967. 'Germanicus and Drusus Caesar', *Latomus* 26, 413–35.

Sutherland, C.H.V., 1951. *Coinage in Roman Imperial Policy, 31 BC–AD 68*. London: Eyre Methuen

——, 1976. *The Emperor and the Coinage: Julio-Claudian Studies*. London: Spink and Son.

——, 1987. *Roman History and Coinage 44 BC–AD 69: Fifty Points of Relation from Julius Caesar to Vespasian*. Oxford: Clarendon Press.

Svoronos, J.N., 1890. *Numismatique de la Crète ancienne*, vols 1–2. Macon: Imprimerie Protat Frères.

Sydenham, E.A., 1917. *Historical References on Coins of the Roman Empire from Augustus to Gallienus*. London: Spink and Son.

Syme, R., 1939. *The Roman Revolution*. Oxford: Oxford University Press.

——, 1986. *The Augustan Aristocracy*. Oxford: Clarendon Press.

Tamm, B., 1963. *Auditorium and Palatium* (Acta Univ. Stock.: Stock. Stud. in Class. Archaeol., no. 2). Stockholm: Almqvist and Wiksell.

Tarn, W.W., 1934. 'Antony and Octavia', in *CAH* 10, 51–5.

Tölle-Kastenbein, R., 1974. *Das Kastro Tigani* (Samos, no. 14). Bonn: R. Habelt.

Touratsoglou, J., 1978. 'The 1976 Patras Hoard of Aurei from the Early Empire', *NomChr* 5/6, 41–52.

Toynbee, J.M.C., 1953. 'The Ara Pacis Reconsidered and Historical Art in Roman Italy', *PBA* 39, 67–95.

——, 1955/8. 'Some Notes on Roman Art at Colchester: VIII. the Glass Medallion (Pl. IX)', *TEAS* 25, 17–23.

——, 1971. *Death and Burial in the Roman World*. London: Thames and Hudson.

——, 1978. *Roman Historical Portraits* (Aspects of Greek and Roman Life). London: Thames and Hudson.

Toynbee, J.M.C. and Richmond, I.A., 1953. 'A Roman Glass Phalera from Carlisle', *TCWA* 53, 40–8.

Treggiari, S., 1973. 'Domestic Staff at Rome in the Julio-Claudian Period, 27 BC to AD 68', *HSRC* 6, 241–55.

——, 1976. 'Jobs for Women', *AJAH* 1, 76–104.

Trillmich, W., 1978. *Familienpropaganda der Kaiser Caligula und Claudius: Agrippina Major und Antonia Augusta auf Münzen*. Berlin: W. de Gruyter.

Trump, D.H., 1972. *Malta: An Archaeological Guide*. London: Faber and Faber.

Tupet, A.-M., 1980. 'Les Pratiques magiques à la mort de Germanicus', in *Mélanges Pierre Wuilleumier* (ed. M.Y. Burnand *et al.*). Paris: Société d'Edition Les Belles Lettres, 345–52.

Turner, E.G., 1959. 'P.Oxy.2435. Acta Alexandrinorum?', in *The Oxyrhynchus Papyri: Part XXV* (ed. E. Lobel and E.G. Turner). London: Egypt Exploration Society, 102–12.

——, 1968. *Greek Papyri: An Introduction*. Oxford: Oxford University Press.

——, 1987. *Greek Manuscripts of the Ancient World* (Bulletin Suppl. no. 46 – 2nd edn, rev. P.J. Parsons). London: Institute of Classical Studies.

Turner, J., 1983. 'Priestesses in Ancient Greece'. Unpubl. diss., University of California, Santa Barbara.

Urdahl, L.B., 1959. 'Foreigners in Athens: A Study of the Grave Monuments'. Unpubl. diss., Chicago University.

Vermeule, C.C., 1968. *Roman Imperial Art in Greece and Asia Minor*. Cambridge, Mass.: Harvard University Press.

——, 1986. *The Cult Images of Imperial Rome* (Stud. to the Mem. of John

Petersen Elder, 1913 to 1985). Privately printed.

Vidman, L., 1982. *Fasti Ostienses*. Prague: Academia Scientiarum Bohemoslovacae.

Villefosse, A.H. de, 1899. 'Le Trésor de Boscoreale', *MonPiot* 5.

Vollenweider, M.-L., 1966. *Die Steinschneidekunst und ihre Künstler in spätrepublikanischer und augusteischer Zeit*. Baden-Baden: B. Grimm.

Wagenvoort, H., 1980. *Pietas* (Stud. in Greek and Roman Religion, no. 1). Leiden: E.J. Brill.

Walker, S. and Burnett, A., 1981. *The Image of Augustus*. London: B.M. Publications.

Wallace, S.L., 1938. *Taxation in Egypt: From Augustus to Diocletian*. Princeton, NJ: Princeton University Press.

Ward-Perkins, J.B., 1981. *Roman Imperial Architecture* (The Pelican History of Art). Harmondsworth: Penguin Books.

Weaver, P.R.C., 1972. *Familia Caesaris*. Cambridge: Cambridge University Press.

Weingärtner, D.G., 1969. *Die Ägyptenreise des Germanicus* (Papyr. Texte und Abh. no. 11). Bonn: R. Habelt.

Wellesley, K., 1954. 'Can You Trust Tacitus?', *G & R* 1 (2nd ser.), 13–33.

West, R., 1933. *Römische Porträt-Plastik*. Munich: F. Bruckmann.

Willrich, H., 1911. *Livia*. Leipzig: B.G. Teubner.

Wiseman, T.P., 1980. 'Josephus on the Palatine (AJ 19. 75–6)', *LCM* 5, 231–8.

——, 1984. 'Cybele, Virgil and Augustus', in *Poetry and Politics in the Age of Augustus* (ed. T. Woodman and D. West). Cambridge: Cambridge University Press, 117–28.

——, 1987. *Roman Studies: Literary and Historical*. Liverpool: Francis Cairns.

Zevi, F. and Andreae, B., 1982. 'Gli scavi sottomarini di Baia', *PP* 37, 114–56.

(C) A SELECTION OF UNCITED BIBLIOGRAPHY

Adams, F., 1955. 'The Consular Brothers of Sejanus', *AJP* 76, 70–6.

Allen, W., 1941. 'The Political Atmosphere of the Reign of Tiberius', *TAPA* 72, 1–25.

Assa, J., 1960. *The Great Roman Ladies* (Eng. tr. A. Hollander). New York: Grove Press.

Avery, W., 1935. 'Julia and Lucius Vinicius', *CP* 30, 170–1.

Baldwin, B., 1972. 'Women in Tacitus', *Prudentia* 4, 83–101.

Balsdon, J.P.V.D., 1951. 'The Murder of Drusus, son of Tiberius', *CR* 1, 75.

——, 1979. *Romans and Aliens*. London: Duckworth.

Bartels, H., 1963. *Studien zum Frauenporträt der Augusteischen Zeit: Fulvia, Octavia, Livia, Julia*. Munich: Feder.

Best, E.E. Jr, 1970. 'Cicero, Livy and Educated Roman Women', *CJ* 65, 199–204.

Bianchi, U., 1976. *The Greek Mysteries* (Icon. of Relig., no. 17:3). Leiden: E.J. Brill.

Birt, Th., 1932. *Frauen der Antike*. Leipzig: Quelle and Meyer.

Bishop, J.D., 1960. 'Dating in Tacitus by Moonless Nights', *CP* 55, 164–70.

Boddington, A., 1963. 'Sejanus, Whose Conspiracy?', *AJP* 84, 1–16.

Boulvert, G., 1970. *Esclaves et affranchis impériaux sous le haut-empire romain rôle politique et administratif*. Naples: Jovene.

Bowersock, G.W., 1965. *Augustus and the Greek World*. Oxford: Clarendon Press.

——, 1969. *Greek Sophists in the Roman Empire*. Oxford: Clarendon Press.

Bowman, A.K., 1986. *Egypt after the Pharaohs: 332 BC–AD. 642 from Alexander to the Arab Conquest*. London: B.M. Publications.

Brelia, L., 1968. *Roman Imperial Coins: Their Art and Technique*. London: Thames and Hudson.

Brilliant, R., 1963. *Gesture and Rank in Roman Art: The Use of Gestures to Denote Status in Roman Sculpture and Coinage* (Mem. of the Conn. Acad. of Arts and Scien., no. 14). New Haven, Conn.: The Academy of Arts and Sciences.

Bulst, C.M., 1961. 'The Revolt of Queen Boudicca in AD 60', *Historia* 10, 496–509.

Carcopino, J., 1958. 'La véritable Julie', *RP* 65, 17–31, 66–80.

Chanler, B., 1934. *Cleopatra's Daughter: The Queen of Mauretania*. London: Putnam

Charlesworth, M.P., 1922. 'The Banishment of the Elder Agrippina', *CP* 17, 260–1.

——, 1927. 'Livia and Tanaquil', *CR* 41, 55–7.

Chisholm, K. and Ferguson, J. (eds), 1981. *Rome: The Augustan Age*. Oxford: Oxford University Press.

Colin, J., 1954. 'Les consuls du César-Pharaon et l'héritage de Germanicus', *Latomus* 13, 394–416.

Crook, J.A., 1951. 'Titus and Berenice', *AJP* 72, 162–75.

Dawson, A., 1969. 'Whatever Happened to Lady Agrippina?', *CJ* 64, 253–67.

Deckman, A.A., 1925. 'Livia Augusta', *CW* 19, 21–5.

Delbrück, R., 1912. *Antike Porträts*. Bonn: A. Marcus and E. Weber.

Deutsch, M.E., 1918. 'The Women of Caesar's Family', *CJ* 12, 502–14.

Donaldson, J., 1907. *Woman: Her Position and Influence in Ancient Greece and Rome, and Among the Early Christians*. London: Longmans, Green.

Dorey, T.A., 1961. 'Adultery and Propaganda in the Early Empire', *UBHJ* 8, 1–6.

Dudley, D.R., 1967. *Urbs Roma: A Sourcebook of Classical Texts on the City and its Monuments*. London: Phaidon

Dudley, D.R. and Webster, G., 1962. *The Rebellion of Boudicca*. New York: Barnes and Noble.

Fraser, P.M., 1972. *Ptolemaic Alexandria*. Oxford: Clarendon Press.

Fullerton, M.D., 1985. 'The Domus Augusti in Imperial Iconography of 13–12 BC', *AJA* 89, 473–83.

Furtwängler, A., 1888. 'Studien über die Gemmen mit

Künstlerinschrift: II. Gemmen mit Künstlerinschrift in verschiedenen Sammlungen', *JdI* 3, 193–224.

Garcia y Bellido, A., 1949. *Esculturas Romanas de España y Portugal.* Madrid: Consejo Superior de Investigaciones Cientificas.

Garnsey, P., 1970. *Social Status and Legal Privilege in the Roman Empire.* Oxford: Clarendon Press.

Giacosa, G., 1974. *Ritratti di Auguste.* Milan: Edizioni Arte e Moneta. (Appeared in English in 1977 as *Women of the Caesars: their Lives and Portraits on Coins.*)

Gill, C., 1983. 'The Question of Character-Development: Plutarch and Tacitus', *CQ* 33, 469–87.

Goodwater, L., 1975. *Women in Antiquity: An Annotated Bibliography.* Metuchen, NJ: The Scarecrow Press.

Gould, J., 1980. 'Law, Custom and Myth: Aspects of the Social Position of Women in Classical Athens', *JHS* 100, 38–59.

Györkösy, A., 1942. 'Review of Rumpf's Antonia Augusta', *ArchPhilol* 66, 114–15. (For other reviews see below Jongkees 1942 and also *The New Pallas* 6 (1942), 45.)

Hallett, J.P., 1984. *Fathers and Daughters: Women in Roman Kinship and Society.* Princeton, NJ: Princeton University Press.

——, 1986. 'Queens, Princeps and Women of the Augustan Elite: Propertius' Cornelia-Elegy and the Res Gestae Divi Augusti', in *The Age of Augustus* (Conference held at Brown University, 1982 – ed. R. Winkes). Providence, Rhode Isl.: Brown University, 73–88.

Heine, S., 1987. *Women and Early Christianity.* London: SCM Press.

Heyob, S.K., 1975. *The Cult of Isis among Women in the Graeco-Roman World* (Etud. Prélim. aux Relig. Orient. dans l'Empire Rom.). Leiden: E.J. Brill.

Hoffsten, R.B., 1939. 'Roman Women of Rank of the Early Empire as Portrayed by Dio, Patercullus, Suetonius and Tacitus'. Unpubl. diss., University of Pennsylvania.

Imhoof-Blumer, F., 1885. *Porträtköpfe auf antiken Münzen hellenischer und hellenisierter Völker.* Leipzig: B.G. Teubner.

Jongkees, J.H., 1942. 'De Hera Ludovisi en Livia', *BABesch* 17, 13–16.

Jordan, R., 1974. *Berenice.* London: Constable.

Jucker, H., 1973. 'Methodisches zur kunstgeschichtlichen Interpretation von Münzbildnissen der Agrippina Maior und der Antonia Minor', *SchMünz* 23, 55–64.

——, 1982. 'Ikonographische Anmerkungen zu frühkaiserzeitlichen Porträtkameen', *BABesch* 57, 100–9.

Kahrstedt, U., 1910. 'Frauen auf antiken Münzen', *Klio* 10, 261–314.

Kiefer, O., 1969. *Sexual Life in Ancient Rome* (Eng. tr. G. and H. Highet). London: Panther Books.

Kornemann, E., 1942. *Grosse Frauen des Altertums.* Heidelberg: C. Winter.

Köstermann, E., 1955. 'Der Sturz Sejans', *Hermes* 83, 350–73.

Lefkowitz, M.R., 1981. *Heroines and Hysterics.* London: Duckworth.

——, 1983. 'Wives and Husbands', *G & R* 30, 31–47.

Lefkowitz, M.R. and Fant, M.B., 1978. *Women in Greece and Rome.*

Toronto and Sarasota: Stevens.

——, 1982. *Women's Life in Greece and Rome: A Sourcebook in Translation*. London: Duckworth.

Leon, E.F., 1951. 'Scribonia and her Daughters', *TAPA* 82, 168–75.

Linderski, J., 1988. 'Julia in Regium', *ZPE* 72, 181–200.

Macmullen, R., 1966. *Enemies of the Roman Order: Treason, Unrest, and Alienation in the Empire*. Cambridge, Mass.: Harvard University Press.

——, 1980. 'Women in Public in the Roman Empire', *Historia* 29, 208–18.

Macurdy, G.H., 1937. *Vassal-Queens and Some Other Contemporary Women in the Roman Empire* (Johns Hopkins Univ. Stud. in Archaeol., no. 22). Baltimore, Md: Johns Hopkins University Press.

Malcovati, H., 1945/6. *Donne di Roma Antica*. Rome: Quaderni di Studi Romani.

Marsh, F.B., 1926. 'Roman Parties in the Reign of Tiberius', *AHR* 31, 233–50.

Mattingly, H., 1961. *The Women of the Roman Empire*. Christ Church: Wilding Memorial Lectures.

McCabe, J., 1911. *The Empresses of Rome*. New York: H. Holt.

McDaniel, W.B., 1910. 'Bauli the Scene of the Murder of Agrippina', *CQ* 4, 96–102.

McDermott, W.C., 1970. 'The Sisters of P. Clodius', *Phoenix* 24, 39–47.

McHugh, J., 1975. *The Mother of Jesus in the New Testament*. London: Darton, Longman and Todd.

Mierow, C.C., 1943/4. 'Germanicus Caesar Imperator', *CJ* 39, 137–55.

Mireaux, E., 1951. *La Reine Bérénice*. Paris: A. Michel.

Neumann, E., 1972. *The Great Mother: An Analysis of the Archetype*. Princeton, NJ: Princeton University Press.

Newell, E.T., 1937. *Royal Greek Portrait Coins*. New York: Wayte Paymond.

Oliver, J.H., 1965. 'Livia as Artemis Boulaia at Athens', *CP* 60, 179.

Oliver, J.H. and Palmer, R.E.A., 1954. 'Text of the Tabula Hebana', *AJP* 75, 225–49.

Ooteghem, J. van, 1959. 'Germanicus en Egypte', *EC* 27, 241–51.

Peradotto, J. and Sullivan, J.P. (eds), 1984. *Women in the Ancient World: The Arethusa Papers*. Albany, NY: State University of New York Press.

Percival, J., 1976. *The Roman Villa: An Historical Introduction*. London: B.T. Batsford.

Phillips, J.E., 1978. 'Roman Mothers and the Lives of their Adult Daughters', *Helios* 6:1, 69–80.

Piana, G. la, 1927. 'Foreign Groups in Rome during the First Centuries of the Empire', *HTR* 20, 183–403.

Picard, G.C., 1961. 'Chronique de la sculpture romaine: l'iconographie à l'epoque d'Auguste et de Tibère', *REL* 39, 275–85.

Pietrangeli, C., 1938. *La famiglia di Augusto*. Rome: Mostra Augustea della Romanita (Tip. Colombo).

Platner, S.B., 1911. *The Topography and Monuments of Ancient Rome* (2nd edn). Boston, Mass.: Alyn and Bacon.

Polacco, L., 1955. *Il volto di Tiberio* (Accad. Patav. di Scien. Lett. e Arti, no. 67). Rome: 'L'Erma' di Bretschneider.

Polaschek, K., 1972. 'Studien zu einem Frauenkopf im Landesmuseum Trier und zur weiblichen Haartracht der Iulisch-Claudischen Zeit', *TrZ* 35, 141–210.

——, 1973. *Porträttypen einer Claudischen Kaiserin* (Stud. Archaeol., no. 17). Rome: 'L'Erma' di Bretschneider.

Pomeroy, S.B., 1973. 'Selected Bibliography on Women in Antiquity', *Arethusa* 6, 125–57.

——, 1976. 'The Relationship of the Married Woman to her Blood Relatives in Rome', *AncSoc* 7, 215–27.

Poulsen, F., 1923. *Greek and Roman Portraits in English Country Houses.* Oxford: Oxford University Press.

Price, M.J. and Trell, B.L., 1977. *Coins and their Cities: Architecture on the Ancient Coins of Greece, Rome, and Palestine.* London: V.C. Vecchi and Sons.

Radford-Ruether, R. (ed.), 1974. *Religion and Sexism: Images of Women in the Jewish and Christian Traditions.* New York: Harper and Row.

Richmond, I.A., 1954. 'Queen Cartimandua', *JRS* 44, 43–52.

Richter, G.M.A., 1948. *Roman Portraits.* New York: Metropolitan Museum.

Rogers, R.S., 1931. 'The Conspiracy of Agrippina', *TAPA* 62, 141–68.

——, 1967. 'The Deaths of Julia and Gracchus, AD 14', *TAPA* 98, 383–90.

Ross, D.O., 1973. 'The Tacitean Germanicus', *YCS* 33, 209–27.

Saller, R.P., 1982. *Personal Patronage under the Early Empire.* Cambridge: Cambridge University Press.

——, 1984. 'Familia, Domus, and the Roman Conception of the Family', *Phoenix* 38, 336–55.

Sandels, F., 1912. 'Die Stellung der kaiserlichen Frauen aus dem Julisch-Claudischen Hause'. Unpubl. diss., Giessen University.

Schwartz, D., 1987. *Agrippa I the Last King of Judaea.* Jerusalem: Zalman Shazar Center (in Hebrew).

Scott, K., 1931. 'Greek and Roman Honorific Months', *YCS* 2, 201–78.

Sealey, R., 1961. 'The Political Attachments of L. Aelius Seianus', *Phoenix* 15, 97–114.

Shotter, D.C.A., 1968. 'Tacitus, Tiberius and Germanicus', *Historia* 17, 194–214.

——, 1974. 'The Fall of Sejanus: Two Problems', *CP* 69, 42–6.

Simon, E., 1986. *Augustus: Kunst und Leben in Rom um die Zeitenwende.* Munich: Hirmer.

Singer, M.W., 1944. 'Octavia Minor, Sister of Augustus: An Historical and Biographical Study'. Unpubl. diss., Duke University.

——, 1947. 'Octavia's Mediation at Tarentum', *CJ* 43, 173–7.

Smethurst, S.E., 1950. 'Women in Livy's History', *G & R* 19, 80–7.

Solin, H., 1981. 'Germanicus in Patrai', *ZPE* 41, 207–8.

Stagg, E. and Stagg, F., 1978. *Woman in the World of Jesus.* Edinburgh: Saint Andrew Press.

Stahr, A., 1865. *Römische Kaiserfrauen.* Berlin: von J. Guttentag.

Stewart, Z., 1953. 'Sejanus, Gaetulicus, and Seneca', *AJP* 74, 70–85.

Strong, E., 1908. 'Antiques in the Collection of Sir Frederick Cook, Bart, at Doughty House, Richmond', *JHS* 28, 1–45.

Sumner, V.G., 1965. 'The Family of L. Aelius Seianus', *Phoenix* 19, 134–45.

Sutherland, C.H.V., 1984. 'Indications of Chronology in the Julio-Claudian Coinages', *RBN* 130, 49–57.

Swidler, L. and Swidler, A. (eds), 1977. *Women Priests*. New York: Paulist Press.

Swift, E.H., 1923. 'Images in Imperial Portraiture', *AJA* 27, 286–301.

Syme, R., 1956. 'Seianus on the Aventine', *Hermes* 84, 257–66.

——, 1978. *History in Ovid*. Oxford: Clarendon Press.

Torelli, M., 1982. *Typology and Structure of Roman Historical Reliefs*. Ann Arbor, Mich.: University of Michigan Press.

Treggiari, S., 1971. 'Libertine Ladies', *CW* 64, 196–8.

——, 1975. 'Jobs in the Household of Livia', *PBSR* 43, 48–77.

Trillmich, W., 1971. 'Zur Formgeschichte von Bildnistypen', *JdI* 86, 179–213.

Vischer, F. de, 1946. 'Un incident du séjour de Germanicus en Egypte', *Muséon* 59, 259–66.

Warner, M., 1976. *Alone of All her Sex: The Myth and the Cult of the Virgin Mary*. London: Weidenfeld and Nicolson.

Warren, L.B., 1973. 'The Women of Etruria', *Arethusa* 6, 91–101.

Weinstock, S., 1957. 'The Image and the Chair of Germanicus', *JRS* 47, 144–54.

——, 1966. 'The Posthumous Honours of Germanicus', in *Mélanges André Piganiol*, vol. 2 (ed. R. Chevallier). Paris: SEVPEN, 891–8.

Wiseman, T.P., 1965. 'The Mother of Livia Augusta', *Historia* 14, 333–4.

Witt, R.E., 1971. *Isis in the Graeco-Roman World* (Aspects of Greek and Roman Life). London: Thames and Hudson.

Woodman, A.J., 1977. *Velleius Paterculus: The Tiberian Narrative (2.94–131)*. Cambridge: Cambridge University Press.

——, 1985. *Tacitus and Tiberius: The Alternative 'Annals'*. Durham: University Inaugural Lecture (read on 14 February 1985).

Worsfold, T.C., 1934. *The History of the Vestal Virgins of Rome*. London: Rider.

Wruck, W., 1931. *Die syrische Provinzialprägung von Augustus bis Traian*. Stuttgart: W. Kohlhammer.

Xuereb, P., 1969. *The Roman Villa in History*. Malta: Msida.

Zanker, P., 1987. *Augustus und die Macht der Bilder*. Munich: C.H. Beck. (English tr. A. Shapiro 1988, *The Power of Images in the Age of Augustus*. Ann Arbor, Mich.: University of Michigan Press.)

REVIEW CHAPTER

A decade since the first publication of Antonia Augusta

Of everything other than thought, there can be no history. Thus
a biography, for example, however much history it contains, is
constructed on principles that are not only non-historical but
anti-historical...

Thus the renowned philosopher of history R. G. Collingwood in
his *Idea of History* (Oxford 1946, 304), advised his readers against
considering biography as a legitimate task for the historian. I have
always found the first sentence of this quotation unacceptable.
There can be no history? But there are infinite historical facts definitely recorded, which cannot be prejudiced by any historian. For
example, a historian cannot intervene in the struggle between
Octavian and Mark Antony in such a way as to affect the result. In
the 'post-Collingwood', or 'post-modern', world in which we have
now regrettably arrived, this kind of extreme scepticism towards
historical knowledege has often led to cynicism and unhealthy neg-
ativity. Nevertheless, the quotation's second sentence, if taken as a
reference to a *complete* or *infallible* biography, must be a true ver-
dict. We should long ago have given up the exercise – for if one
simply cannot know everything about oneself, how can one
attempt to know everything about someone else? In a parallel way,
Fergus Millar stated in the foreword to this book:

> None the less the material is not nearly sufficient to allow a real
> biography, and Nikos Kokkinos neither pretends to be able to
> offer that, nor seeks to provide some semi-fictional substitute.
> Instead he does something quite different, which is to look at the
> way in which the figure of Antonia is reflected, and made visi-
> ble to us, through a remarkable variety of types of evidence...

Fergus wrote this early in 1988, when he had seen the original version of my work. I felt his comment was appropriate. In no place
had I claimed to have achieved (or indeed that it was generally
achievable) to write a 'real' biography of an individual in antiquity. A few years later, on receiving a copy of the book from the pub-

lishers, Fergus sent me a congratulatory letter (4/12/1992), in which he said:

> In spite of my guarded words in the Preface, it actually comes out pretty well as a biography, one of the very few female biographies which will be possible from the Ancient World.

So it seems that by examining the broadest variety of primary materials available, it is possible to achieve something 'close' to a biography (in a non-Collingwood sense), or at least a reflective biographical framework. Such framework, with all the dangers that it entails, deriving from an interdisciplinary approach to literary, documentary and archaeological evidence, I have proposed in the Preface for other ancient figures. I am pleased to note that my suggestion has not fallen on deaf ears. Near-biographies, at least of other women, utilising more diverse sources than was usual hitherto, have now been written, such as of the last wife of Claudius by Anthony Barrett (*Agrippina*, London 1996) or, at a level focussing largely on the public images, of all Julio-Claudian women by Susan Wood (*Imperial Women*, Leiden 1999).

Antonia has been read widely and much cited in the last decade, and it has been included in the bibliographies of several important manuals, such as *The Cambridge Ancient History*, vol. 10 (new edn. by A. K. Bowman *et al.*, Cambridge 1996); *Der Neue Pauly: Enzyklopädie der Antike*, vol. 1 (ed. by H. Cancik & H. Schneider, Stuttgart 1996); and *The Book of Acts in its Graeco-Roman Setting*, vol. 2 (ed. by D. W. J. Gill & C. Gempf, Carlisle 1994). While it is difficult at this stage to compile a full list of reviews the book has received, several will be discussed briefly below. Some criticisms may need a reply. Next, and hopefully more usefully, I shall make an attempt to highlight new discoveries and interpretations bearing on Antonia, without pretending to have had the time to be informed about every aspect concerned in all the fields of study I was rash enough to involve myself originally! To re-collect, re-analyse and re-conclude on the entire body of evidence, as it exists today for Antonia (rather than in the mid–1980s), would mean to re-edit the book extensively or perhaps even re-write it completely. But having had a good impact, the book, I feel, stands well as it is and especially in the light of this chapter. Finally, I can only be restricted to a few points missed before 1992 (or really

1988 – see first Preface), and to a selection of relevant publications which have appeared since.

REFLECTIONS ON THE REVIEWS

Marie-Thérèse Raepsaet-Charlier, author of a now standard female prosopography of Rome, in a review of recent research ("La femme, la famille, la parenté à Rome: thèmes actuels de la recherche", *L'Antiquité Classique* 62 [1993], 247–53), mentions *Antonia* favourably for its interdisciplinary approach, noting that "L'originalité... réside dans la place accordée aux différentes catégories de sources...". Similarly, Susan Treggiari in her review (in *Echos du Monde Classique/Classical Views* 38 [1994] 435–8) states that "the methodical collection of evidence (inscriptions, papyri, coins, sculpture, minor arts, architecture) provides a model of how to explore documentation of the best-attested women of the imperial family". Dietmar Kienast (in *Historische Zeitschrift* 259 [1994], 770–1) also stresses the collection's usefulness, "Das Material... jetzt bequem bereitgestellt", while the conclusion of Thomas Wiedemann about *Antonia* in his subject review of Roman history (in *Greece & Rome* 39 [1992], 239–44), concurs firmly in that "the evidence collected here will be essential to future studies both of Julio-Claudian women, and Julio-Claudian politics".

Christer Bruun (in *Arctos* 29 [1995], 212–3) very kindly writes that "it is no mean feat to master such a variable collection of sources", and goes on to offer comments with the intention to further understanding of the Latin epigraphical evidence, an area in which he excels. Indeed, his elucidation of the graffiti at Pausilypon is interesting. Macrinus was the steward (*dispensator*) of Pollius Felix's estate in AD 65 (see pp. 64–5). From the abbreviated texts, it "appeared" to me that his father, an administrator (*procurator*) named Diadumenus Antonianus, could have been a freedman of Antonia: MACRINUS DIADUMENI AUG. L. PROC. ANTONIANI DISP. Bruun explains that the *agnomen* 'Antonianus' would indicate that he was a slave of Antonia, who became freedman only after being acquired by the Emperor – so AUG(*usti*) rather than AUG(*ustae*) in extension (cf. B.39–41). Therefore Macrinus, presumably unfree according to Bruun in AD 65, was the son of an imperial freedman Diadumenus, who had been a slave of Antonia before AD 37 (when she died). Now, as a freedman Diadumenus would have served the Emperor in the position of 'administrator' conceivably in a nearby villa, but could he have held this or a similar position (as a slave) under Antonia as I suggested? Macrinus' employment at Pausilypon (opposite Bauli), does not impress Bruun enough to see that his father could have worked locally – e.g. in Antonia's villa in the area. He also does not seem enthusiastic about my observation that the names 'Macrinus' and 'Diadumenus' are otherwise attested among Antonia's workforce (though I have claimed no direct relationships). But as no evidence to the contrary has been produced, I may continue to believe that it is possible for the people at Pausilypon, involving an ex-slave (as corrected by Bruun) of Antonia, to have had a connection with Bauli across the Bay of Puteoli.

B. Campbell ("A Great Lady", *The Classical Review* 47 [1994], 129–30) finds the registers of the book "excellent" for providing help to teachers guiding their students "to a wider understanding of the role of the imperial family in the early empire". Yet, at the same time he does not favour my "enumerative" approach, because the subject in his opinion is not sufficiently important (whatever the logic in this association). According to Campbell, Antonia was not as important a figure in Roman society as I have presented her to be, and while accepting that she was "a central figure in the transition from republic to empire", he would attribute this to a mere accident of birth. It seems that Campbell would have Rome rather devoid of female power, because Livia's importance (the only other woman really comparable to Antonia) would then be an accident of marriage, and of course no female of common birth can ever be considered. But how about the involvement of Antonia in politics? Campbell recognises only one appearance of Antonia in matters of state, that is in the uncovering of Sejanus' plot, the validity of which he doubts by claiming that Josephus' source Agrippa I, being a friend of Antonia, would have exaggerated her role. At such a simplistic level we could easily doubt almost any historical source with which our model is in conflict. However, history is not written this way. Campbell is actually unaware of Josephus' real source ('Thaumastus'), of which one can read in my book *The Herodian Dynasty* (Sheffield 1998, particularly pp. 274–5). Also he does not seem to realise the fact (quite apart from the evidence I have gathered from Josephus and Dio, not to mention my interpretations of Honestus, the Tiberian dupondii, the Victory coin of Thessalonica, the papyrus of Pallas etc.) that Tacitus' *Annals* book 5 is lost to us! This is where he would have given his version, and we do not know what the details were. Further, it is difficult to understand why it was "misleading" to mention that Sejanus and Livilla (Antonia's daughter) were lovers, for following on from my position (and re-reading the *Fasti Ostienses*) it has now been argued by Jane Bellemore ("The Wife of Sejanus", *ZPE* 109 [1995], 255–66) that Sejanus may even have married Livilla! Finally, while acknowledging my reservations regarding some sculptural identifications, Campbell concludes that "we have no way of knowing how people reacted to the iconography of Antonia, how popular and well-known she really was, and how far her celebration in the visual arts was merely routine". This would make Plutarch jump! The Greek biographer calls her nothing less than *periboêton* – "far famed" (Anton. 87.6). But so defeatist a conclusion not only ignores a large part of what the book has revealed about the daughter of famous Mark Antony (including her extensive inscriptional record, massive Egyptian holdings, divine personifications, shrines, priests, and private *lararia* – see fig. 109), but also what Fergus Millar said in *Antonia*'s Foreword about Paul Zanker's book *The Power of Images in the Age of Augustus* that "our view of how to understand the early Empire has been transformed". In the opinion of Treggiari, *Antonia* "is the first biography of a Roman in English to use visual evidence so effectively. The lessons of Zanker or, in Roman social history, of Kampen and Kleiner or, in early modern history, of Simon Schama and Linda Colley have not been lost."

In his review Peter Herz (*Gnomon* 68 [1996], 171–3) finds the collection of material in the book a significant achievement, though not without criticisms – some expressed in the over-confident German style, which can often be misplaced. While he does correct two factual mistakes (p. 26, where the number "31" was printed twice for the date of Sejanus' execution on 18 October AD 31; and p. 171, where the genealogical tree has the name of M. Vinicius spelled "M. Vicinius"), several of his objections are debatable. For example, he thinks that I am wrong in saying that Gaius Caesar visited Jerusalem because Suetonius presumably states the exact opposite: *quod Iudaeam praetervehens apud Hierosolyma non supplicasset* (*Aug.* 93). But strictly speaking this Latin phrase ("not offering prayers at Jerusalem as he passed by Judaea") does not refer to Gaius not visiting Jerusalem, but only not sacrificing there. Herz cites in his support H. Halfmann's work on the imperial journeys, but this cannot decide the matter if Timothy Barnes' review of Halfmann is ignored. Independently, Barnes ("Emperors on the Move", *Journal of Roman Archaeology* 2 [1989], 251) also suggests that Gaius would have visited Jerusalem where he should have ignored the cult. Further, Suetonius' precise assertion that Augustus highly praised (*conlaudavit*) Gaius for abstaining from sacrifice in this city, sounds very odd. We know that Augustus himself commanded daily sacrificies in the Temple of Jerusalem at his own expense (Philo, *Leg.* 157, 317; cf. Jos., *Apion* 2.77), and he, his wife Livia and other members of his household, had showered the place with votive offerings and gifts (Philo, *Leg.* 157, 319; Jos., *War* 5. 562–3).

Another objection of Herz is that the inscriptions mentioning Antonia from the province of Asia (which I put forward to suggest that she may have accompanied Germanicus in a part of his eastern journey), "nicht zwingend die physische Präsenz der geehrten Person gerade an diesem Ort voraussetzen muß". This view is echoed in other reviews and discussions, for example, more strongly, in Campbell's words: "Inscriptions from places on Germanicus' route through the east in AD 18 celebrating Antonia as 'benefactress', cannot demonstrate that she was there in person, since petitions may have been forwarded to her through her son". Although I have nowhere claimed that the epigraphical record "demonstrates" Antonia's participation in Germanicus's tour (for indeed inscriptions can record thanks for benefits received by remote control), a negative approach to the evidence will not do either. The timely dedications from Asia may not prove that she visited the province, but they do clearly support my suggestion that she may have done. In any case petitions would not have been forwarded to Antonia through Germanicus, as Campbell thinks, because Antonia's son never returned to Rome. In sharp contrast to Herz and Campbell, Greg Rowe in his review (in *Bryn Mawr Classical Review* 5.3 [1994], 222–5) finds my suggestion "compelling", calling it an "important new fact for political history", and so seems to be the opinion of Thomas Watkins (in *The Classical World* 88 [1994], 144–5) and of M. Cebeillac Gervasoni (in *Latomus* 55 [1996], 230–1) among others. Described as "remarkable and provocative" by Susan Wood (*op. cit.*, 145), my view that the eastern journey in AD 18/19 of Germanicus and family was probably much more important than has previously been appreciated, needs to be seen in context. The death of Augustus was still fresh in the memory. The timing of the move is very significant, marking, as it did, the 'half-centenary' anniversary of the defeat of Mark Antony at Actium in 31 BC. Its itinerary, beginning at Nicopolis, is also indicative. The extremely enthusiastic reception by the Greek world of the Antonian family – which would now have included *three* generations of descendants – comes as a complete surprise. Its disastrous conclusion with the death of Germanicus sent waves of panic in all directions and back to Rome. There can be no doubt that there were many people who believed that Tiberius was to blame, even though it is unlikely that he was directly involved – if only because of Antonia's subsequent protection of him. We must not forget that Tiberius continued to be the brother of her beloved, dead husband Drusus. From his part Tiberius, long appreciating Antonia for her chastity, and now obviously for her wisdom in this matter (unlike that of Agrippina's), held her in high regard. Josephus (*Ant.* 18.182) tells us that his esteem for the lady reached even higher points after AD 31, which is a natural consequence in my reconstruction of her uncovering of Sejanus' plot.

Finally Campbell, not unexpectedly, defends Tacitus saying: "if Tacitus has little to say about Antonia, that may be due not to ignorance but to his historical judgement"! It is strange that there are scholars still around who are prepared to defend *every* judgement that Tacitus made, despite repeated demonstrations from external evidence that some of his conclusions were ill-conceived (cf. support for my position by Harriet Flower, *Ancestor Masks and Aristocratic Power in Roman Culture*, Oxford 1996, 251–2). Without having to refer to irrelevant events for this book (such as his various misunderstandings of circumstances in the history of the Eastern Empire), Tacitus is precisely confused about the two Antonias in Rome itself. He declares that L. Domitius chose to become the husband of Antonia Minor (*Ann.* 4. 44: *Ipse delectus, cui minor Antonia, Octavia genita, in matrimonium daretur...*), and that Domitia Lepida was Antonia Minor's daughter (*Ann.* 12.64: *... quia Lepida minore Antonia genita...*)! Had these passages been the only evidence at our disposal, who would have dared to raise his voice against the 'infallible' historian Tacitus? But his ignorance in this matter I have also shown in my interpretation of the *Tabula Siarensis* (pp. 37–9) – not only about

Antonia's contribution to the ceremonies of Germanicus' funeral (*contra* Tac., *Ann.* 3.3), but also about the dating of Agrippina's return to the capital in December AD 19 rather than in AD 20 (*contra* Tac., *Ann.* 3.2). My dating, moreover, surprisingly anticipated the discovery of an extremely important document, the publication of which marked the field of Roman studies in the 1990s: the complete text of the Senate's judgement in the trial of Piso (*Senatus Consultum de Cn. Pisone Patre*)! I shall briefly discuss this later. In sharp contrast to Campbell, in one of the most pleasing comments I have received in a review so far (which can also be read on the website of *Bryn Mawr Classical Review*), Rowe wrote:

> It is a pity that K. was unable to take account of the *SC de Pisone* in his book. But it is one of the book's merits that it contributes so signally to our understanding of the new document.

BACK TO THE BEGINNING

Already in the introduction there are things that could be said to complement my written thoughts. The myth of the amazons, with which I began, according to recent understanding (and against what classicists have always believed) may have been built around a historical core! Though there is still no evidence as such for a matriarchal society in antiquity, the graves of female warriors (about 25% of all graves with weapons) now dug up in an area extending from the southern Ukraine through the steppes of southern Russia to the borders of Kazakhstan, strongly suggest a high if not an equal standing of women in these societies (see J. Davis-Kimball, "Warrior Women of the Eurasian Steppes", *Archaeology* 50:1 [Jan./Feb. 1997], 44–51; cf. L. Webster Wilde, *On the Trail of the Women Warriors*, London: Constable, 1999). Let us hope that we are not going to have to deal next with any archaeological discoveries pertaining to Lemnos' mariticidal women who wiped out the entire male population of the island, with the exception of King Thoas, who was saved by his heroic daughter, Hypsipyle! But more down to earth, among the examples of brave Greek women I mentioned in the introduction, I could have included the vengeful Pheretime, mother of the murdered tyrant of Barca in Cyrenaica, who had those involved in the death of her son crucified around the city walls (Herod., 4.201). I could also have noted the daughter-in-law of Polypherchon, an unstoppable female called

Kratesipolis ("conqueress of cities"), who put down a rebellion in Sicyon, near Corinth, and had about thirty of its inhabitants also crucified (Diod. 19.67.2).

Aristotle's description of the warlike nations beyond the Celts as "governed by women" (*gynaikokratoumenoi*), can also be compared with the description of Tacitus (*Germ.* 45.9) about the Sitones, living somewhere in Scandinavia, among whom "the woman rules" (*femina dominatur*). Whatever exaggeration might be assumed in the travellers' accounts that reached the Greeks and Romans, taken together with the recorded existence of 'foreign' laws on female rights (see p. 1), suggest that the position of women beyond Greece and Rome to the north was by comparison noticably enhanced. This may then indicate that the Anglesey parallel I have given and the appearance in the political scene of British queens such as Cartimandua and Boudicca would not have been accidental. As for the involvement of Roman women in writing, and particularly in poetry, I should have mentioned at least the six surviving elegies of a Sulpicia under Augustus (see Jane McIntosh Snyder, *The Woman and the Lyre: Women Writers in Classical Greece and Rome*, Bristol 1989, 128–36), and the four epigrams inscribed on one of the Memnon Colossi in Egyptian Thebes attributed to a poetess Julia Balbilla under Hadrian (see now Emily A. Hemelrijk, *Matrona Docta: Educated Women in the Roman Élite from Cornelia to Julia Domna*, London 1999, 164–70).

Further, when it came to 'real' power, as defined in my quotation of S. Dixon (pp. 2–3), and in reference to the exceptional period of the Early Empire, I should have put forward the example of Calvia Crispinilla – if for no other reason than that she was not even a member of the ruling family. Of high rank, nevertheless, she became a kind of chamberlain in Nero's palace, taking care of Sporus (named commonly "Sabina") the boy-mistress of the Emperor. Practising systematic extortion, Crispinilla grew vastly rich – enough to be able to set off from Italy after Nero's death. On a daring adventure in Africa she managed to rouse the legionary commander to revolt, in an attempt to bring famine on the Roman people! Despite her treason against the state, she succeeded in remaining unpunished in Rome by manipulating a former consul into marrying her, and by convincing the then emperor (probably Otho) to defend her against loud clamour. Making heavy use of her economic power (and conceivably mind and body), she went on instead to extend her influence throughout the capital. Crispinilla remained prominent for a long time (Tac., *Hist.* 1. 73; Dio 62.12.3–4). 'Real' power was also enjoyed by the women of Roman governors posted abroad, an issue debated in the senate where note was taken of their ordering people about, their engaging in intrigues, and of their practising extortion (Tac., *Ann.* 3.33.3f.). A lengthy study of such women was published by Mika Kajava ("Roman Senatorial Women and the Greek East: Epigraphical Evidence from the Republican and Augustan Period", in H. Solin & M. Kajava [eds], *Roman Eastern Policy and Other Studies in Roman History*, Helsinki 1990, 59–124).

The amount of research in recent years that has gone into the subject of women in general has been phenomenal. All periods of history have now been covered over an extensive geographical area. There is space here to note only a few books broadly pertinent to our subject. Collections of papers worth mentioning are *Women in the Classical World* (ed. by E. Fantham *et al.*, Oxford 1994), *Women in Antiquity: New Assessments* (ed. by R. Hawley & B. Levick, London 1995), and *Grenzen der Macht: Zur Rolle der roemischen Kaiserfrauen* (ed. By C. Kunst & U. Riemer, Stuttgart 2000). A recent exhibition in the British Museum has produced a lavish volume on *Cleopatra of Egypt from History to Myth* (ed. by S. Walker & P. Higgs, London 2001). Roman women, and especially those of the Julio-Claudian period, have been looked at more thoroughly than ever before – collectively in books such as Richard Bauman's *Women and Politics in Ancient Rome* (London 1992) and Susan Wood's *Imperial Women* (*op. cit.*), or individually such as Werner Eck's *Agrippina* (Cologne 1993), Anthony Barrett's *Agrippina* (*op. cit.*) and Claudia-Martina Perkounig's *Livia Drusilla-Iulia Augusta: Das politische Porträt der ersten Kaiserin Roms* (Vienna 1995). Other monographs of individual matrons, focussing on iconography, will be mentioned later. Beyond Rome in the north, a new edition appeared of Graham Webster's *Boudicca* (London 1999), whereas a part of the Near East has been covered more generally by Tal Ilan's *Jewish Women in Graeco-Roman Palestine* (Tübingen 1995). From a later context I should at least refer to Richard Stoneman's *Palmyra and its Empire: Zenobia's Revolt Against Rome* (Ann Arbor, MI, 1992), to Jan Drijvers' *Helena Augusta* (Leiden 1992), and to Maria Dzielska's *Hypatia of Alexandria* (Cambridge, MA, 1995).

REVIEW CHAPTER

LITERARY SOURCES

When *Antonia* was first published, it seemed as if the chapter examining her history had exhausted all the literary sources which bore any relevance. Yet a few more references could have been utilised had I noticed them a little sooner. First Ovid. In one of his poems sent from Tomis, his place of exile on the Black Sea, dated during the time of Tiberius' operation against the Germans after Varus' defeat in AD 9, Ovid praised the members of the 'Augustan House' (*Domus Augusta*, as expressed for the first time in history). I now realise that he must be hinting at Antonia (*Tristia* 4.2.11–14):

Livia too with her good *daughters-in-law* may be making for her
son's safety
the offerings she will always make to the well-deserving gods;
likewise the matrons and the chaste ones
who preserve the sacred hearths with their perpetual virginity...

First among the "good" (*bonis*) "daughters-in-law" (*nuribus*) of Livia was of course Antonia (p. 16) as the poet imagines her to be – although this unfortunately has not been appreciated (see inconsistencies between the translator of the Loeb edition and more recent examinations of the passage such as in Nicholas Purcell, "Livia and the Womanhood of Rome", *PCPhilS* 212 [1986], 84, Fergus Millar, "Ovid and the 'Domus Augusta': Rome Seen from Tomoi", *JRS* 83 [1993], 12–13, and Marleen Flory, "The Meaning of 'Augusta' in the Julio-Claudian Period" *AJAH* 13 [1997], 115–6). But who was Livia's other daughter-in-law? This can also be deduced. Apart from Livia's son, Drusus the Elder, who provided Livia and Augustus with a 'daughter-in-law' in the person of Antonia (and excluding Tiberius' married life as not relevant at this period), another 'daughter-in-law' was provided by one of their grandsons and adopted sons, Gaius Caesar. The unlucky young man had been married to Antonia's daughter Livilla (see pp. 13 and 191, note 24, where the reference Tac., *Ann.* 40.4.4 is missing). Her subsequent second marriage to Drusus the Younger (Tiberius' son) further made her a 'granddaughter-in-law' of Livia and Augustus. Therefore, Ovid's use of the plural makes good sense: Antonia and her daughter Livilla were both Livia's daughters-in-law as well as living together in the same house on the

251

Palatine (see p. 148). Ovid's past experience, when in Rome, of what Livia was doing in circumstances similar to the one described, for example during a previous celebration of Tiberius' victory against the Dalmatians and Pannonians in 9 BC (Dio 55.2.4), would have fed his imagination. The presence of Antonia at Livia's side in c. AD 10–12 during public ceremonies and private functions cannot be disputed. I have already suggested that Antonia should have participated in the rededication in the name of Tiberius and his brother Drusus the Elder of the Temple of Concord in AD 10 (p. 192, note 34). But as it happened the occasion expected by Ovid in connection to Germany at this time did not take place.

Unfortunately, in note 24 (mentioned above) further mistakes crept in. Another reference concerning the marriageable age was dropped: Dio 54.16.7. This is important for giving "twelve years in full" as the acceptable minimum. Livilla's wedding to Gaius, which must have taken place in c. 2 BC (wrongly given as "1 BC" on p. 13, following the arbitrary marginal note of Loeb's edition, and also wrongly as Dio "65.10.18" in note 24, and parallel note 47, which should be 55.10.18), means that she would not have been born later than 13 BC in inclusive reckoning. In fact even the end of 14 BC may be an appropriate time for her birth to be accommodated. This now dictates that Livilla must have been too young to be carried in the tiring procession of the Ara Pacis on 4 July 13 BC, where Germanicus is the only child of Antonia shown (pp. 115 and 202, note 16). Incidentally, Antonia is also not shown pregnant (see new photos in Diane Atnally Conlin, "The Reconstruction of Antonia Minor on the Ara Pacis", *JRA* 5 [1992], 209–15). Livilla, an inadequately studied member of the family, has not attracted attention in the literature, even though an interesting article on her must be mentioned by Patrick Sinclair ("Tacitus' Presentation of Livia Julia, Wife of Tiberius' son Drusus", *AJP* 111 [1990], 238–56).

From slightly later (apparently before the Illyrian triumph was celebrated by Tiberius on 23 October AD 12), when Ovid was becoming desperate for support from the capital, comes his letter to his friend Messalinus in which I also now discover another hint at Antonia (*Ex Ponto* 2.2.69–74):

The time is right for prayers. He [Augustus] is flourishing, and sees

that your strength, Rome, that he built up himself, is flourishing
too.
A wife [Livia] in good health guards her couch;
his son [adopted Tiberius] pushes forward the western front.
Germanicus is older than his years in spirit [twenty-six years
old];
the vigour of Drusus [Tiberius' son] matches his nobility.
Add a pious *daughter-in-law* and granddaughter, and grandsons
with sons,
and that all the members of the Augustan house are in good
health.

Ovid here was pointing out to Messalinus that Augustus' household was going through happy times and therefore it was appropriate to make petitions – such as for a grant which could terminate his exile. The "pious" (*pia*) "daughter-in-law" (*nurum*) must
of course be Antonia already famous for her piety (unfortunately
misunderstood also in another article of Flory, "Dynastic Ideology,
the 'Domus Augusta', and Imperial Women: A lost Statuary Group
in the Circus Flaminius", *TAPA* 126 [1996], 294). We have seen
Antonia as Pietas on coins (pp. 95–6), as well as the "worthy"
(*digna*) "daughter-in-law" (*nurus*) of Livia in the *Consolatio* sometimes attributed precisely to Ovid (p. 150). But who is the "granddaughter"? Following on from the *Tristia* discussion above she
should again be Livilla – meant as granddaughter[-in-law] in this
poem (the pairing of the two will be seen later also in the new epigraphical evidence). However, this time I must not be too confi-
dent. Augustus had an actual granddaughter in the person of
Agrippina, the daughter of Julia the Elder. (His other granddaughter Julia the Younger was now in exile.) It is therefore possible that
Antonia and Agrippina, rather than Livilla, are referred to by Ovid
in the celebration which, unlike that in *Tristia*, was soon to take
place indeed.

In the more than 25 years between the death of Antonia's husband Drusus (9 BC) and that of her son Germanicus (AD 19),
when our literary sources dry up completely in regard to her
actions, I have speculated that she would have observed several
important events relating to her family (pp. 16 and 192, note 35).
The occasion alluded to by Ovid in which she must have participated has now been added. Another event which would have

affected her in this period is the revision of the *Lex Voconia* in AD 9. According to this law no woman could inherit property to the value of more than 100,000 sesterces, but Augustus decided to permit some matrons to do precisely that (Dio 56.10.2). It is certain that the first two ladies among them, who were closest to the Emperor, that is Livia and Antonia Minor, would have benefitted. This must have assisted immensely the private economy of Antonia, who was already a 'free agent' (p. 192, note 34) and who was to inherit later, among other wealth, that of the Herodian princess Berenice I. But the timing was perfect also for Livia who was to receive in c. AD 10 (almost immediately after the revision of *Lex Voconia*) a substantial inheritance upon the death of Berenice's mother Salome I, sister of Herod the Great (pp. 72 and 198, note 12; see now also my *Herodian Dynasty*, 190–2).

The documentation I have provided has shown that several doctors looked after Antonia on her 'off days' (pp. 33, 61). From the literary sources we even know of two remedies she tried – an eye ointment referred to by Galen, and a salve by Scribunius Largus. But there is yet another medicine connected to Antonia which I missed. A little-used source, *De Medicamentis* by one Marcellus Empiricus from Bordeaux, dated around AD 400, contains more than 2500 prescriptions, one of which (35.9) evidently remained well-known for a long time as having been used repeatedly by both Livia and Antonia (*Acopum, quo fere semper Liuia Augusta et Antonia usae sunt*). With ingredients no less unusual than those of Galen, it is a long recipe which is supposed to have worked against chills, arthritis, and all kinds of nervous pain. We cannot be sure for which of the symptoms Antonia found it soothing, but the basic authenticity of the text may not be doubted. There does not seem to be enough reason to assume that this or the other medicines attributed to imperial women are all fabrications belonging to a hostile tradition which aimed at presenting the matrons as creators of weird potions with which they harmed the male members of their families (cf. N. Purcell *op. cit.*, 95). Even if some women did get involved in actual poisoning, they would have done this through the expertise of the same employees who were supplying them with 'beneficial' ointments and salves. In any case the remedies to which Antonia's name was attached, were all said to have been *used* by her, and there is no known slur on record that she ever attempted to poison anyone (unlike some other matrons).

Of the Roman writers who did not come to be registered in my notes of the chapter on Antonia's history, I regret only one: Velleius Paterculus. Though he does not refer to Antonia directly (thus his absence), he should have been referred to at least in relation to Drusus the Elder. Velleius 2.95 is supporting evidence in note 19 attesting to his campaign against the Raetians in 15 BC, and Velleius 2.97 supports note 12 in regard to Drusus' career as well as note 28 about his death. The cause of death is given quite unspecifically as "unkind fate" (*fatorum iniquitas*), in contrast to "a riding accident", "a disease" or "poisoning" mentioned in the note. Of sources in note 9, showing that Antonia's mother Octavia had provided high quality education for her children, I have given only Strabo who says that a philosopher Nestor was teacher to her son Marcellus. A supporting source may be Suetonius (*Gram.* 18) who reveals that a grammarian Lucius Crassicius had tutored Iullus Antonius, the son of Antony and Fulvia, who was also raised by Octavia.

Finally, the ambiguous passage in Suetonius' *Life of Claudius* 11.2 needs further comment (p. 93). Upon becoming Emperor in AD 41, Claudius showered with honours first his grandmother (*avia*) Livia, and then his father Drusus and his mother Antonia – *matri... et cognomen Augustae ab viva recusatum.* That is to say, on his mother he conferred the surname *Augusta* "which she had declined during her lifetime". I have omitted to note that the crucial word *viva* in the text is an emendation by Lipsius, but one which is universally accepted. Suetonius could not have written what we find in the existing codices *ab avia recusatum* ("which had been declined by his grandmother"), for Claudius' grandmother never refused her title and she had already been dealt with earlier in his text. So given the necessity of this emendation, what does the passage again tell us? I have used it to raise the following question: is it possible that Antonia had declined the title of *Augusta* under Tiberius, who would have offered it to her after AD 29 (at Livia's death) or better after AD 31 (at Sejanus' execution)? This would have seemed a natural assumption, had it not been for another passage that complicates the issue. We are also told that Caligula had bestowed on Antonia all honours previously enjoyed by Livia (Suet., *Cal.* 15.2) and "by a single decree of the senate" (*uno senatus consulto*). Now the question becomes one of timing: when exactly was Caligula's decree voted upon and when did Antonia die? Tiberius' funeral took place in Rome on 3 April AD 37, after which we are told Caligula went straight to the islands near Campania to retrieve the ashes of his mother and brother (see pp. 36–7). Any imperial decisions, following his proclamation, would have waited his return, hardly earlier than the middle of the month under adverse weather conditions. Antonia commited suicide on 1 May. She thus lived under her grandson's direct command effectively only for about two weeks at the end of April. In this short period everything must have happened: the voting of the decree appointing her Augusta, her offer of advice to the Emperor who replied by threatening her life (Suet., *Cal.* 29.1), and her subsequent decision to put an end to it. Meanwhile, her title had already appeared inscribed in Latin (*not* Greek, reflecting the Roman colony) on an inscription found in Corinth (pp. 46–7). It is to be wondered whether she had the time or indeed the choice to refuse to be called *Augusta*. And could her refusal in the days she remained alive under Caligula have lasted long enough for it to become as recognised a fact as that provided by Suetonius? Could two weeks be implied in the phrase "during her lifetime" rather than a much longer period? Would not Suetonius have specified "just before she died" instead of "during her lifetime"? In conclusion, I still regard it as possible that Caligula was forcing on Antonia a title which she had already declined earlier in her life. It may even be significant that her wishes this time were not respected.

Alhough, of course, ambiguity will remain, based on the literary evidence alone, I have offered my interpretation of the Salus coin supporting the suggestion that Antonia may have been granted the rank of Augusta by Tiberius (pp. 91–93). Flory (*op. cit.*, 123, 136 note 38) says that I have provided "no documentation", presumably herself unwilling to enter into a discussion of my numismatic interpretation. Her view has been echoed in other recent works, such as in the important book by Hemelrijk (*op. cit.*, 296, note 61). Flory points out that Antonia appears without a title in the *Fasti Ostienses* recording her death on 1 May (see A.11), and that this confirms Antonia's refusal to accept it at this time. But the death, by definition, had to be recorded posthumously (even if only by a day), so any wish she might have had would currently not matter. We saw that the title appeared in Latin at Corinth in April when Antonia was still alive, and soon on Latin coins from the same colony (see F.6), as well as later in Rome in the *Acta Arvalium* in

connection with her birthday on 31 January AD 38 (see A.13).
Thus no confirmation of the type sought by Flory can be found,
and in any case it does not follow that the absence of the title
would confirm Antonia's refusal as being a 'recent' one. The
refusal may have been known and respected for a long time. On
the contrary, the records in Ostia may suggest that the town was
informed faster about Antonia's death than about Caligula's decree
– in which case what was being respected was precisely her 'old'
wish not to be called *Augusta*. And if one were to argue here that
perhaps the decree, after all, was just a posthumous one (though
unlikely in view of Antonia's manner of death and Caligula's indifference towards her funeral, see p. 28), this would actually prove
that Suetonius' "during her lifetime" cannot refer to this decree but
to one under Tiberius! But multiple hypotheses aside, what is more
important to remember is that in Tacitus' *Annals* we lack both,
almost the entire narrative of AD 29–31, and almost the entire narrative of AD 37–47. My suggestion dismissed, we will have to continue believing that, despite the existence of a perfect candidate and
for some unexplained reason, the established position of Augusta
was allowed to remain vacant in the crucial period between AD 29
and 37.

EPIGRAPHY

By far the most important discovery of the last decade in the area
of Roman inscriptional evidence has been the decree on Gnaeus
Calpurnius Piso – the complete text of the decision of the Senate in
the trial of the Governor of Syria who was held responsible for the
death of Germanicus in AD 19 (W. Eck, A. Caballos & F.
Fernández, *Das senatus Consultum de Cn. Pisone Patre*, Munich
1996). Six (or perhaps seven) copies of the decree – one practically complete at 176 lines – inscribed on bronze (like the *Tabula
Siarensis*, p. 38) were found in the late 1980s near the Spanish city
of Seville in the Roman province of Baetica. The central question
as to whether Piso was charged with murder remains unclear,
though it is thought that it was subsumed under the political
charge of treason (*maiestas*) by which Piso was condemned (he had
abandoned his province and then tried to retake it by force). This
would not contradict Tacitus, who claims that the charge of murder could not be proved in the trial (*Ann.* 3.14. 1), but the decree,
nevertheless, does record the fact that Germanicus "himself bore

witness that Piso was the cause of his death" (line 28).

This raises questions for which there is yet no answer. How exactly was the opinion of Germanicus, the Emperor's adopted son, evaluated by the Senate if it was not necessary for Piso to be charged with murder in view of the overriding charge of treason? If the evaluation itself was superfluous under the circumstances why was it mentioned at all?

In any case, as I would have expected, this precious document (despite discouragement from Tacitus) does indeed mention Antonia, as well as her daughter Livilla, and in a way which confirms several points claimed in this book:

> And further the Senate expresses its great admiration of Antonia, the mother of Germanicus Caesar, whose only marriage was to Drusus the father of Germ(anicus), and who, through the excellence of her moral character, proved herself to the divine Augustus worthy of so close a relationship. And of Livia the sister of Germ(anicus) Caesar whom her grandmother and her father-in-law, who is also her uncle, our Princeps, hold in the highest esteem – whose esteem, even if she did not belong to their family, she could deservedly vaunt and can do so all the more as she is a lady attached by such family ties: the senate greatly admires these ladies in equal measure for their most loyal grief and their moderation in that grief.
> (Lines 139–142; translated by Miriam Griffin in "The Senate's Story", *JRS* 87 [1997], 253).

The admiration of the Senate for Antonia, notwithstanding formalities, is now, as a result of my suggestions, not a surprise. Her "single marriage" (*unum matrimonium*) and her "moral character" or "moral principles" (*sanctitas morum* – literally "the integrity" or "the sacredness of her morals") are stressed, proving that I was not over-enthusiastic in emphasising them before the publication of this document (pp. 15–6 etc.). Antonia's morals were, indeed, highly esteemed in Rome and throughout the Empire. As I had already concluded, Antonia "dared, in an affluent and corrupt society, to become a *univira*!" (p. 163). This was something extraordinary and precisely so noted, despite Tacitus. Her moral principles, in the understanding of the Senate, reflected directly on her relationship to "the divine Augustus", which is close enough to my translation of the difficult Greek text from Ilium (pp. 43–5, 196, note 29; not improved upon by Ulrike Hahn, *Die Frauen des römischen Kaiserhauses und ihre Ehrungen im Griechischen Osten anhand epigraphischer und numismatischer Zeugnisse von Livia bis Sabina*, Saarbrücken 1994, 119–20). The meaning there, in my opinion, has to do with Antonia's "abundant and greatest principles" (*pleistas kai megistas archas*) as reflected on "the most divine family" (*tou theiotatou genous*). Worthy Antonia became the source of providing (*paraschousan*) the integral morals of the family of Augustus. To have gone a step further, which could never be spelled out clearly at Ilium or anywhere, would have been to say that it was she who had provided the Domus Augusta with most morals! Would there have been any great morality displayed by the Julio-Claudian family were it not for Antonia? The prominent citizen who commissioned the text at Ilium, as much as the members of the Senate who issued the decree at Rome, must have known that their message was easily understood.

The appearance of Livilla (called Livia) together with her mother in the decree on Piso, is again unsurprising from the perspective of this book. Tiberius, the Princeps, is Livilla's uncle (*patruus*), being the brother of her father Drusus the Elder. He is also her father-in-law (*socer*), as father of her husband Drusus the Younger. Livilla has now changed from being Augustus' "daughter-in-law" to being Tiberius' "daughter-in-law" – remembering Ovid's poetry. It is also significant that it was "the most loyal grief" (*dolorem fidelissumum*) of both ladies, mother and daughter, towards the departed that was singled out and registered by the Senate. Could Tacitus have been reading the same document (pp. 23–4)? Following him we should believe that Antonia and Livilla hid themselves away, shedding not a single tear seen by anyone in Rome, and failed to participate in any of the funeral ceremonies! Their son and brother Germanicus meant little to them according to Tacitus, or at least to the plot he is trying to make up.

As I have mentioned earlier the dating in this decree has been anticipated here (p. 38). The editors (Eck *et al.*, *op. cit.*) do not acknowledge my observation, although they do refer laconically to *Antonia* in a footnote. Their reference diverts the reader to a secondary article by Simonetta Segenni ("Antonia Minore e la 'Domus Augusta'", *Studi Classici e Orientali* 44 (1994), 297–331), which makes extensive use of the material collected here and at least in one article (Kokkinos 1990). But unlike the appreciative tone and good use of *Antonia* made for example by Wood (*op. cit.*) and by Hemelrijk (op. cit.), all Segenni had to say was: "Il lavoro più recente... che raccoglie la documentazione... ma dal quale dissento in più punti nell' interpretazione" (p. 298, note 3). She is, of course, entitled to her own interpretations. But more irritatingly than the editors of the decree on Piso, the editors of the survey of Romans inscriptions 1991–95 (in *JRS* 87 [1997], 213, n. 92) prefer to refer to Segenni for "a discussion of the estates of Antonia Minor, esp. in Egypt". Segenni has almost nothing to say about Antonia's estates in Egypt – all of the papyrological work is to be found here (pp. 68–86 and C–D). Nevertheless, the latter editors felt obliged to mention my publication elsewhere (p. 220, note 168), irrelevant to Antonia, of the Greek inscriptions from Mount Hermon (*PEQ* 124 [1992], 9–25), for which I should thank them.

As *Antonia* was being published in England, another interesting text relating to her was appearing in print in Italy (Géza Alföldy, "Un dono delle due Antonie nel Forum Augustum", in *Studi sull' Epigrafia Augustea e Tiberiana di Roma*, Rome 1992, 35–38, pl. VI, nos. 22–3). From past excavations in the Forum of Augustus, a fragmentary inscription (in two pieces) had come to light that remained until now unedited. It reads: [...]*o Duarum [A]ntoniaru[m]*. This is undoubtedly the two young Antonias, as we have seen in what I called "a unique document" (though it is not any longer) bearing on the history of Antonia. Among the 'indirect' inscriptions (pp. 53–5), one referred to "the Basilica of the Two Antonias" (*Basilica Antoniarum Duarum*). I have suggested looking for this building in the vicinity of the Circus Flaminius, and there is no reason to change my mind (despite my learning since of an older suggestion by R. E. A. Palmer, "Roman Shrines of Female Chastity from the Caste Struggle to the Papacy of Innocent I", *Rivista Storica dell' Antichita* 4 [1974], 139). The Basilica would have been dedicated to the girls, probably by Octavia their mother, who had also built a library to her son Marcellus. The recording of the names in the new text serves a different purpose, although again connected to a building programme.

Alföldy suggests that the sisters themselves have contributed in some way to the embellishment of the Temple of Mars the Avenger (*Ultor*). This is possible, but in my opinion only if the contribution was made at an earlier occasion than the actual inauguration of the

Temple in 2 BC. We know that the building remained incomplete for many years. I am saying this because the formula "Antoniarum Duarum", in the context of Antonia's history as we now know it, seems to presuppose a time when Antonia Minor and Major were young and still living together. There is no evidence that after Antonia's marriage to Drusus in c. 18 BC the sisters kept a very close relationship or common goals, and the formula itself is unknown in texts thereafter. If this does not satisfy Alföldy, then we should be looking for an edifice in the Forum of Augustus other than the Temple of Mars, such as the porticoes. It is interesting that later, in AD 19, an arch was dedicated by the side of this temple when the news arrived that Antonia's son Germanicus had appointed Zeno to the throne of Armenia (p. 39). But the discovery is significant whatever the location. If Alföldy is right that this is not another dedication to the Antonias by a third person, here we have two women being involved in a building project. This would naturally follow the established tradition of their great mother Octavia. Moreover, such women who were largely disregarded before the publication of *Antonia*, are now seen to have been parading as active public benefactors and, significantly, to have been thought worthy of such a parade.

The continuing work at the wonderful site of Messene, in the southwest of the Peloponnese, has produced more fragments (now put together with those found previously) of a local decree inscribed on a monumental stele (P. Themeles, "Anaskaphê Messênês", *Praktika* 1990 [1993], 87–91 = *SEG* 41 1991 [1994], no. 328). Originally connected to the city's Sebasteion, the text acknowledges the death of Augustus in AD 14 and honours Tiberius the new Emperor. Belonging to a period from which little evidence for Antonia could be gathered, the mention of her in one of the fragments is a very welcome addition. In fact, it is interesting that the only members of the Imperial family referred to in the surviving parts (but evidently in the entire document), apart from the past and present emperors, are Livia, Antonia and Livilla. We have already seen the togetherness of this company recognised in other texts. Also from the Greek world, and slightly later, it is worth noting at least one inscription bearing on Antonia's son Germanicus and the journey of AD 18. Discovered at Perge in Pamphylia, and assumed by its editor to indicate that the city was visited by the imperial group, it has caused a re-assessment of the

Asia Minor route taken during this journey (S. Şahin, "Germanicus in Perge", *Epigraphica Anatolica*, 24 [1995], 28). The new map should be compared with the respective part of the more complete but more tentative one presented here (p. 24, fig. 15).

Two other inscriptions have been thought to refer to Antonia. Her name is restored in a fragment from the theatre of Tyndaris in Sicily, which refers to the mother (*matr[i]*) of an emperor believed to be Claudius (G. Manganaro, "Iscrizioni latine nuove e vecchie della Sicilia", *Epigraphica* 51 [1989], 162, no. 3 = *AE* 1989, 338b). Tyndaris has already appeared in this book as a place from which a possible head of Antonia belonging to the 'youthful and individualised' replica series has come (pp. 111, 168, no. 45). If the restoration of the inscription is sound then there may be reason for it to be re-examined. But its identity may not be ascertained; for, as we shall see below under iconography, recent studies have rejected many portraits of 'Antonia' beginning with this particular series, taking us effectively back to the position of the 1970s. Another inscription, this time in Verona, has been assumed for Antonia. The discovery of a plaque dated to AD 44, belonging to the monumental facade of the city gate, has shown that there must have been a dedication in three parts to the Emperor Claudius, mentioning the members of his family (G. Cavalieri Manasse, "L'imperatore Claudio e Verona", *Epigraphica* 54 [1992], 9–41 = *AE* 1992, no. 739a–c). Celebrating the return of Claudius from Britain, the second part of the text – which has not been retrieved – should have mentioned his mother Antonia. As a comparison, the inscription of Antonia once attached to the Arch of Claudius in Rome, also celebrating the conquest of Britain, may be pointed out (pp. 39–42).

Finally, an important new publication on Roman inscriptions of early imperial dynasties is that of the collection of those from the Mausoleum of Augustus (H. von Henner & S. Panciera, *Das Mausoleum des Augustus: Der Bau und seine Inschriften*, Munich 1994). Having suggested that Caligula may have allowed Antonia's ashes to be deposited in the Mausoleum (p. 28), despite the circumstances of her death, which apparently annoyed him, this volume was of interest to me. Of course I knew that no tombstone of Antonia had been found in this monumental round building, but this does not mean that it did not exist originally. Indeed, Panciera does not list Antonia among the people who had been directly excluded from burial here – a discussion on her is included under the heading of the 'Possibili' (84–87). In fact, even if Caligula was too upset to give permission for her inclusion in the Augustan tomb (which does not make sense in that the honours conferred on her were not revoked), Claudius later would not have hesitated to transfer his mother's remains to the proper place. As we have seen, this is precisely what Caligula had done for his mother Agrippina the Elder. Could Antonia not have been allowed (whether by Caligula, the Senate, or Claudius) to be reunited in the Mausoleum of Augustus with her eternal husband, Drusus, for whom she stayed a *univira* for a lifetime? I think she should have been allowed.

NUMISMATICS

A major publication on coins of the Early Empire has been the first volume (in two parts) of *Roman Provincial Coinage: From the Death of Caesar to the Death of Vitellius, 44 BC–AD 69*, vol. 1 (ed. by A. Burnett, M. Amandry & P. Pau Ripollès, London and Paris 1992). Concerning Antonia, no provincial city has appeared in this volume which I have not managed to record (having also had the benefit of the work of Trillmich 1978). On the contrary, I have listed at least one coin, that from Aezanis (pp. 104, 201, note 49), which does not seem to be included in *RPC* (see 734, index on Antonia) – probably because it remains unpublished. But *RPC* has detailed descriptions of all variations, 26 in total, against the "main" 11 provincial types listed here for Antonia (p. 97 & F). Among them a puzzling issue from Thessalonica, in three variations, presents new evidence that will be discussed below. Further, while *RPC* includes (with a question mark) the coin minted under Caligula at Carthago Nova with *Sal(us) Aug(usta)* as referring to Antonia, being co-written by Burnett for obvious reasons it excludes the Panias one (because he does not believe it belongs to Antonia). These two coins will also be discussed below.

First the issue from Thessalonica. In his corpus of this city's coinage, Ioannis Touratsoglou listed three small examples of leaded bronze and of a copper-based alloy carrying the effigy of Antonia (*Die Münzstätte von Thessaloniki in der römischen Kaiserzeit*, Berlin 1988, nos. 47–9). That it is Antonia depicted is certain, if only because the reverses show the same motifs of the Nike/Victory and of the Horse known from the other

Thessalonican coins clearly attributed to her (see here p. 98; cf. *RPC* 1, nos. 1581–7). The mystery is that the Greek legend now reads *Markia*. No explanation for this name is available, other than the fact that Antonia was Mark Antony's daughter. What makes it more peculiar is that the coins according to Touratsoglou date to AD 41/42 under Claudius. The parallel series with the same reverses have the inscription *Antônia*, without any title, which is partly the reason why I have placed them (with a question mark) under Tiberius in the period AD 32–37. They now have to be reckoned as Claudian too following Touratsoglou. In the epigraphical record we have seen Antonia being called *M(arci) F(ilia)*, "daughter of Marcus", only once at Ulia in Spain as early as 12 BC, and perhaps at Cemenelum in Alpes Maritimae under Tiberius (p. 35 & A.1, 3). We have also seen that an 'improbable' papyrus from Egypt mentioning an Antonia *thygatêr*, "daughter", would better suit the daughter of Claudius (p. 86 & D.1). So it is unusual for Antonia to be called daughter of Mark Antony after her marriage, let alone at the time of Claudius, or as *Markia*.

The solution to this problem may lie elsewhere. The cutting of this die must anyway have been an *ad hoc* decision by the minting authorities at Thessalonica, but one which reflected what may be thought of as Antonia's *praenomen* – her full name after her father being "Marcia Antonia". Some issues, then, carried *Markia* and some *Antônia*. Be that as it may, the chronology of these coins needs re-assessment in the future. The omission of her main title of 'Augusta' under Claudius is an extremely rare phenomenon – in fact, there is only a single example, which can be explained away. The Claudian coin from Crete has a plain *Antônia* (F.12), but it is easy to understand the reason. She is depicted face-to-face with Drusus, and his legend could not carry such a title under the circumstances. It must have seemed proper to drop hers. At all events, Thessalonica now holds the record for striking the most coins for Antonia (10 types, as against 6 known from Alexandria, which is second among ten or a few more provincial cities in my count). Yet why? Presumably Antonia never visited Thessalonica. Was Antony still so famous in Macedonia? Or were there local dignitaries who had extensive dealings with Antonia in Rome, and who subsequently influenced the city's mint? The lady's connection with the motifs chosen for the coins (p. 98), particularly the 'Victory on Globe', cannot fail to remind us again of the 'Augusta who saved the whole world' (p. 42). Whether dated under Tiberius after AD 32 or as late as the accession of Claudius in AD 41/42, if this victory does not celebrate the one Antonia won over Sejanus, which does it celebrate?

The subject of this victory brings me to the decision of the *RPC* editors to mention the Carthago Nova coin of AD 37 as possibly (even if uncertainly) representing Antonia, which is encouraging in view of my suggestion that Antonia personified Salus also on the notorious coin from Rome (pp. 90–4). The Spanish coin is further taken as representing Antonia by Tomasz Mikocki (*Sub Specie Deae*, Rome 1995, 33) though he allows that the portrait may have changed soon to that of Caesonia – an old theory that has never seemed possible since Caligula married Caesonia only at the end of AD 39 (Dio 59.23.7; and see worse below). But once we accept that, at least in Spain under Caligula, Antonia could be equated to Salus we come close to recognising the possibility that she could also have done so in Rome. My suggestion has been rather ignored by those working in iconography, evidently because it spoils conventional classifications (see for example Rolf Winkes, *Livia, Octavia, Iulia: Porträts und Darstellung*, Providence, R.I 1995; and generally Lorenz Winkler, *Salus vom Staatskult zur politischen Idee*, Heidelberg 1995). Yet, as I have noted, some distinguished numismatists, such as H. Mattingly, E. A. Sydenham and M. Grant, allowed the Roman dupondii to be struck for many years without changing their date of AD 22/23 (referring to the decree of the Senate in this year). I have suggested that the example inscribed with 'Salus Augusta' may have been struck in AD 31/32 as a result of the fall of Sejanus, and would therefore have celebrated Antonia's bringing of 'Safety' and 'Salvation' to Rome. This evidently links well with the discussion of the title *Augusta* above, as well as the coins from Thessalonica.

Despite the caution I have expressed concerning the coin from Panias, support for Andrew Burnett's theory of '[*Caes*]*onia*' has continued unabated (pp. 101–3). For example, C. B. Rose (*Dynastic Commemoration and Imperial Portraiture in the Julio-Claudian Period*, Cambridge 1997, 235–6, note 105) says that: "Meshorer… and Kokkinos… have argued that the obverse represents Antonia II. Meshorer's reading has not been accepted by the editors of *RPC* and it is difficult to reconcile an Antonia identification with the legend." Then, using my observation, made in fairness in support of Burnett, he continues: "The word 'Sebastos' alone refers to the reigning emperor, and because the coin is securely dated to AD 41, it must represent Caesonia". Unfortunately, things are not as clear as Rose perceives them to be, and Burnett's theory has real problems. First, it must be recognised that we are dealing with a restoration. Second, the coin actually dates between October AD 40 and September AD 41 (Agrippa I's 'Year 5'), and since Caligula died on 24 January AD 41, it must have been struck by the end of AD 40. Third, although Caesonia had been acknowledged as Caligula's wife at the beginning of AD 40 when his daughter was born (Dio 59. 23. 7, 28.7; Suet., *Cal.* 25.3), we are told that he had forbidden the awarding of distinctions to the people close to him (Dio 59.22.9). Fourth, Caesonia would almost certainly not be the woman depicted on the obverse of the Panias coin, for she is totally unknown in art and coinage. Fifth, Caligula's daughter cannot be the woman depicted on the reverse, because Drusilla was killed as a baby, her brains dashed out against a wall (Suet., *Cal.* 59; Dio 59.29.7).

On the other hand, the theory that the coin reads '[*Ant*]*onia*' has much in its favour – so I can afford to ignore the evidence of a copy which had been reported to me (p. 102) with the reading: [...]*tonia*, for this may only be evaluated when it is published. Antonia is, of course, well-known in art and coinage. Agrippa I had many reasons to commemorate her, as she had been like a 'second mother' to him. The selection of depictions on the Panias coin makes very good sense: Caligula's 'beloved' grandmother (Antonia) and 'beloved' sister (Drusilla), both now *dead*, are each connected here to his 'beloved', *dead* ancestors – the wife (*gynê*) of his famous grandfather (Drusus), and the daughter (*thygatêr*) of his famous father (Germanicus). In this way all the dead members of Caligula's family were honoured, while each male was embellished with a title (*Sebastos*) which he did not have but he deserved nevertheless. The only apparent problem with this theory is the presence of this title: Drusus the Elder and Germanicus were both officially only 'sons' of *Augusti*. But I have explained the difference of the title's use in East and West, and proof has been attested (p. 201, note 46). Besides, we must be realistic: would Caligula, who craved for honours and regarded himself a god, have demured had he learnt that his father and grandfather were coined as 'Sebastoi' in Syria? Can we forget that Caligula was actually awarding superior titles to himself, such as *Optimus Maximus Caesar*, and that he was pleased to be hailed even as 'Jupiter Latiaris' (Suet., *Cal*. 22. 1– 2)?

ICONOGRAPHY

The area of iconography for Antonia continues to be by far the most productive (p. xv). New attempts at classification have gone hand in hand with the publication of new portraits. Since the appearance of *Antonia* enormous strides have been taken towards understanding many details relating to her presentation in sculpture, often using the book as a launching-pad. This means that the chapter "Antonia and Sculpture" could, in theory, be extensively revised. However, directions followed by the experts have varied, and, since it now seems that there will never be a consensus on the identification of all the portraits concerned, there seems no reason to argue for or against any particular piece, or even revise or update my lists. Some of Antonia's portaits still look certain, but beyond them lies a world of hypotheses. Despite confidence on 'secure' effigies, the problem continues to be the lack of a clear example (excluding coins) of the Roman lady directly accompanied by an original inscription identifying her.

While I have been satisfied with much of the progress done recently in this area of research, I remain sceptical about certain theories as well as some of the 'new' directions followed. A major change that needs to be adressed here, affecting a whole part of my chapter, is the currect rejection of the entire replica series classified as 'youthful and individualised' (pp. 109–13). This move, seemingly supported by most experts, is not new – it goes back to the work of Karin Polaschek (1973). Although I could see that physiognomy (or in this case physiognometry) presented an apparent problem for the attribution of this series to Antonia, I have decided to support it for various reasons, not least chronology. The people rejecting this series are happy to deprive Antonia of any portraits early in her life, even if we know from inscriptions that they existed! With the important exception of the Ara Pacis, we are now left with only 'mature' effigies. Further, the insistence (for example by Rose, *op. cit.* 69) that Antonia was never seen in public with a row of little curls around her forehead is manifestly misleading. Coins not only in Alexandria but also in Corinth show Antonia with just such curls (F.6, 8). In fact, even some specimens of her famous dupondius from Rome (E.6) have curls high on the forehead (for example one in the collection of the Berlin Museum) – as opposed to the couple of curls between the temple and the ear featured in Polaschek's *Schläfenlöckchentypus*. We seem to forget that the portraits on the coins are in fact inscribed – they do not need to be identified! To attribute the entire 'youthful' series to Antonia's daughter Livilla (as suggested by Polaschek), whose looks would have been similar to her mother's, is to fail to explain how so many portraits survived belonging to a person upon which *damnatio memoriae* was placed early in AD 32 (Tac., *Ann*. 6.2). But even if a later member of the family is chosen for such a sweeping reassignment – for example Julia Livilla, daughter of Germanicus (as suggested by Rose) – new problems are created. The portrait from Lepcis Magna, which hardly dates after AD 24 (and it could belong to an earlier dedication), shows a young lady "in her late teens or early twenties" (p. 110) and probably the latter. Since Julia was born in AD 18 (Tac., *Ann*. 2.54), a Caligulan date must be sought at all costs for the portrait. But this is not possible. Although the inscription at Lepcis refers to later work at the Temple of Augustus and Rome, it talks only about a restoration, not about the addition of portraits or indeed of Julia in particular. Besides, Julia (unlike her sister Drusilla) never became famous enough to deserve such a long replica series. Caligula had not honoured, or even had affection for, this sister (Suet., *Cal*. 24), whom he actually banished – an event mentioned by Dio (59.3.6) under AD 37, but which took place in AD 39 (Dio 59.22. 8). To commemorate Julia individually, instead of Drusilla, at Lepcis at the beginning of Caligula's reign, does not make any sense. Moreover, to reattribute this well-defined series to another lady not yet thought of, one would still need to produce some early portraits for Antonia (and some with curls on the forehead as well). Where are they?

Therefore, it will be best here to record only a few 'possible' portraits, which either I decided not to mention originally or which have been published since, and then to list some new books for further study. The reader may follow the different schools of thought as he or she pleases. A statue retrieved from the theatre of Falerii in Etruria, and now in Berlin, had once been attributed to Antonia (Siri Sande, "Römische Frauenporträts mit Mauerkrone", *Acta ad Archaeologiam et Artium Historiam Pertinentia* 5 [1985], 173–82), but its facial characteristics were not very convincing.

However, because of its approximate date and general style, representing the goddess Fortuna wearing a diadem with the beaded
wool band, this piece may deserve a future re-examination. It clearly compares with the 'Juno Ludovisi' head and its parallels (pp.
121–2; an older article on the Warsaw head [I.9] ought to have
been mentioned – Anna Sadurska, "Un portrait idéalisé d'Antonia
Augusta au Musée National de Varsovie", in C. Kumaniecki [ed.],
Acta Conventus XI 'Eirene', Vratislava 1971, 499–506). The statue from Falerii has recently been compared with the coins of
Antonia, 'under the cloak' of Constantia holding a cornucopia (p.
88), by T. Mikocki (*op. cit.*, pp. 32, 172, no. 147, pl. XI). A head
identified as Antonia from the Forum of Lucus Feroniae in Latium
may also need more attention (A. Sgubini Moretti, "Statue e ritrati
anorari da Lucus Feroniae, *RendPondAcc* 55/6 [1985], 71–109),
as seem to do two heads from Velia in Campania (M. Fabbri & A.
Trotta, *Una scuola-collegio di età augustea: l'Insula II di Velia*,
Rome 1989, p. 84, no. 4 & p. 90, no. 8). The latter, discovered in
the cryptoporticus of a large building, were apparently connected
to a school of medicine or association of doctors – an interesting
combination in view of Antonia's interest in medicine.

The best head of Antonia produced in the last decade has been
a new acquisition by the University of Alberta in Canada, which
initiated an important iconographic study by Alastair M. Small ("A
New Head of Antonia Minor and its Significance", *MdI* 97 [1990],
217–34, pls 60–6). The head falls into the 'plain' type (Polaschek's
schlichter) with the characteristic frontal fillet (see pp. 121–5).
Small compares it carefully with nine other portraits (see here
J.10–12, 14, 17, 19, 21–23), thus recreating a secure (if not identical) replica series. The group is headed by the specimen in the Fogg
Art Museum, one of the finest of all known portraits of Antonia (p.
125, fig. 83). The work of Small has even helped to solve a little
mystery. Since the Alberta example had come from London with
unknown history and provenance, in a letter to Small (20/11/1993)
I suggested the challenging task of learning more about a portrait
– once thought to be of 'Antonia' – missing from London for
almost a century, to see whether the two might be one and the same
(see p. 206, note 26). The information I provided was not specific
enough, but after months of research and travel Small succeeded in
bringing the missing portrait back to light! Ultimately it turned out
not to be Antonia ("Lucien Bonaparte's Excavations at Tusculum

and the History of a Female Portrait Head", in G. R. Tsetskhladze *et al.* [eds], *Periplous: Papers on Classical Art and Archaeology Presented to Sir John Boardman*, London 2000, 291–7).

I have talked about the level of popularity Drusus and Antonia enjoyed west of Italy, through the provinces of the Alps Maritimae to Gallia Narbonesis, in the cases of portraits from Cemenelum and Baeterrae (see pp. 121–4, 168). Since then a cluster of relevant sites has begun to be created in this area, with the publication or re-publication of two more portraits. Both fall into the category of Polaschek's *Schläfenlöckchentypus* (pp. 125–6): one, partly damaged, came from the Chiragan villa in Martres-Tolosane (François Queyrel, "Antonia Minor à Chiragan", *Revue Archéologique de Narbonnaise* 25 [1992], 69–81); the other, very fragmentary, came from the theatre of Vienne (Emmanuelle Rosso, "Un portrait d'Antonia Minor au théâtre antique de Vienne (Isère)", *RA* 2000, 311–25). The example from Vienne wears both the diadem and the beaded headband of the 'Priestess of the Divine Augustus', while it is colossal in size. We are reminded again of the colossal 'Juno-Ludovisi' portrait (pp. 119–20), identified here with Antonia, in disagreement with the opinion of Renate Tölle-Kastenbein ("Juno Ludovisi: Hera oder Antonia Minor", *MdI* (Ath. Abt.) 89 [1974], 241–53, pls. 91–96). Clearly there was an iconographic programme (sponsored by public and private funds) on Antonia west of Italy, now attested in four sites, which must have been connected to the Imperial Cult. Even deeper into France, there may be another site with a possible portrait of Antonia, if the one discovered as early as 1821 in the area of Mont-Auxois coming from ancient Alesia of Gallia Lugdunensis, and now kept in Dijon, has been correctly identified (F. Queyrel, "Une princesse julio-claudienne à Alesia", *Revue Archéologique de l'Est et du Centre-Est* 44 [1993], 411–28).

The number of works that can be consulted on the iconography of Antonia has grown significantly in 1990s. Apart from those already mentioned (particularly Small, Mikocki, Rose and Wood), a brief report on Antonia by Dietrich Boschung ("Die Bildnistypen der iulisch-claudischen Kaiserfamilie: ein kritischer Forschungsbericht", *JRA* 6 [1993], 51–2) provides a summary of the field, while Walter Trillmich's entry in the new *Enciclopedia Dell'Arte Antica* (vol. 1, Rome 1994, 263–5 "Antonia Minore") is a compact and useful guide. But a leading corpus of Antonia's portraits is now given in the substantial article by Susanna Künzl ("Antonia Minor – Porträts und Porträttypen", *Jahrbuch des Römisch-Germanischen Zentralmuseums Mainz* 44 [1997], 441–95, pls. 47–62). This work has made positive use of *Antonia* and presents an array of possibilities regarding iconographic detail, as well as some additional little-known effigies – such as a bronze statue from Herculaneum, a statue from Villa Doria Pamphilj in Rome, and a head from Gortyna on Crete. Finally, works on the iconography of other imperial women, such as Livia and Agrippina the Elder, are in many ways helping our perspective of Antonia – for the first see Winkes (*op. cit.*) and Elizabeth Bartman (*Portraits of Livia,* Cambridge 1999), and for the second see Raffaella Tansini (*I ritratti di Agrippina Maggiore*, Rome 1995). Research on relevant goddesses or divine female representations of state virtues are also becoming useful supplements, for example on Salus by Winkler (*op. cit.*) or Ceres by B. S. Spaeth (*The Roman Goddess Ceres,* Austin, Tx., 1996). It would be nice to see more such goddesses being treated individually and in depth using all available sources (literary, documentary and archaeological) as Antonia has now been suggested to have (or conceivably have) personified many (p. 162): Venus, Vesta, Diana, Ceres, Juno, Salus, Iustitia, Pietas, Constantia, Pax, Cybele, Victoria, and now possibly Fortuna.

In the department of minor arts, in my original research I just missed the opportunity to make use of an important collection of cameos by Wolf-Rüdiger Megow (*Kameen von Augustus bis Alexander Severus*, Berlin 1987). Although he lists 11 items under Antonia (288–91, D.2–12), only three are given as securely identified (D.3–5), two of which are listed here as K.2 (the topaz intaglio from Florence) and L.9 (the chalcedony head showing Antonia as the 'Priestess of the Divine Augustus' now at Malibu). The one I missed (D.4; a lapis lazuli in Cologne) is not provided with a photo by Megow. Of the eight cameos which are presented with a question mark, four (D.9–12; two in Paris, one in Florence and one in Prague) should not be doubted as showing Antonia. Very interestingly, she is crowned in a similar way to the 'Juno Lodovisi' head. In fact, Künzl (*op. cit.* 491–2) was quick to list all of them in her corpus. Another cameo in Megow's collection, strangely listed under Livilla (D.30; a sardonyx in Paris), makes good sense for Antonia, and it had so been identified in the past by Babelon and Chabouillet. The important feature is that she is represented with the wings of the goddess Nikê/Victoria (a point not missed by Mikocki, *op. cit.* 174, pl. 36, no. 160). This commemorated victory, like the coins of Thessalonica, would hardly be any other than that won by Antonia over Sejanus, as we have seen in many contexts throughout this book.

A new discovery that has also come to my attention is a small portrait-head in a green, translucent hardstone, broken off a figurine or bust. Measuring 23 mm in height, this tiny but valuable piece belongs to a private collection and has recently been identified as 'Antonia' in Oxford (Martin Henig & Robert Wilkins, "A New Portrait of Antonia Minor", *Oxford Journal of Archaeology* 15 [1996], 109–11). It has been compared with the chalcedony head at Malibu mentioned above, though it is unveiled and crowned only with an unusually thin diadem. The chalcedony head, by the way, has now been republished by J. Spier (*Ancient Gems and Finger Rings*, Malibu 1992, 156, no. 432). The new green portrait-head has also been compared by one of the two authors with a cornelian cameo in high relief in the Content Family Collection (M. Henig, *The Content Family Collection of Ancient Cameos*, Oxford 1990, 39, no. 65).

Finally, in respect to minor arts and under the various secondary objects discussed at the end of the chapter (pp. 143–5), prominence was given to the discs known as *phalerae* – even if none of the surviving examples depict Antonia. But what was just missed in this discussion was a fundamental study by Dietrich Boschung ("Römische Glasphalerae mit Porträtbüsten", *Bonner Jahrbücher* 187 [1987], 193– 258) which I am glad to note here. As for the silver libation dish (*patera*) from which the small bust, tentatively attributed to Antonia, was broken off, it was said to have come from Boscoreale (p. 143). For more information on this place in connection with the discovery of its famous cups, but also with a broader iconographical perspective, there is now a lengthy study by Ann L. Kuttner (*Dynasty and Empire in the Age of Augustus: The Case of the Boscoreale Cups*, Berkeley, Cal., 1995).

ARCHITECTURE

In marked contrast to the conditions under which one had to work in the mid-1980s when it came to gathering archaeological information related to specific topographical and architectural questions in the city of Rome, life has changed completely from the mid-1990s. The difference is largely due to the appearance of the magisterial publication of the *Lexicon Topographicum Urbis Romae* in five volumes (plus an index volume), edited by Eva Margareta Steinby (Rome 1993–2000). For any individual site or building, information is now available conveying the conclusions of research and excavation in the last 30 years – a very productive period indeed. For example, my discussion of the House of Livia/Antonia (pp. 147–53) can be enriched by reading in *LTUR* (vol. 2, 130–2) the entry of "Domus: Livia" by I. Iacopi. The archaeology of the city has also been the subject of a book which covers a broad range of topics with new topographical maps, edited by Jon Coulson and Hazel Dodge (*Ancient Rome: The Archaeology of the Eternal City*, Oxford 2000). But our visualisation of the Roman capital as a whole is now being transformed by the combination of archaeology and the electronic revolution. In terms of imagining the Augustan Rome in which Antonia lived most of her life, a fresh publication by Diane Favro (*The Urban Image of Augustan Rome*, Cambridge 1996) offers fascinating reading.

For at least two of the areas frequently referred to in *Antonia* I should also note separate studies, even if everything can now be checked in *LTUR*: the Palatine Hill (where Antonia woke up every morning) has seen an interesting book by M. A. Tomei (*Il Palatino*, Rome 1992), while the Campus Martius (where Antonia may have been cremated) has received a professional account by F. Coarelli (*Il Campo Marzio*, Rome 1997). Two of the relevant arches discussed in *Antonia* also happened to have been built in the general area of Campus Martius: the Arch of Claudius on the ancient Via Lata (pp. 39–42), and the Arch of Germanicus which I assumed to have stood by the Porticus Octaviae on the spot shown in a fragment of the Forma Urbis (pp. 39, 54, fig. 34 arrow). The Arch of Claudius has been treated in detail by Anthony Barrett ("Claudius' British Victory Arch in Rome", *Britannia* 22 [1991], 1–19), offering a more plausible reconstruction of the edifice. This article, following a similar understanding of the coin evidence, greatly adds to my brief comments. The Arch of Germanicus indeed is now said to have been relocated in the Circus Flaminius by the Porticus Octaviae (Emilio Rodriguez-Almeida, "Alcuni appunti su due Archi di Roma: L'Arco di Germanico in Circo Flaminio e l'Arco di Gallieno sull'Esquilino", *Bollettino di Archeologia* 9 [1991], 1–4).

A bas-relief uncovered nearby, showing a legionary standard of an eagle surrounded by the city walls and towers, seems to belong precisely to this arch.

CONCLUSION

This review chapter has shown that since the original research on Antonia in the 1980s much new evidence has appeared, particularly in the areas of epigraphy and iconography. The major discovery of the decree of the Senate on Piso, and the inscription mentioning the two Antonias from the Forum of Augustus, came to light almost concurrently with several new portraits of Antonia in sculpture, such as the Alberta head, and in minor arts, such as the Paris cameos. But even in numismatics a welcome addition has been the identification of the coins from Thessalonica mentioning *Markia*. The reassessment of old evidence has also added perspective, as in the identification of Antonia in two poems of Ovid included in the collections of *Tristia* and *Ex Ponto*, besides the uncovering of yet another medical prescription named after her and found in the work of Marcellus Empiricus.

Reflecting on the reviews *Antonia* received, and while accepting some corrections of fact and interpretation, the main criticisms would seem to have been given adequate replies. Suggestions such as Antonia's possible participation in a part of Germanicus' eastern journey in AD 18, her active presence in the deliberations of her son's funeral in AD 19, her political involvement in the uncovering of Sejanus' plot up to AD 31, and her possible refusal of the title 'Augusta' subsequently under Tiberius, can still be defended. If anything, the new evidence has strengthened my overall reconstruction, particularly in showing that Tacitus could err. Antonia's possible journey to the East in AD 18 may not be supported by direct literary evidence, but almost the same is the case with her journey to the West in 10 BC. Had it not been for the indirect information that Claudius was born at Lugdunum on 1 August 10 BC, would one not be in trouble in suggesting that Antonia may have gone to Gaul?

The new evidence also strengthens the picture I have drawn of Antonia's character and status. In the original conclusion, perhaps unwisely, I compared Antonia with Livia in a final attempt to show her importance. Greg Rowe (*op. cit.* 223) remarked that "it is difficult to imagine the scale for such an evaluation, or to see the need for one." As I may have failed to provide clear definitions the point is taken, even if some of my statements seem to have tried to explain what was involved in the evaluation – for example, "Antonia not only equalled Livia in status in the later part of her life, but on many counts (social, political, economic) even surpassed her" (p. 4). Yet, the fact remains that Antonia has hitherto been extremely underrated, for which we should partly blame Tacitus. Even in the case of Ovid, as I have shown, most recent studies would rather not admit that the poet refers to Antonia when using favourable epithets. But thanks to Josephus and to the new inscriptional and archaeological discoveries I may now have succeeded in restoring some overdue respect to this extraordinary Roman lady.

INDEX

This index is primarily one of ancient and modern names of people, buildings and places, with a selection of topics and key Latin and Greek words. The foreword, preface and registers have not been indexed, and the notes only partially. Very repetitive words such as Rome/Roman, Greece/Greek have been excluded. Latin names are listed by the *gentilicium* (family name), except of those people known in familiar forms, such as the Emperors (e.g. Tiberius for Tiberius Claudius Nero, or Caligula for Gaius Julius Caesar). Patronymics of ordinary individuals do not appear separately. Numbers in square brackets indicate implied references.

INDEX

Pausanias 190
Pausilypon 52, 64, 168; *see also*
 aqueduct
Pax *see* personification
Peloponnese 31
Persephone *see* Libera
Persia/Persian 22; *see also* Parthia
personification: of Constancy
 (Constantia) 31, 88, 134, 162;
 of Duty (Pietas) 16, 42, 90–1,
 94–6, 119, 159, 162, 200, *see*
 also altar; of Justice (Iustitia)
 42, 90–1, 94–5, 104, 121, 159,
 162; of Peace (Pax) 104, 136,
 162; of Safety (Salus) 42, 90–3,
 104, 111, 115, 159, 162; *see also*
 Concord; Victoria
Pertinax 199
Petermouthis son of Heracleus
 77–8, 79, 80 (fig. 56)
Petesouchus son of Labatatos 75
Petra 20
Petrie, F. 82
Petronius Honoratus, Marcus
 80–1
phalera 143
Pharos 21
Philadelphia (in Egypt) 73
Philadelphia/Philadelphian (in
 Lydia) 48
Philo 32, 199
Philo son of Apollonius 43, 196
philosophy/philosopher 11, 16,
 26, 33, 199
Philoteris 84
Phoebe 139, 162, 204
Phoenicia/Phoenician 5, 133
Phrygia 52, 104
Pietas *see* personification
Pindarus (doctor) 33, 61, 67; *see*
 also Antonius Pindarus
Piso, Gnaeus 22–3, 96, 128, 159
Plancina 22
Pliny (the elder) 28, 33, 119, 146,
 153
Pliny (the younger) 31, 155, 191
Plutarch 118, 190
poetry/poet/poem 2, 10, 11, 33,
 [52], 191; *see also* epigram

poisoning, K. 15, 22, 26 28
Polaschek, K. 120, 121, 125, 127
Pollius Felix 64
Polydeukia 84
pomerium 96
Pompeii/Pompeiian 47, 72 (fig.
 52), 141, 143, 153, 156 (fig.
 107)
Pompeius Saturninus 191
Pompey 26; *see also* house,
 theatre
Pontus 192
Porta Appia 60 (fig. 38); Latina
 60 (fig. 38); at Lepcis 46 (fig.
 28), 109, 146; Pia 57, 58; of
 temple at Jerusalem (gates) 198
portico 49, 129, 129 (fig. 87),
 130, 133, 146; of Livia [163],
 166; of Octavia 53, 54 (fig. 34),
 163, 166
Postumius, Quintus 53
Postumius Helenus, Gaius 53
Poulsen, V.H. 111, 112, 121, 126
Praeneste 10 (fig. 5)
praetor 13, insignia of 31
Praxiteles 41
prefect 25, 26, 81, 102
priest/priestess 1, 35, 49, 55, 57,
 64, 96, 98, 105, 113, 140, 149,
 161, 197; *see also sodalitas*
princeps/principate 26, 70, 79, 159
proconsul 16, 26, [192]
procurator 32, 64, 70, 73, 154
propaganda 31, 87, 105–6, 115,
 131–2, 140–1, 158
Protos 32, 194, 198
Psenyris 73, 79
Psosneus 75
Ptolemais (in Cyrenaica) 35, 45,
 168
Ptolemais (in Palestine) 194, 198
Ptolemais Nea 73
Ptolemy (son of Juba II) 25
Ptolemy Philadelphos 6, 10
ptotomê 129, [129 (fig. 87)]
Puteoli (Pozzuoli) 64, 116, 144–5,
 153, 155
Pylades 140–1, 143, 162
Pythagoreion 121

287

Pythodoris 11, 192

Qedar, S. 102–3
quaestor 11
quarries at Carrara 120
Quinctilius Varus 68
Quintia 64, 153

Raetia/Raetian 13
Ramesses II 21–2
Ravenna 168; *see also* museum, Ravenna
relief 10 (fig. 5), 12 (figs 6, 7), 13, 39, 62 (fig. 41), 63 (fig. 45), 72 (fig. 51), 111, 129, 129 (fig. 87), 130; *see also* museum, Ravenna
replica series 108, 111f.
restoration series 16, 90, 95
Reynolds, J.M. 49, 201
Rhodes 18
Richmond, O.L. 143
river: Elbe 13; Nile 20, 72 (fig. 52), 74 (fig. 53), 75, 78 (fig. 55), 84, 160; Rhine 13, 39; Scamander 44 (fig. 26); Tiber 27, 155; Yssel 13
rogator 59
Rolfe, J.C. 194
Romania 98
Rostovtzeff, M. 73
rostra 18 (fig. 11), 147
Rumpf, A. 119
Rusellae 121, 157, 168

Salamis 134
Salome I 72, 194, 198
Salus *see* personification
Samaria/Samaritan 5
Samnium 157
Samos 112, 121, 126, 146, 161, 168
Samothrace 18
San Benedetto 46
Sappho 2
sarcinatrix 59
sarcophagus 64 (fig. 44), 126 (fig. 84)
Sardis/Sardian 35, 47–9, 50, 168
Sartius Secundus 193

satire/satirist 2, 27, 100–1, 164
Saturninus 132
Scalae Gemoniae 27
Schliemann, H. 43
Schlüter, M. 138
school 53
Scribonius Largus 33
Scythia/Scythian 22
sea, Bithynian 22; Black 99; Euxine 18; Illyrian (Adriatic) 17; Ionian 17; Lycian 22; North 13
Sejanus 25–7, 30, 32, 42, 46, 57, 84, 91–5, 96, 102, 128, 153, 159, 160, 193, 194, 196
Semiramis 1
senate/senator 2, 3, 16, 20, 25, 26, 31, 36, 39, 64, 113, 161, 195, 200; *consulta* of 34, 37, [38], [90], 91, [95]; *see also* house
Seneca 26
Servilia 2
Severus/Severan 55
shrine of Antonia 55, 57, 112, 144, 146, 161, 162; of Drusilla 197, 203
Siarum (near Seville) 35, 37, 168; *see also Tabula Siarensis*
Sibaris 57
Sicily 70, 111, 116 (fig. 76), 121, 126; *see also* mountain
signature 26, 76, [131], 132 (fig. 88), [134], 135, 135 (figs 90–1); *see also* graffiti
Silas 102
silver plate [31], [45], 140–3
simpulum 90
Sinope 18
slave/slave-girl 5, 26, 32, 37, 59, 61, 65–7, 75–6, 84, 144, 159
Sminthe *see* Apollo
Smith, R.R.R. 130
Smyrna (Izmir) 7 (fig. 1), 98, 104
sodalitas 106, 162; *see also* priest
Soknopaiou Nesos 79, 84
Sophocles 140
Spain 13, 24, 35, 37, 38 (fig. 22), 43, 95, 113, 122, 159